Puzzling Passages in Paul

Puzzling Passages in Paul

Forty Conundrums Calmly Considered

Anthony C. Thiselton

CASCADE *Books* • Eugene, Oregon

PUZZLING PASSAGES IN PAUL
Forty Conundrums Calmly Considered

Copyright © 2018 Anthony C. Thiselton. All rights reserved. Except for brief quotations in critical publications or reviews, no part of this book may be reproduced in any manner without prior written permission from the publisher. Write: Permissions, Wipf and Stock Publishers, 199 W. 8th Ave., Suite 3, Eugene, OR 97401.

Cascade Books
An Imprint of Wipf and Stock Publishers
199 W. 8th Ave., Suite 3
Eugene, OR 97401

www.wipfandstock.com

PAPERBACK ISBN: 978-1-5326-5054-3
HARDCOVER ISBN: 978-1-5326-5055-0
EBOOK ISBN: 978-1-5326-5056-7

Cataloging-in-Publication data:

Names: Thiselton, Anthony C., author

Title: Puzzling passages in Paul : forty conundrums calmly considered / Anthony C. Thiselton.

Description: Eugene, OR : Cascade Books, 2018 | Includes bibliographical references.

Identifiers: ISBN 978-1-5326-5054-3 (paperback) | ISBN 978-1-5326-5055-0 (hardcover) | ISBN 978-1-5326-5056-7 (ebook)

Subjects: LCSH: Bible—Epistles of Paul—Criticism, interpretation, etc. | Paul—the Apostle, Saint. | Bible—Hermeneutics.

Classification: LCC BS2650.2 T46 2018 (print) | BS2650.2 (ebook)

Manufactured in the U.S.A.   10/19/18

To my wife Rosemary,
for her tireless support and help

Contents

Preface | xiii

I Paul and the Law

Chapter 1
Are Christians antinomians? | 3
   (Romans 7:6; 10:4)

Chapter 2
Did God give the law to increase sin? | 7
   (Romans 5:20)

Chapter 3
"If it had not been for the law, I would not have known sin" yet "I delight in the law" | 9
   (Romans 7:7, 22)

Chapter 4
How can Paul claim to be "as to righteousness under the law, blameless"? | 12
   (Philippians 3:6)

II Paul and Jesus

Chapter 5
What is the meaning of "in Christ all things hold together" and related Christological titles? | 19
   (Colossians 1:17, 15–16)

Chapter 6
How can Christ be a curse for us? | 23
   (Galatians 3:13)

Chapter 7
Is Christ's work not "finished" and all-sufficient? | 30
 (Colossians 1:24)

Chapter 8
Did Christ descend "into the lower parts of the earth"? | 34
 (Ephesians 4:10)

III Paul and Salvation

Chapter 9
Has everything old passed away and everything become new? | 41
 (2 Corinthians 5:17)

Chapter 10
Baptism for the dead? | 44
 (1 Corinthians 15:29)

Chapter 11
Will all Israel be saved? | 48
 (Romans 11:26)

IV Paul, Women, and Men

Chapter 12
Should women not be permitted to speak? | 55
 (1 Corinthians 14:34; 1 Timothy 2:11–12)

Chapter 13
Why should women choose their head-covering "because of the angels"? | 64
 (1 Corinthians 11:10)

Chapter 14
Should wives be expected "to be subject" to their husbands? | 68
 (Ephesians 5:22)

Chapter 15
Can childbearing ever relate to salvation? | 72
 (1 Timothy 2:15)

Chapter 16
Is it really "well for a man not to touch a woman"? | 78
 (1 Corinthians 7:1)

Chapter 17
What is the "appointed time" that suggests people should live as if they had no spouse? | 81
   (1 Corinthians 7:29)

Chapter 18
Is an abandoned Christian spouse free to remarry? | 85
   (1 Corinthians 7:10–15)

Chapter 19
How can Christians be mismatched with unbelievers? | 90
   (2 Corinthians 6:14)

V   Paul and Moral Concerns

Chapter 20
How can the God of love also reveal his wrath against all ungodliness and wickedness? | 95
   (Romans 1:18)

Chapter 21
What are a wounded conscience and a weak conscience? | 99
   (1 Corinthians 8:12)

Chapter 22
Does love involve utter incredulity? | 102
   (1 Corinthians 13:7)

Chapter 23
Loveless brass and a flourish of cymbals? | 104
   (1 Corinthians 13:1)

Chapter 24
Curses by Paul | 107
   (1 Corinthians 16:22; Galatians 1:8–9)

Chapter 25
"Heaping burning coals on their heads"—Is this a Christian sentiment? | 111
   (Romans 12:20)

Chapter 26
Death-penalty for immorality with no second chance? | 113
   (1 Corinthians 5:5)

Chapter 27
Is the epistle to Titus incurably racist? | 117
   (Titus 1:12–13)

Chapter 28
Is obedience to the state unconditional? | 123
   (Romans 13:1)

Chapter 29
Remaining in Slavery? | 128
   (1 Corinthians 7:17–24)

Chapter 30
Who inherits the kingdom of God? | 132
   (1 Corinthians 6: 9–11)

VI   Paul and Christian Worship

Chapter 31
Self-examination before communion and "not discerning the Lord's body." | 141
   (1 Corinthians 11:28–30)

Chapter 32
Should all Christians speak in tongues? | 145
   (1 Corinthians 14:5)

Chapter 33
What kind of thing is prophesying in Paul? | 155
   (1 Corinthians 14:1, 3, 29–40, and 1 Thessalonians 5:20)

VII   Paul's Power in Weakness

Chapter 34
Why boast about "being let down in a basket through a window in the wall"? | 161
   (2 Corinthians 11:33)

Chapter 35
Why not boast about visions and being caught up in the third heaven? | 164
   (2 Corinthians 12:1–2)

Chapter 36
What was Paul's "thorn in the flesh"? | 168
   (2 Corinthians 12:7)

VIII   Puzzling Passages in Paul

Chapter 37
Bland, progressive optimism about everything? | 173
   (Romans 8:28)

Chapter 38
Who is the "god of this world"? | 175
   (2 Corinthians 4:4)

Chapter 39
Who is "the lawless one" and what is "the mystery of lawlessness"? | 179
   (2 Thessalonians 2:3, 7)

Chapter 40
Bewitched? Or Rational and Logical? | 188
   (Galatians 3:1)

Bibliography | 193
Index of Names | 207
Index of Main Biblical Passages Discussed in Canonical Sequence | 213

Preface

I first began teaching in Bristol in 1963. I specialized in the theology of Paul. Over the intervening forty-five years I have been conscious of how many people imagine that there are irresolvable puzzles in Paul when careful attention to context and argument might have shed new light on his thought. I have not found any example of these supposed puzzles that cannot be resolved if sufficient care and patience is devoted to these passages.

After I had long begun this work I discovered that Manfred Brauch had written *Hard Sayings of Paul* (London: Hodder & Stoughton, 1990). Many but not all of his examples overlap with mine, and I have not adopted his approach to many passages. I have attempted a much more far-reaching level of scholarship and detail. His book, however, remains helpful, and I acknowledge that it has sometimes triggered productive thoughts of my own.

As before, I am indebted to Revd. Stuart Dyas for many improvements in content, clarification, and style. He gave of his time while on holiday in Greece. I am also deeply indebted to Dr. Robin Parry of Wipf & Stock for extremely helpful suggestions for re-ordering the chapters of this book under thematic headings and for his excellent rewording of the sub-title.

I hope that this volume may clear away many perplexities about Paul and reveal him as an acute and ever relevant thinker.

Anthony C. Thiselton, D.D., FKC, FBA
Emeritus Professor of Christian Theology, University of Nottingham and
Emeritus Canon Theologian of Leicester and Southwell and Nottingham

I

Paul and the Law

Chapter 1

Are Christians antinomians?

(Romans 7:6; 10:4)

In Romans 7:6, Paul says, "Now we are discharged from the law, dead to that which held us captive," and in Romans 10:4, he says, "Christ is the end of the law." Don't these verses suggest that Christians are entirely free from the law, or, in modern theological terms, that Christians are antinomians? N. T. Wright observes on the word "end" (Greek, *teleios*) in 10:4: "usually translated 'end,' this can, like the English 'end' itself, mean both 'cessation, termination,' and 'goal, fulfilment.' At this point lexicography can offer us options, but exegesis must decide which better fits the flow of thought."[1]

How can Paul assert what he does in Romans 7:6 and 10:4, and yet write in Romans 7:12, "The law is holy, righteous, and good"? How can he also say that the law "comes from God" and "leads to life" (7:10 and 22)? Paul appears to reflect an ambiguity that also occurs in the Gospels. In Matthew 5:17, Jesus says, "Do not think that I have come to abolish the law and the prophets; I have not come to abolish but to fulfill. For truly, I tell you, not one stroke of a letter will pass from the law until all this is accomplished. Therefore, whoever breaks one of the least of these commandments and teaches others to do the same will be called least in the kingdom of heaven." On Paul, D. E. H. Whitley asserts:

> St. Paul's statements about the Law would appear to be in flat contradiction with each other. In its favour, he says that it is one of the

1. Wright, "The Letter to the Romans," 655.

1 Paul and the Law

privileges of Israel (Rom. 9:4), and that it has been a kind of tutor (*paidagōgos*) in charge of us till Christ should come (Gal. 3:24). Against it, he urges that it intruded, to multiply [i.e., with the effect of] law-breaking (Rom. 5:20), and that those who rely on obedience to it are under a curse (Gal. 3:10).[2]

How can Christians simultaneously be obliged to obey the law and also be told that they are free from the law, which leads only to death? In broad terms, the Lutheran tradition regards the law as a negative force. In this tradition, the New English Bible (NEB) translates, "Christ ends the law," and (perhaps ironically, for a Catholic translation) the Jerusalem Bible (JB) translates, "the Law has come to an end with Christ." Likewise, the King James Bible/Authorized Version (KJV/AV) and the English Standard Version (ESV) both favor "end." On the other hand, the Calvinist tradition regards the law as largely positive. The New Jerusalem Bible (NJB) translates, "The law has found its fulfilment in Christ," and the New International Version (NIV) translates, "Christ is the culmination of the law." N. T. Wright comments that after a period of huge popularity, the Lutheran interpretation is now declining in favor, partly because of Paul's intensely Jewish background, and partly because of the varied meanings of *telos*. How convincing is this recent reaction against the traditional view?

Part of the answer is that "the law" is used to convey different meanings in both Paul and the other New Testament texts. Israel regarded God's revelation of the law to them as the greatest possible privilege. The law, after all, revealed what conduct was pleasing to God. A supreme example of this is the Ten Commandments. Exclusive worship of the one God and utter loyalty to him is what God expects from his covenant people, as the first three commandments assert; so is the fourth commandment, namely to observe one day in seven as a day devoted to him.

The fifth to the tenth commandments are likewise revelations of God's will for humankind. To honor one's parents, to refrain from murder, adultery, theft, and false testimony also reflect his will for human beings. To covet, as Paul later expounds, is to engage in a very deep source of dissatisfaction that leads to various kinds of sin. In as far as obeying "the law" signifies obedience to the declared will of God, Christians are no more freed from the law than Israel. My uncle, Dr. Ernest Kevan, wrote a book that he entitled *The Grace of Law*. He argued that grace and law amounted to

---

2. Whiteley, *The Theology of St. Paul*, 76.

the same thing, citing especially the Puritan Anthony Burgess (1600–1663) and other Puritans in defense of the moral law for Christians.

Other examples of this positive use occur in Paul. Whiteley, again, writes: "In respect of content the *Torah* included stirring accounts of what God had done for Israel. The fact that the legal ordinances were set in the framework of the Exodus makes it fair to say that the law was not mere 'moralism,' but included the moral requirements of God, placed in a framework of salvation-history, and in particular of God's covenants with his people."[3] The law, he continues, was the expression, whether oral or written, of Israel's daily way of life, and was the means of keeping alive their sense of God. After the exile, much changed. With the destruction of the temple and its sacrifices, only one thing remained: the law and its regulations. The law seemed to become "*the* link with God."[4] Paul the Rabbi never lost sight of these two differing conceptions of the law.

But "law" has other meanings also. W. D. Davies, in his essay "Paul and the Law" identifies four distinct meanings of the law: (i) the commandments (*mitzōt*); (ii) accounts of Israel's history; (iii) the cosmic function of Torah, especially in the Wisdom tradition; and (iv) Torah as an expression of total culture, the whole of the revealed will of God in the universe, nature, and society.[5] Sometimes the law is further used almost metaphorically to mean "principle" or "rule." Paul can speak of "the law of the Spirit of life" (Rom 8:2). In Romans 7:21 the NJB actually translates: "So I find this rule: 'that for me, where I want to do nothing but good, evil is close at my side.'" The New Revised Standard Version (NRSV) renders the same verse: "So I find it to be a law that when I want to do what is good, evil lies close at hand." Clearly here "law" means "rule" or "principle" as the NJB implies. "Law" in Romans 7:23 repeats this use.

A mass of scholarly literature witnesses to Paul's varied uses of "the law." These include, for example, F. F. Bruce, James D. G. Dunn, Heikki Räisänen, E. P. Sanders, H-J. Schoeps, Graham Stanton, M. Winger, and many others.[6] All demonstrate Paul's varying concepts and attitudes to the law.

---

3. Whiteley, *The Theology of St Paul*, 77.
4. Whiteley, *The Theology of St Paul*, 78.
5. Davies, "Paul and the Law," 4.
6. Bruce, "The Curse of the Law"; Dunn, *Theology of Paul the Apostle*, 128–61; Dunn (ed.), *Paul and the Mosaic Law*; Räisänen, *Paul and the Law*; E. P. Sanders, *Paul, the Law, and the Jewish People*; Stanton, "The Law of Moses and the Law of Christ: Gal. 3:1—6:2"; and Winger, *By What Law? The Meaning of Nomos in the Letters of Paul*.

I Paul and the Law

In Romans 7:14–25 we see what Fitzmyer calls, "The cry of human beings enslaved by the law."[7] But even here on this one specific subject Paul betrays two opposing attitudes to the law. In 7:14, he calls it "spiritual," in 7:16 it is "good," and in 7:22, Paul "delights" in it (Fitzmyer's translation, and NRSV). Yet the law produces an internal conflict, which makes Paul exclaim: "Wretched man that I am! Who will rescue me from this body of death?" (v. 25). Through the law, humankind or Israel is "in bondage to sin" (7:14, Fitzmyer's translation; "sold into slavery under sin," NRSV), and "I do not do what I want" (7:20). Paul expounds the victory through Christ in chapter 8, where it is clear that the Holy Spirit becomes the positive and effective personal force that takes over from the negative, if originally unintended, effects of the law. Through the Spirit, God has done what the law could not do (Rom 8:1–7).

Wright concludes, "In 10:4 Paul does not intend to declare the law's abrogation in favour of a different 'system,' but rather to allow the Messiah himself to be the climax of the long story of God and Israel, the story of told tales, in which it plays a vital, though puzzling part."[8] This appears to do justice to the various meanings and nuances that Paul appears to ascribe to the law. It also coheres with the verdict of W. D. Davies: "It was only a messianic event of revelation and cosmic significance that could have induced Paul to reassess the Law as he did."[9] The conclusion is that Paul in no way encouraged Christians to ignore the law of God, even though Davies admits (perhaps with tongue in cheek), "To Christians in Galatia Paul would have appeared to be an antinomian, but to those in Corinth a disciplinarian, if not an incipient legalist!"[10]

---

7. Fitzmyer, *Romans*, 472–79.
8. Wright, "The Letter to the Romans," 658.
9. Davies, "Paul and the Law," 8.
10. Davies, "Paul and the Law," 9.

Chapter 2

Did God give the law to increase sin?
(Romans 5:20)

Paul writes, "But law came in, with the result that the trespass multiplied; but where sin increased, grace abounded all the more" (Rom 5:20). The puzzle is how to square this with Paul's statement elsewhere that "The law is holy, and the law is spiritual" (Rom 7:12, 14). Increasing sin does not seem like a "holy" or "spiritual" purpose. I have elsewhere in this book addressed the varied meanings of "the law" (e.g., in Rom 10:4, "Christ is the end of the law").[1] However, even Paul's contrasting declaration, "Where sin increased, grace abounded all the more" (Rom 5:20b) seems to confirm that the purpose of the law being given was so that "sin increased."

The NRSV translation "came in" is said to represent the Greek term *pareisēlthen*, allegedly a double compound indicating the intervention of an interloper. Danker proposes "to slip in," "to come in as a side issue," and Sanday and Headlam suggest "to come in as a sort of afterthought."[2] Jewett comments, "Sin is a usurper, but grace is triumphant."[3] Cranfield, however, disputes the negative overtone of the word. It simply reports, he says, "the undisputed fact that the law was given at a later date than Adam's fall."[4]

The key point, however, is that what the law increased was *not sin* but the *awareness* of sin *as sin*. Paul explicitly writes: "What should we say?

---

1. "Are Christians antinomians?" (chapter 1).
2. Danker, *BDAG*, 774; and Sanday and Headlam, *Epistle to the Romans*, 139.
3. Jewett, *Romans*, 389.
4. Cranfield, *Epistle to the Romans*, 292.

I Paul and the Law

That the law is sin? By no means! Yet, if it had not been for the law, I would not have known sin. I would not have known what it is to covet if the law had not said, 'You shall not covet'" (Rom 7:7). Paul describes the dilemma that faces humankind: "If I do what I do not want . . . sin dwells within me" (7:20). Before the arrival of the law of Moses, even the narrative in Genesis 1–3 illustrates the point that until God's command came to them our first parents would not have been conscious of sin *as sin*. In Cranfield's phrase, one purpose of the law was that "sin might be known as sin . . . in the sense of becoming manifest as sin . . . [as] conscious and willful disobedience."[5]

N. T. Wright comments, "What 'sin' would have meant in the early dawn of the human race it is impossible to say" other than a turning away from obedient relationship with the loving Creator.[6] But with the coming of the law of Moses, it became clear that "[t]o be a 'sinner' is, to be sure, more than a mere status. It involves committing actual sins."[7] By contrast, he continues, Christ's active obedience "deals with people's sins." Anders Nygren comments, "It is God's will that, where there is sin, it be made manifest (Gal. 3:19)."[8] But he then adds concerning "Where sin increased, grace abounded all the more" (v. 20), "[t]hereby the situation is entirely changed."[9] Finally, Käsemann clinches the point. He writes, "Paul finds in the law no legitimate answer to the question of eternal life. . . . The pious who set themselves under it also stand under the reign of Adam. . . . To this there corresponds afresh the eschatological extravagance of grace in the hyperbolical [Greek] *hyperperisseuein* [superabound]."[10]

---

5. Cranfield, *Epistle to the Romans*, 293.
6. Wright, "The Letter to the Romans," 526.
7. Wright, "The Letter to the Romans," 529.
8. Nygren, *Commentary on Romans*, 226.
9. Nygren, *Commentary on Romans*, 227.
10. Käsemann, *Commentary on Romans*, 158.

Chapter 3

"If it had not been for the law, I would not have known sin" yet "I delight in the law"

(Romans 7:7, 22)

This passage overlaps with our discussion of Romans 5:20 (the law came in . . . to multiply the trespass),[1] where the puzzle is closely parallel. How can Paul say that the law brings knowledge of sin, but that he delights in the law, and that it is spiritual, holy, and good? It also further partly overlaps with Romans 7:6,[2] but it still needs attention in its own right.

Romans 7:7–13 addresses the provocative effects of the law. In his diatribe (or debating) style, Paul asks of an imaginary or real opponent, "Is the law sin?" and at once replies, "Perish the thought!" or "By no means!" (NRSV, v. 7, Greek, *mē genoito*, rare optative mood). The key contrast is between the notion that the law *causes sin*, and the idea that the law *makes us aware of sin*. Paul gives an example, namely of the law "You shall not covet" (v. 7). To covet means to desire what is not "mine," i.e., to desire wrongly, or to have a wrong desire. In Judaism and in Paul this constitutes a special example of sin, because desire, when it is wrong, is, as Augustine stressed, the root of sinful thought and action.

In Romans 8, Paul insists that part of the work of the Holy Spirit is to provoke internal, spiritual, conflict and consciousness of sin, as Jesus'

---

1. See puzzling passage 2.
2. See puzzling passage 1.

1 Paul and the Law

sayings in John also indicate. The Spirit or Paraclete "will prove the world wrong about sin" (NRSV; traditional translation, "convict" or "convince" of sin; 16:8), and "will guide you into all the truth" (John 16:13), where "all truth" includes knowledge of sin (see also below). Here the law and the Holy Spirit share the same function. But the law alone brings death because "I died" (Rom 7:10). The "I" here is emphatically not autobiographical; it describes the corporate state of unregenerate Israel.

It is true that many of the church fathers assumed that Paul's "I" referred to his personal pre-Christian experience. Today, however, commentators are virtually unanimous in rejecting this interpretation. Wright comments, "The point of the 'I' as a rhetorical device . . . could be used for the purposes *other than* literal descriptions of *one's own actual experience*. . . . It is a way of not saying 'they,' of not distancing himself from the problem, from the plight of Israel."[3] In our modern era, Bultmann, Dodd, Kümmel, Cranfield, Käsemann, Leenhardt, Barrett, Black, and Fitzmyer are among the myriads of writers who adopt this view.[4] Wright adds that "Sin deceived me" refers not to someone's experience as such, but to the historic narrative of Genesis 3:13.

Paul is so eager to distinguish the law from sin that he emphasizes that the law is "holy, just, and good" (7:12). In verse 11 sin has a starting-point or "handle" (Greek, *aphormē*). As we argue elsewhere in this book,[5] the law states God's will for humankind, and its covenant relation with God.

The past tense of 7:7–13 stands in contrast to the present tense of 7:14–25. Here Paul describes a divided and discordant state even of the Christian life. Only a Christian, in Paul's perspective, can delight in the law of God. The conflict is because the law is "spiritual" (7:14), while "I" am of the flesh (Greek, *sarkinos*), "sold . . . under sin" (v. 14). Nygren points out that the Christian "belongs at the same time to both the new and the old aeons (or ages)."[6] Cranfield is most helpful here. He writes: "The more seriously a Christian strives to live from grace . . . *the more sensitive he becomes to the fact of his continuing sinfulness.*"[7] Luther likewise comments that the wise and spiritual person "is displeased with himself, and praises the law of

---

3. Wright, "A Commentary on Romans," 533 (my italics).

4. E.g., Leenhardt, *Epistle to the Romans*; Barrett, *Epistle to the Romans*, 152; Black, *Romans*, 101; Fitzmyer, *Romans*, 463.

5. Puzzling passage 2.

6. Nygren, *Commentary on Romans*, 296.

7. Cranfield, *Epistle to the Romans*, vol. 1, 358 (my italics).

"If it had not been for the law, I would not have known sin" yet "I delight in the law"

God, which he recognizes because he is spiritual."[8] Calvin acknowledges that Christians find that "remnants of the flesh are wholly contrary to the law of the Lord, while the spirit would gladly obey it."[9]

This entirely explains, "I do not do what I want, but I do the very thing I hate" (v. 15). Cranfield comments, "Verses 15–23 as a whole . . . explain what it means to be 'sold under sin.'"[10] Although the Greek for "I do not know," *ou ginōskō*, can mean "know," the word may also mean "I do not understand" (as NRSV). The "I" is intellectually "puzzled" by its behavior.[11] 7:16–17 then recounts Paul's aversion to his sinful acts. The force that pulls at the Christian is now "external." In himself he approves of God's law. Dunn comments, "The ambivalence of the imagery reflects the ambivalence of the experience of sin."[12] This is less a contrast between two selves, than between will and action. In verses 19–20 Paul prepares for his need for the Holy Spirit to bring the solution, which is expanded in Romans 8.

In verses 21 and 23, however, Paul uses the term "law" in a different sense. Here it means "principle" (as NEB and JB). Danker, Denney, Murray, Whiteley, Black, and Fitzmyer, all agree on this.[13] I argued for this in expounding three or four distinct meanings of "the law" in Paul, with reference to Romans 7:6.[14] Finally, verses 24–25 constitute a bridge to the joyous contrast of chapter 8. Paul has called the divided state of humans "wretched." But Nygren argues that this is not a cry of despair because of what follows it.[15] Only God can and will free us from "this body of death" (v. 24), i.e., the old human nature.[16] The supposed puzzle of the seeming paradox of 7:7 and 7:22 disappears partly in the light of different meanings of "the law," and partly in the light of humankind's twofold nature and perspective. As we commented on Romans 7:6, humankind is decisively freed from the law, but still lives under the influence (even if the decreasing influence) of the old nature.

---

8. Luther, *Commentary on Romans*, 112.
9. Calvin, *Romans*, 191.
10. Cranfield, *Romans*, vol.1, 358.
11. Wright, "Commentary on Romans" 566.
12. Dunn, *Romans 1–8*, 390.
13. E.g.. Fitzmyer, *Romans*, 476.
14. See puzzling passage 1, "Are Christians antinomians?"
15. Nygren, *Romans*, 301–2.
16. Barrett, *Romans*, 151.

Chapter 4

How can Paul claim to be "as to righteousness under the law, blameless"?

(Philippians 3:6)

From certain writers, a claim to be "blameless" in terms of Israel's law might not seem wholly surprising. But from *Paul*, and in this letter in particular, such a claim seems to constitute a deep puzzle. In this chapter, we shall set out four themes that need to be considered.

First, on one side of this conundrum, Paul is notorious for stressing the *seriousness and depth* of human sin, alienation from God, and unrighteous attitudes, as we'll see. Second, this passage does not appear to correspond with the spirit of the meekness of Christ, when it seems to imply moral superiority to others. In 2:3b, Paul wrote: "In humility regard others as better than yourselves." Third, as Krister Stendahl and very differently Wolfhart Pannenberg (both discussed later) argued, Paul does not seem to regard *individual* and *personal acts* of sin as the most serious aspect of sin. Rather, he stresses that sin concerns in the first place corporate and communal attitudes of humankind, even if the heart and will concern individuals. Where Paul seems to claim that he is "blameless," this refers only to *individual* sin; whereas Paul's "serious" statements about the power and consequences of sin are those passages that regard sin as a universal and cosmic phenomenon. Fourth, we need to consider more carefully Paul's use of polemical rhetoric, especially when this may allow irony or hyperbole. (Though see also the last paragraph of this chapter.)

How can Paul claim to be "as to righteousness under the law, blameless"?

To discuss the first and third points together, Paul speaks primarily not of individual sin, but of *corporate, communal,* and *structural,* sin. To cite one of many possible examples, D. E. H. Whiteley calls attention to three passages in Paul that, he says, represent current versions, so to speak, of the human "fall" in Genesis.[1] Paul argues in Romans 1:18–32 that both Jew and gentile share the same *universal* condemnation. This passage may reflect overtones of a standard synagogue sermon, but Paul's overriding point is that "God gave them up" (Rom 1:24 and 26). Sin, as G. Stählin and others have expressed it, is itself an *effect* of sin. For example, sin brings blindness or bondage, which places constraints on further action, leading to further sin. Romans 2:1 begins, "Therefore you have no excuse, whoever you are." The gentiles may be condemned for their idolatry and immoral practices, but Jews have no more excuse, for "in passing judgement on another, you condemn yourself." In Romans 1:22 "this echo became stronger."[2]

Whiteley's second example of human "fallenness" occurs in Romans 5:12, which he calls "Paul's fundamental teaching." It was, Paul says, "through one man that sin came into the world, and death came through sin, and so death spread to all, because all have sinned."[3]

Whiteley's third passage is Romans 7:7–13, where Paul speaks of selfish desire, or covetousness, as the *root of sin*, as Augustine would later do. The Apocalypse of Moses 19:3 asserts, "Desire (Greek *epithymia*) is the origin of every sin." Dunn declares, "The use of the Adam story once again to speak of the general condition of humankind seems clear beyond dispute."[4] In this passage, Paul declares, "If it had not been for the law, I would not have known sin" (Rom 7:7). "The law is holy" (v.12), but incapable of bringing life (v. 13). The following verses, "I do not do what I want" (v. 15) should be interpreted not as Paul's autobiography, but more probably as the corporate experiences of Israel.[5]

---

1. Whiteley, *The Theology of St. Paul*, 50–53.
2. Dunn, *The Theology of Paul the Apostle*, 91; cf. Dunn, *Romans 1–8*, 60.
3. Admittedly Augustine translated the Greek *eph hō* not as *because* but (following the Latin Vulgate) as *in whom*. (Taking Paul to mean that all later humans, as they descended from Adam, were present "in" him when he sinned and are consequently shared in the guilt for his sin.) Today scholars accept that the Latin is not a faithful translation of the Greek.
4. Dunn, *The Theology of Paul the Apostle*, 99.
5. See a balanced discussion in Cranfield, *The Epistle to the Romans*, vol. 1, 354–61; Wright, *Paul and the Faithfulness of God*, vol. 2, 10, 16–21; Dunn, *The Theology of Paul the Apostle*, 472–77; and Fitzmyer, *Romans*, 472–79.

I Paul and the Law

Paul does not restrict the fallen condition of humankind and the universality of sin to these three passages. In Romans 3:9 he declares, "All, both Jews and Greeks, are under the power of sin." He adds, "As it is written, 'There is no one who is righteous, not even one'" (3:10). Most importantly, he speaks of *alienation* from God. In Romans 5:10, he writes: "While we were enemies, we were reconciled to God"—and reconciliation presupposes a prior alienation. Other Epistles add their voices: "You were dead in trespasses and sins" (Eph 2:1); "If we say that we have no sin, we deceive ourselves" (John 1:8).

In the patristic era, Augustine (354–430), following Paul, pointed to the universality of ignorance, concupiscence, weakness, suffering, *indifference to God, and the inevitability of death*. The work of Jesus Christ and of the Holy Spirit, through the sheer unmerited grace of God, could overcome what human beings alone could not overcome. Augustine's view of the *nature and universality* of sin was virtually endorsed by Leo I (d. 461) and Gregory I of Rome (c. 540–604). Bede of Jarrow and Alcuin of York also endorsed it in the medieval period.

In the Reformation era, Martin Luther (1483–1546) wrote, "It is no small thing when a man is said to be ignorant of God, and to despise him; for this is the fountain-head of all iniquities. . . . Here is unbelief, disobedience, sacrilege, blasphemy towards God, cruelty and mercilessness."[6] In Romans 8:5, Paul sums up this attitude as "the mind of the flesh" (cf. Rom 8:9).[7]

John Calvin (1509–64) also underlined Augustine's doctrine. He wrote, "Sin is the hereditary corruption to which early Christian witnesses give the name 'Original Sin,' meaning by the term the depravation of a nature formerly good and pure."[8] He noted that this term was controversial, even in his day. Today Karl Rahner notes the difficulty of using the term "original sin" but insists on retaining what it genuinely denotes. Calvin rejects the notion that Adam's sin affected only himself. He called this "a profane fiction," devised by Pelagius. He cites Psalm 51:5, "I was born guilty, a sinner when my mother conceived me." Humankind is therefore "a seed-bed of sin and cannot but be odious and abominable to God."[9]

---

6. Luther, *The Bondage of the Will*, 282.
7. Luther, *The Bondage of the Will*, 299.
8. Calvin, *Institutes of Christian Religion*, 2.1.5 (Eng., vol. 1, 214).
9. Calvin, *Institutes of Christian Religion*, 2.1.8 (Eng., vol. 1, 217).

How can Paul claim to be "as to righteousness under the law, blameless"?

Like Luther and Paul, Calvin regarded humankind as under "the dominion of sin."[10] His use of the term "total depravity" meant "depraved in all aspects of one's humanity," *not* "depraved in every action." He conceded that many had promoted stronger views of "freedom," but pointed to Paul's use of the word *slave*, to underline Luther's view. Admittedly Augustine, Luther, and Calvin, represent only one major tradition of Christian theology. We could cite a largely different tradition in Origen, Bernard, Anselm, Peter Lombard, and Aquinas, who counterbalance Augustine and Luther with a stronger emphasis on human freedom. On the other hand, we refer to a tradition that especially derives from Paul.

Here it is especially relevant to refer to the assessments of Wolfhart Pannenberg, when he stresses the affinity of Augustine to Paul. He writes: "The decay of the doctrine of original sin led to the anchoring of the concept of sin in *acts* of sin, and the concept was reduced to the individual act."[11] He continues, "The classical significance of Augustine for the Christian doctrine on sin consists in the fact that he viewed and analysed the Pauline link between sin and desire more deeply than Christian theology had hitherto managed to do."[12] Pannenberg rightly urges that the tradition of Augustine and Luther genuinely reflects the outlook of Paul.

As Pannenberg and others point out, Paul draws on the biblical vocabulary of sin. Of the three main Hebrew terms, *khātā, peshaʿ*, and *ʿāwōn*, broadly translatable into English respectively as (i) *missing the mark*, or *making a mistake*, (ii) as *rebelling* or *seeking independence*, and (iii) as *distortion*, or *having a damaged nature*. The word *ʿāwōn* denotes a human state of nature or character; *peshaʿ*, a defiant or self-centered stance; and *khātā*, less crucial acts of omission, failure, or error.[13] Paul takes account of *all* these dimensions.

To return now to our *second* main point, Krister Stendahl has helpfully clarified this theme. On one side, Stendahl observed, "No one could ever deny that *hamartia,* sin, is a crucial word in Paul's terminology, especially in Romans. . . . Romans 1–3 sets out to show that all—both Jews and Gentiles—have sinned." But, he added, "It is much harder to gauge how

---

10. Calvin, *Institutes of Christian Religion,* 2.2.1(Eng., vol. 1, 223).
11. Pannenberg, *Systematic Theology,* vol. 2, 234.
12. Pannenberg, *Systematic Theology,* vol. 2, 243.
13. Brown, Driver, and Briggs, *The New Hebrew and English Lexicon,* 306–10; and Thiselton, *Systematic Theology,* 148–51.

Paul experienced the power of sin in his life."[14] For example, he said, "I am not aware of anything against myself" (1 Cor 4:4). Stendahl also cited our passage: "As to righteousness under the law, blameless" (Phil 3:6). He concluded that on a personal, individual, sin-as-act level, Paul had a "robust" conscience. He may speak in part more lightly of sin of this kind because here he does not speak of sin as a state of heart, attitude, or habit in relation to God. But sin is not merely an individual action.

We come, finally, to what constitutes the fourth main consideration of our argument. This concerns Paul's use of rhetorical irony or hyperbole. Manfred Brauch tends to major almost exclusively on this, but helpfully compares the passage with 2 Corinthians 10–12, Galatians 1–3, and Philippians 3:2–6.[15] In Philippians 3, he is careful to define sin *in the terms used by his opponents*. Pride in birth and upbringing was a typical quality prized by Pharisees but rejected by Paul during his Christ-following period. He assessed this supposed badge of honor as sheer "loss" in comparison with the surpassing "gain" of knowing Christ (Phil 3:7–8).

These four distinct reasons are more than sufficient to explain and to demystify the supposed puzzle of Philippians 3:6. Paul might be "blameless" only within the frame of reference marked out by the legalists and his opponents. He may be "blameless" if sin is always defined in terms of individual and outward actions. However, like Jesus Christ, Paul does not regard this as the primary nature of sin, which is an attitude of the heart and more than individual. Further, he is also making a point about his past, which will add force to his words. He was "a member of the people of Israel, of the tribe of Benjamin, a Hebrew born of the Hebrews, as touching the law, a Pharisee, as to zeal, a persecutor of the church; as to righteousness under the law, blameless" (Phil 3:5–6).

---

14. Stendahl, "Paul and the Introspective Conscience on the West."
15. Brauch, *Hard Sayings*, 224.

II

Paul and Jesus

Chapter 5

What is the meaning of "in Christ all things hold together" and related Christological titles?

(Colossians 1:17, 15–16)

The Greek word for "hold together" is *synestēken*, from *synistēmi*, which means "to bring together," "to put together," "to hold together," or "to put in a condition of coherence."[1] In Christ, Paul says, the universe (literally "all things") finds its coherence, meaning, or intelligibility (Col 1:17). This language and theme also reflect what Jewish writers said about God's pre-existent Wisdom and God's Word. In Ben Sirach 43:26 we read: "By his word all things hold together" (Greek, *en logo autou sygkeitai ta panta*). In Philo of Alexandria, the Jewish exegete and philosopher who was a near-contemporary with Paul, this phrase occurs at least four times.[2] In Paul, Wisdom, God, Christ, and Spirit appear to be merged into one as the sustaining principle of a coherent and intelligible universe.

To adequately appreciate Paul's Christology in Colossians 1:17, we need to examine Colossians 1:15–17 (or even 1:15–20) as a whole, as well as the problem of false teaching that the church at Colossae faced. Many writers consider verses 15–20 to be non-Pauline. But Lohmeyer, Dibelius, Moule,

---

1. Danker, BDAG, 972–73.

2. Philo, *The Heir of Divine Things*, 23.188 (Eng. Loeb Library vol. 4); *On Flight and Finding* 112 (Eng. Loeb Library vol. 5); *On the Life of Moses* 2.133 (Eng. Loeb Library vol. 6).

II Paul and Jesus

Bruce, Kümmel, Caird, and Dunn argue for Paul's authorship, even if Paul is using a pre-Pauline hymn. In Colossians 1:15, Paul says, "He [Christ] is the image of the invisible God, the firstborn of all creation" (Greek, *ho estin eikon tou aoratou, prōtotokos pasēs ktiseōs*). The contrast between visible and invisible comes from Plato and numerous earlier Greek writers. Paul agrees that God is invisible, but Christ, he stresses, is the *visible manifestation of the God who is beyond human sight*. In canonical terms, we may compare the enfleshment of the Divine Word in John 1:1–5, 14. Puzzling at first is the phrase "the firstborn of creation." Without its broader context it might seem as if Christ is simply the first (chronologically) among created beings or things. The NEB and REB use "primacy over creation" to avoid this mistaken interpretation of "firstborn."

However, we need to go back further, to understand the contours of the main problem that faced the church in Colossae, which past generations often called "The Colossian Heresy." Today this term is often regarded as misleading, not least because, as Dunn points out, it presupposes that Christology in the Christian church had reached a relatively well-defined stage by the date at which this epistle was written, rather than existing perhaps in various diverse, or at least fluid, forms.[3] Certainly this thesis should not be exaggerated, but it carries some weight. It is clear from other passages in Colossians that false teachers or leaders in the church underestimated the status and cosmic significance of Christ. Dunn argues that the problematic group did not strive to undermine the gospel, for in comparison with Galatians "the mood of Colossians is surprisingly relaxed."[4] Yet there was an insidious "philosophy" at Colossae, which stressed "the elements of the universe" (2:8, 20), veneration of angels (2:18), cosmic powers (2:10, 15), and a *plērōma* ("fulness" as in 2:8–9, but in a technical sense, perhaps *divine emanations,* according to opponents' use of the term).

Lohse and Bornkamm regarded this system of belief as a gnosticizing syncretism, which represented a corruption of Christian belief. Other writers, however, looked to the corrupting influence not of gnostic tendencies but of tendencies within Judaism. The Jews were a strong minority in the cities of the Lycus valley, which included Colossae. Laodicea featured in such Diaspora Jewish customs as the payment of the temple tax, Jewish food laws, and rights of assembly, according to Josephus.[5] Whether we

---

3. Dunn, *Epistles to the Colossians and to Philemon*, 24–35.
4. Dunn, *Epistles to the Colossians and to Philemon*, 26.
5. Josephus, *Antiquities*, 14.241–42; Dunn, *Epistles to the Colossians and to Philemon*,

What is the meaning of "in Christ all things hold together"?

point to Gnosticism, to Judaism, or to both, a plausible picture emerges of a threat to a genuinely adequate view of Christ. This becomes all the more credible in the light of Christological passages, especially in 2:8–20, as well as in 1:15–20. Paul writes, first of all: "In him [Christ] the whole fullness of the deity dwells bodily, and you have come to fullness in him, always the head of every ruler and authority" (vv. 8–9).

Paul resumes in this section: "You were raised with him through faith in the power of God, who raised him from the dead" (v. 12). Further, "He [Christ] disarmed the rulers and authorities and made a public example of triumphing over them in it" (v. 15). Again, "Do not let anyone disqualify you insisting on self-abasement and worship of angels" (v. 18). Finally, "If with Christ you died to the elemental spirits of the universe, why do you still live as if you still belonged to the world?" (v. 20).

This also sets the scene for our understanding of Colossians 1:15–17: "Christ is the image of the invisible God . . . in him all things in heaven and on earth were created, whether thrones or dominions or rulers or powers—all things have been created through him and for him. He himself is before all things, and in him all things hold together." These take on a new sense in the light of the threat to the Colossians' view of Christ. We can now understand more about how Jesus Christ can be the image of the invisible God. Moule writes, "Christ is claimed to gather up in his own person that manifestation of the invisible God which was to be found both generally in nature (Rom. 1:20) and more particularly in man. If man is 'in the image of God' (Gen. 1:26; 1 Cor. 11:7; 2 Cor. 3:18; Col. 3:10) . . . then so is Christ *par excellence*."[6] Further, through Christ the otherwise unknown God becomes known. Martin correctly writes, "The objectivization of God in human life, the 'projection' of God on the canvas of our humanity . . . is revelatory, more than ontological"; in other words, "It tells us what Christ does (to reveal God) rather than what he is in himself."[7]

The phrase "firstborn of all creation" (v. 15) was interpreted by the Arians to mean that Christ was included among created things. But such an interpretation would be inconsistent with much else in Colossians and in Paul in general. "Firstborn" cannot be a temporal term, but it means "the one who is supreme over all creation."[8] In O'Brien's language, "Christ

---

30.

6. Moule, *Epistles to the Colossians and to Philemon*, 62.
7. Martin, *Colossians and Philemon*, 57.
8. Moule, *Epistles to the Colossians and to Philemon*, 64.

is unique, being distinguished from all creation.... He is both prior to and supreme over that creation since he is its Lord."[9] He continues that the next verse gives explicit interpretation of this by saying "In him (Greek, *en autō*) all things were created" (v. 16). Many commentators understand "in" as an instrumental case, "*by him.*" But, O'Brien states, more than this is implied. Dunn points out that such terms as "from, by, through, in, and to" were widespread in talking of God's relation to the world. This says that "the powerful action of God... is now to be seen as embodied in Christ."[10] Also, Christ bridges "the gulf between the Creator and created."[11] He is both prior to and superior over that creation since he is its Lord."

Further, the addition of "thrones or dominions" may perhaps disrupt a more balanced sequence of lines, but dominions (Greek, *kyriotētes*) are probably "to be taken as referring to heavenly powers in the light of Eph. 1:20–21."[12] In 1:17 Christ's ultimacy in relation to "all things" is continued. In Platonic-Stoic cosmology, it was believed that rationality (*logos*) pervaded the universe, and Paul identifies this with Christ. The cumulative *from, by, through*, and *to* underlines this point. This reaches its redemptive climax in Paul's statement that God purposed "to reconcile all things through him [Christ]," (Greek, *di' autou apokatallaxai ta panta eis auton*).

---

9. O'Brien, *Colossians, Philemon*, 45.
10. Dunn, *Epistles to the Colossians and to Philemon*, 91.
11. Dunn, *Epistles to the Colossians and to Philemon*, 90.
12. Dunn, *Epistles to the Colossians and to Philemon*, 92.

Chapter 6

How can Christ be a curse for us?
(Galatians 3:13)

Betz comments on Galatians 3:13, "The concept of 'curse of the Law' is strange and occurs only here in Paul," and asks, "What does he mean by it?" He replies, "The law becomes a curse for those who seek justification before God 'by the works of the law,' because by doing so they deprive themselves of the blessing of Abraham given to 'men of faith' (3:9)."[1] This takes us part of the way, but does not entirely or sufficiently seem to explain the puzzle of this verse. Burton does not take us much further by his repeated contrast between "the curse of the law" and the curse of God, as if God had not given us the law.[2]

We make progress, however, when we consult the commentary by F. F. Bruce. He comments, "The curse of the law is the curse pronounced on the law-breaker in Deut. 27:26, quoted in 3:10, above. From this curse Christ has redeemed his people, says Paul, by becoming a curse on our behalf (Greek, *genomenos hyper hēmōn katara*)."[3] Christ, Bruce continues, remained immune from the curse because he continually kept the law, as Paul indicated in such texts as 2 Corinthians 5:21. He therefore bore the curse "for us." The circumstances of his death brought a curse, according to Deuteronomy 21:22–23. That verse enjoined that any person punishable

---

1. Betz, *Galatians*, 149.
2. Burton, *Epistle to the Galatians*, 172.
3. Bruce, *Epistle to the Galatians*, 164.

II Paul and Jesus

by death should be buried the same day, so that the land be not defiled or polluted.

Most importantly, Bruce suggests: "It is not improbable that the argument of vv. 10–13 was worked out in Paul's mind at the beginning of his Christian career." The root of his hostility to the followers of Jesus, Bruce says, is not easy to uncover, but since the Messiah enjoyed the unique blessing of God, whereas a crucified person, according to the law, died under the curse of God, "[t]he identification of the crucified Jesus with the Messiah was [i.e. seemed] a blasphemous contradiction in terms."[4] Paul faced the problem of how and why Jesus the Messiah had died under the divine curse. The solution set forth in verses 10–13 probably came to him sooner rather than later: "Christ had endured the curse on his people's behalf (by being hanged on a tree) in order to redeem them from the curse pronounced on those who failed to keep the law."[5]

Bligh is also helpful. He compares two possible interpretations of "being made a curse for us." The first is the notion of drawing out or absorbing the sting of the law and taking away its curse. (We shall see that this is Whiteley's favored explanation.) But Bligh rejects this.[6] He argues, rather, that sinners undergo with Christ the curse of the law, but the pain and shame of it are borne by Christ. That will explain why elsewhere St Paul says, "Christ is the end of the law," not only for all Jews but for those who believe (Rom. 10:4).

Perhaps surprisingly, often the most detailed comments on this verse come not from Galatians commentaries but from books on the theology of Paul. Many writing on Pauline theology perceive this verse as a foundational biblical passage for a particular doctrine of the atonement, one which is often described as a theology of substitution, or even penal substitution. In this passage, the death of Christ is certainly perceived as sacrificial, probably as expiatory or propitiatory. We shall consider these words further shortly.

D. E. H. Whiteley, to select one of several examples, considers Galatians 3:13 twice in his *Theology of St Paul*. The first comes in his section on the law. He at once refers to Deuteronomy 21:23, "For a hanged man is accursed by God" (his translation). He then comments, "This passage has

---

4. Bruce, *Epistle to the Galatians*, 166.
5. Bruce, *Epistle to the Galatians*, 166.
6. He also rejects the view that the law is weak because it was mediated by angels, not directly from God.

often been regarded as a foundation stone of the substitutionary theory of the Atonement."[7] He adds, "It has been supposed that the task He undertook was to free mankind from sin and guilt and therefore from death."[8] However, he then comments critically, "This problem was not in Paul's mind. . . . St Paul is here describing not how Christ saved mankind from sin, but how he saved the Gentiles from the Law, and not the Gentiles only but the Jews also."[9] Christ caused the curse of the law, he concludes, to be "fulfilled," and therefore "exhausted."

For partial support for this interpretation he turns to the Jewish scholar Hans-Joachim Schoeps. Schoeps argues that according to Deuteronomy 21:13 a corpse must not be left on a tree all night, lest it defile the land. Christ has incurred the curse of the law and exhausted its power. Paul's concern is victory *over the law*, not victory over sin.[10]

Whiteley repeats this argument in his second discussion, this time on the work of Christ. He says, "Christ bought us freedom from the curse of sin by becoming for our sake an accursed thing."[11] Again, he refers to Deuteronomy 21:23. This time he discusses whether "we" and "us" refers to Jews only, or also to gentiles; he follows the latter, partly on the basis of verse 14. He speaks of Christ's *solidarity* with us, the self-identification of the Savior with us. He is happy to say that Christ stood *in solidarity* with sinners, and even that he "purchased" sinners (Greek, *exagorazein*) from slavery. But he rejects the view that this constitutes a "propitiation" (Greek, *hilastērion*) directed towards God.[12] Again, we noted that Bligh argued, "Paul does not mean that Christ destroyed the curse itself. V.10 shows that those who put their trust in the works of the law are still under the curse of the law."[13]

Dunn represents a second approach. In view of his close association with the movement in Pauline studies known as the "new perspective on Paul," which stresses Paul's close relation to the Jewish law and Judaism, we might expect that Dunn would be sympathetic to Whiteley's notion of redemption from the *law, rather than from sin*. In many ways he is, but this is not all that he does. Dunn includes a special section on "The curse of the

---

7. Whiteley, *The Theology of St. Paul*, 83.
8. Whiteley, *The Theology of St. Paul*, 83.
9. Whiteley, *The Theology of St. Paul*, 83–84.
10. Whiteley, *The Theology of St. Paul*, 85.
11. Whiteley, *The Theology of St. Paul*, 137.
12. Whiteley, *The Theology of St. Paul*, 338–39.
13. Bligh, *Galatians*, 265.

law," where he accepts that "the curse falls on those who fail to obey the law."[14] But, like Bruce, he sees "the centre of gravity" of Paul's theology as "expiation for sins past and present."[15] Indeed, he comes close to repeating what Bruce says about the early formulation of Galatians 3:13. He writes, "A crucified/cursed Messiah was no doubt a contradiction in terms," and featured early in Paul's thought.[16] Galatians 3:13 then becomes the "starkest" manifestation of this feature in Paul's thought.[17] The wording of "curse," he says, is another way of saying "being under the power of sin and death."[18]

Dunn also relates Deuteronomy 21:23 with Deuteronomy 27:26, which is quoted in Galatians 3:10, as Bruce does. Bruce argues that Paul alludes to both texts on the basis of the Rabbinic exegetical principle known as *gezerah shawah*, or "equal category," where two texts share a common term in a way that allows each text to shed light on the other.[19] Dunn comments, "This ties in with the understanding of curse as implying rejection and expulsion; and in the Deuteronomistic setting particularly with the warning of divine curses on covenant breakers, which entails their expulsion from the land of the covenant-inheritance (Deut. 29:27–28; 30:1)."[20] In Christ, Dunn concludes, "The blessing was no longer restricted to those who abide by all that has been written in the book of the law to do it" (Gal 3:10). Nor were gentiles cut-off from it by the barrier of the law. That was why the gospel could be good news to gentiles, as also for Jews who did not cling to covenant prerogatives.[21]

Dunn concludes, "Paul uses a rich and varied range of metaphors in his attempt to spell out significance of Christ death. We have highlighted the most important ones—representation, sacrifice, curse, redemption, reconciliation, conquest of the powers. . . . No one metaphor is adequate to unfold the full significance of Christ's death."[22] He adds that the variety of metaphors would hardly have been living and fruitful metaphors had they not corresponded to experiences of conscience set at rest, of release and

---

14. Dunn, *The Theology of Paul the Apostle*, 226.
15. Whiteley, *The Theology of St. Paul*, 208.
16. Whiteley, *The Theology of St. Paul*, 209.
17. Whiteley, *The Theology of St. Paul*, 225.
18. Whiteley, *The Theology of St. Paul*, 225.
19. Bruce, *Galatians*, 165.
20. Dunn, *The Theology of Paul*, 226.
21. Dunn, *The Theology of Paul*, 227.
22. Dunn, *The Theology of Paul*, 231.

liberation, and of reconciliation. In this respect Dunn follows the earlier example of the New Testament scholar Jeremias and others.[23]

As our third main approach, we may consider the work of an older conservative writer, James Denny, and that of a more recent one, Leon Morris. Denney begins with the earlier contexts in Galatians where Paul speaks of redeeming us from this present world and his *anathema* (curse) on those who fail to maintain the centrality of the cross of Christ (Gal 1:4, 8–9). Paul has spoken of Christ as one "who loved me and gave himself up for me," and uttered passionate words against those who acted as if Christ had died for nothing (2:20–21).[24] Denney writes, "The aim of the Epistle to the Galatians is to show that Christianity is contained in the cross."[25] On Galatians 3 and 4, like Whiteley, he emphasizes the role of the law, and Christ's self-identification with others.[26] But unlike him, he stresses, that Christ "made our doom his own."[27] He argues that to say "He became a curse for us" is exactly the same as to say "He was made sin for us" (2 Cor 5:21) or "He died for us" (Rom 5:6).[28]

We may bracket Denney with Leon Morris. Morris makes precisely the same point as Denney, namely that being made a curse for us is equivalent to being made sin for us: "He bore our sin and its consequences so that the latter will mean that he bore our curse."[29] Morris quotes J. S. Stuart with approval when he wrote, "Not only had Christ by dying disclosed the sinner's guilt, not only had he revealed the Father's love: He had actually taken the sinner's place. This meant, since 'God was in Christ,' that *God* had taken that place."[30] Morris concludes, "Substitution is not some external process which takes place with God no more than a spectator. He is involved. He involves himself in this business of saving mankind."[31]

The remaining factor that we have not yet covered is the controversy about expiation and propitiation. This rare word in Greek, which translates

---

23. Jeremias, *The Central Message of the New Testament*, 31–50.
24. Denney, *The Death of Christ*, 150–52.
25. Denney, *The Death of Christ*, 152.
26. Denney, *The Death of Christ*, 155 and 158–62.
27. Denney, *The Death of Christ*, 156.
28. Denney, *The Death of Christ*, 156.
29. Morris, *The Cross in the New Testament*, 222.
30. L. Morris, *The Cross in the New Testament*, 223; and Stewart, *A Man in Christ*, 240–41 (Stewart's italics).
31. Morris, *The Cross in the New Testament*, 224.

either or both terms, is *hilastērion* (Rom 3:25; cf. 9:5). The word is translated as "propitiation" in the KJV/AB and 1662 Book of Common Prayer. The NRSV and NIV evade the controversy by translating the word "sacrifice of atonement," and the NJB avoids it by translating "sacrifice for reconciliation." But the REB and NEB have "the means of expiation in sin," and RSV has "expiation." The Greek of the Septuagint translates the Hebrew *kappōreth* (from the verb *k-p-r*, to cover/conceal) in the Hebrew Bible/Old Testament as *hilastērion*. In purely lexicographical terms Danker favors "means of expiation" or "sacrifice of atonement" in Romans 3:25, although he accepts "place of propitiation" in the sacrificial context of Hebrews 9:5. However, he quotes T. W. Manson and others as defending "propitiation" in Romans 3:25.

What precisely is the difference? "Expiation" denotes *a means of dealing with sin*. C. H. Dodd perhaps rather crudely compares it with disinfecting a stain. "Propitiation" is a more *personal* word, denoting an action directed towards *God*. Those who, like Dodd and Whiteley, wish to avoid this term do so because they fear it might smack of trying to appease an angry God into being gracious by means of a sacrificial gift. But in the New Testament, God is always the subject of the verb, as well as its object. In modern thought, David Hill has rightly insisted that propitiation and expiation are not equivalent terms, because "Propitiation is primary and directly orientated towards a deity or offended person."[32] He makes the point that the Greek *hilastērion* denotes action within a *personal* relationship. He writes that the word concerns "the personal nature of the breach with God caused by sin."[33]

From all this we must conclude that there are distinct advantages to retaining *both* terms. On the one hand, a scholar as responsible as C. K. Barrett rejects "propitiate" and sympathizes with "expiate," because of the dangers of misunderstanding on the basis of pagan religions. On the other hand, it seems foolish to reject the term "propitiation" because this would *depersonalize* a highly personal relationship between God and humankind.

Other writers have suggested various ways of overcoming this dilemma, such as translating the difficult term as *mercy seat*. But this term is not well-known in contexts outside a familiarity with the Old Testament and so would not communicate well to modern readers. It seems best to explain the advantages of both "expiation" and "propitiation" and to retain both.

32. Hill, *Greek Words and Hebrew Meanings*, 23.
33. Hill, *Greek Words and Hebrew Meanings*, 57.

We cannot therefore endorse the view of Dodd and Whiteley that the term "propitiation" is necessarily damaging as long as the term is fully explained.

This now goes a long way towards explaining the puzzling reference to Christ becoming "a curse for us" in Galatians 3:13. If we accept that Paul is using themes of substitution and sacrifice, there is no need to make heavy weather of this passage, or to regard it as a puzzle.

Chapter 7

Is Christ's work not "finished" and all-sufficient?

(Colossians 1:24)

Many have taken assurance and confidence from belief in "the finished work of Christ." Christ's perfect atonement, most Christians believe, has done everything for us that is needed. Augustus Toplady's hymn "Rock of Ages" says it all: "Nothing in my hand I bring, simply to thy cross I cling." Similarly, Charles Wesley wrote, "Plenteous grace with thee is found, grace to cover all my sin." In another hymn ("And Can It Be"), he wrote, "No condemnation now I dread; Jesus, and all in him, is mine." When the hymn was published in 1739, it was entitled "Free Grace." Yet in Colossians 1:24 Paul wrote, "In my flesh I am completing what is lacking in Christ's afflictions for the sake of Christ's body, that is, the church."

Does not this knock the bottom out of every attempt to sing or to say that Christ's work is absolutely finished and complete? Dunn comments, "The words have caused bewilderment to generations of translators and commentators."[1] The REB renders the verse: "I am completing what still remains for Christ to suffer in my own person"; the NJB: "In my own body to make up all the hardships that still have to be undergone by Christ"; and the NEB: "This is my way of helping to complete, in my poor human flesh, the full tale of Christ's afflictions still to be endured." Almost every English version translates "I am completing what is lacking" (NRSV, Greek,

---

1. Dunn, *Colossians and Philemon*, 114.

antanaplērō ta hysterēmata tōn thlipseōn tou Christou). H. A. W. Meyer points out that the double compound *antanaplērō* is more graphic than the simple *anaplērō*, indicating the filling of what is otherwise incomplete.[2]

In the history of interpretation, Hans Windisch (1881–1935) saw Paul's sufferings as actually completing the unfinished work of Christ. He wrote that Paul bore away the sufferings "which Christ could not carry away completely."[3] But Windisch regarded Jesus as a "divine man" in the "history of religions" tradition, and readily saw contradictions within the New Testament, and this view is almost universally discredited today.

Peter O'Brien distinguishes five ways of interpreting this verse, describing it as "an exegetical crux since earliest times."[4] Vincent Taylor flatly asserts: "In these words there is no suggestion that the work of Christ is incomplete."[5] Similarly, C. F. D. Moule writes, "One thing is clear—that St Paul, like other new Testament writers, regarded the actual death of Jesus as efficacious and complete and once for all."[6] He cites Colossians 2:11 and 12, to go no further. Here Paul writes that in Christ "you put off the body of our flesh": "You were buried with him in baptism, were also raised with him through faith in the power of God, who raised him from the dead." He finds, says Moule, no incompleteness or lack (Greek, *hysterēmata*). Quoting J. B. Lightfoot, he adds "St Paul would have been the last to say that [Christians] bear their part in the atoning sacrifice of Christ."

How then might the contrary view have arisen? Against the many diverse interpretations, Moule selects two chief alternatives. First, Christ's sufferings are necessarily shared by Christians, who are "in Christ." Their union with him "involved their participation in his sufferings." "What is lacking" might then constitute "what is yet to be shared, what is still due to us—no Christian still in this life having yet completed the tale of suffering which his union with the Suffering Servant implies."[7] Second, a closely related view argues that there is a "quota" of sufferings that the messianic community, the church, is destined to undergo before the purposes of God are complete. Accordingly, the more the apostle suffers in the cause of Christ, and in the course of ministry, the greater his contribution to

---

2. Meyer, *Philippians and* Colossians, 319.
3. Windisch, *Paulus und Christus*, 244; cf. 236–50.
4. O'Brien, *Colossians, Philemon*, 75 and 77–78.
5. Taylor, *The Atonement in New Testament Teaching*, 104.
6. Moule, *Colossians and to Philemon*, 75.
7. Moule, *Colossians and Philemon*, 76.

II Paul and Jesus

the coming of the End: he is thereby hastening "the Day." Moule himself is willing to combine two interpretations, even if the second is "more uniformly probable."[8]

James Dunn and Peter O'Brien share broadly similar views. Dunn writes, "Christian existence is a lifelong process in which dying with Christ leads to a share of his final resurrection (Rom. 6:5; 8:11, 23; Phil. 3:11)."[9] O'Brien argues, "Clearly any satisfactory explanation of the passage ... must take the words *ta hysterēmata* seriously without suggesting that Christ's sufferings were insufficient to redeem, and explain why Paul's sufferings can be linked with those of the Messiah."[10] O'Brien points to the Jewish and Jewish apocalyptic conception of the afflictions of the end time and the words of Jesus the Messiah, in which the people of God will be called upon to suffer horrors and cosmic disorders that reach their appointed limit, after which the End may come.[11] To support this view, he cites a mass of scholarly writers, including Ernest Best, E. Lohse, Ralph Martin, F. Zeilinger, and others, together with numerous apocalyptic references, including Daniel 12:1; Matthew 24:8; 1 Enoch 47:1–4; and 2 Baruch 30:2.[12] Martin observes that Paul takes over this notion of the end-time suffering of God's people from Jewish apocalyptic, and bends it to his purpose.

D. E. H. Whiteley also argues that "This verse does not mean that the work of Christ was in any sense imperfect or incomplete."[13] In his work on Paul, he uses a number of analogies to explain difficult passages. One of Whiteley's themes is the "participatory" nature of Christ's work in Paul. As Christian believers, he says, "We participate in death and resurrection with Christ."[14] The death of Christ, he continues, is once-for-all. But he then suggests an analogy: "The moon is not an independent source of light, which makes good the shortcomings of the sun; it reflects the light of the sun. In the same way, Calvary is reflected ... in the suffering of the church."[15]

---

8. Moule, *Colossians and Philemon*, 76.
9. Dunn, *Colossians and Philemon*, 115.
10. O'Brien, *Colossians, Philemon*, 78.
11. O'Brien, *Colossians, Philemon*, 78–79.
12. For example, Best, *One Body in Christ*, 136; Martin, *Colossians and Philemon*, 70.
13. Whiteley, *The Theology of St Paul*, 148.
14. Whiteley, *The Theology of St Paul*, 148.
15. Whiteley, *The Theology of St Paul*, 149.

Is Christ's work not "finished" and all-sufficient?

L. S. Thornton has a similar idea: Paul "boldly declares that his afflictions are 'the afflictions of the Messiah.' They are messianic afflictions which declare an identity of life between the Messiah and his apostle. That is what gives him joy."[16] Hermann Olshausen emphasizes that the all-sufficient work of Christ reconciles to God "the universe in its restoration and perfection."[17] As Dunn comments, rejoicing in suffering, especially sharing Christ's suffering, is a common Pauline theme (e.g., in Rom 8:17; 2 Cor 1:5; 4:10–11; Phil 3:10–11). He concludes, "Christian existence is a lifelong process in which dying with Christ leads to a share of his final resurrection (Rom. 6:5; Gal. 2:19; 6:14)."[18]

---

16. Thornton, *The Common Life in the Body of Christ*, 35.
17. Olshausen, *Galatians, Ephesians, Colossians and Thessalonians*, 306.
18. Dunn, *Colossians and Philemon*, 115.

Chapter 8

Did Christ descend "into the lower parts of the earth"?

(Ephesians 4:10)

Ephesians 4:10 is puzzling both in terms of its literal meaning and as an explication of an Old Testament quotation (Psalm 68:18) with a lengthy subordinate clause. The clause is offered to provide an "explanation" of the words of the psalm just quoted. To unpack the complicated clause, the NRSV says, "When it [the psalm] says, 'He ascended,' what does it mean but that he had also descended into the lower parts of the earth? He who descended is the same one who ascended far above all, so that he might fill all things." The NRSV puts the whole clause into brackets, but there are no brackets in the Greek text. A further puzzle is that Paul hardly ever mentions the ascension of Jesus to substantiate his exaltation, preferring to emphasize his resurrection.

What is all this talk of ascending and descending about? A frequently employed interpretation is suggested by Mitton: "For there to be an ascension at all, he [Paul] argues, there had to be a previous 'descent,' as Phil. 2:6–9 so movingly expressed it: 'though he was in the form of God . . . he emptied himself. . . . Therefore, God has highly exalted him.'"[1] Mitton sees the "descent" in our text as the *incarnation*. Westcott, however, concedes that the words of verses 9–10 are beset with difficulties."[2] To what does

---

1. Mitton, *Ephesians*, 147.
2. Westcott, *Saint Paul's Epistle to the Ephesians*, 61.

Did Christ descend "into the lower parts of the earth"?

"he descended" (Greek *katebē*) refer, he asks, and what are "the lower parts of the earth"? "The descent," Westcott continues, has been taken by some to refer to the incarnation, by others to refer to a descent to Hades, and by yet others to a descent through the Holy Spirit at Pentecost. In the same way, some have interpreted "the lower parts of the earth" as the earth itself (if the descent is the incarnation) while others see a reference to the regions lower than the earth (if the descent is to Hades).[3] Snodgrass discusses the same options.[4]

Among the few who argue that "descent" refers to Pentecost are G. B. Caird, Andrew T. Lincoln, and W. H. Harris.[5] These writers urge that the imagery of Psalm 68 fits well with the descent of the Holy Spirit in Acts 2:32–33.[6] Harris argues that in the Targum to the Psalms, Moses first ascends to receive the law, and then brings it down to the people, while Pentecost reflects this tradition.

An answer to these questions, Westcott believes, can be found only by considering the scope of the whole passage. To see this, we must understand the relation of the ascension to Christ's gifts. Jesus learnt all the needs of humankind in his incarnation, death, and resurrection: "He ascended to resume in his glorified humanity, his place on the Father's throne; . . . his personality is throughout unchanged. As Son of Man, still truly God, still truly man, he passed through all the scenes of man's life; as the Son of God, still truly man, he ascended far above all the heavens, that he might bring all things through man, their appointed representative and head, to the end proposed for them in the counsel of creation."[7]

On "the lowest parts of the earth," Westcott considers it unlikely that this phrase could be used to describe the earth. The Greek has simply "this lower earth," so the proposal is reasonable, but theologically unlikely. "Hades" is more probable, not least on the basis of Ephesians 1:10 ("to gather up *all* things in him") and the Hebrew text of the psalm, which the Greek reflects. On the other hand, Snodgrass dissents from the "Hades" interpretation, arguing that if we appeal to 1 Peter 3:18–22 (as Westcott does)

---

3. Westcott, *Saint Paul's Epistle to the Ephesians*, 61.

4. Snodgrass, *Ephesians*, 201.

5. Caird, "The Descent of Christ in Eph. 4:7–11"; Harris, *The Descent of Christ*; and Lincoln, "The Use of the O.T. in Ephesians"; and Lincoln, *Ephesians*, 246–47.

6. Harris, *The Descent of Christ*, 159–69.

7. Westcott, *Ephesians*, 61.

II Paul and Jesus

it is doubtful whether 1 Peter refers to Hades at all.[8] Certainly, he is correct to say that the emphasis here is on the ascent, not the descent. On the other hand, Mitton understands 1 Peter 3:19 to refer to a "descent into hell," whatever Paul intended in Ephesians.[9]

We come then, in verses 11 onwards, to the endowment of his ministers, and bringing all things to completeness (i.e., to "give reality to all that the universe of created things presented in sign and promise").[10] The quotation from the Old Testament brings no special problem. Armitage Robison writes: "The Psalmist pictures to himself a triumphal procession, winding up the newly-conquered hill of Zion, the figure being that of a victor, taking possession of the enemy's citadel, and with his train of captives and spoil following him in triumph."[11] The "tribute" would become gifts to his followers. Paul simply makes two minor changes to the LXX of Psalm 68:18 (and perhaps also Psalm 138:15), when he is perhaps guided by an old Jewish interpretation in the words "he gave." According to S. R. Driver, the Targum and Peshito Syriac hint at Paul's small changes.[12] Robinson comments, "The descent is to the lowest, as the ascent is to the highest."[13]

In the Greek, the plural "heavens" is rare except in the New Testament, where it reflects the plural in Hebrew. Paul amplifies this by saying, "*filling* (Greek, *plērōsē*) the universe." Like Westcott, Robinson also refers to Ephesians 1:10, where Christ sums up or completes (Greek, *anakephalaiōsasthai*) all things or the universe. The next verse (v. 11) refers to the apostles and prophets, who were part of Christ's gift as triumphant victor. "Apostles" would include the Twelve and Paul, but the term was not confined to them. "Prophets" may also include all who preach with application, as I have argued elsewhere in this book. Pastors (Greek, *shepherds*) and teachers are also included. A number of scholars have suggested that this allusion seems to confirm that the emphasis in Ephesians is on a post-Pauline theme of "early catholicism." But it is natural to assume that in his late epistles Paul would turn his attention to what today we might call the "infrastructure" of the gospel. Moreover, the epistle develops what was earlier expounded

---

8. Snodgrass, *Ephesians*, 202.
9. Mitton, *Ephesians*, 147.
10. Westcott, *Ephesians*, 61–62.
11. J. Armitage Robinson, *St Paul's Epistle to the Ephesians*, 179.
12. J. Armitage Robinson, *St Paul's Epistle to the Ephesians*, 180.
13. J. Armitage Robinson, *St Paul's Epistle to the Ephesians*, 180.

in embryo in 1 Corinthians 12:27–31. Ministers are all agents to build the church to maturity.

We conclude that while we cannot exclude the possibility that Paul speaks of Christ's descent into Hades or "hell," this interpretation is unlikely. The emphasis of the passage is on Christ's ascension and his giving gifts as triumphant victor. We also cannot exclude a reference to the descent of the Holy Spirit, with gifts for the church. We should not be frustrated with uncertainty. This uncertainty allows for several possibilities of interpretation.

III

Paul and Salvation

Chapter 9

Has everything old passed away and everything become new?

(2 Corinthians 5:17)

In 2 Corinthians 5:17, Paul declares, "If anyone is in Christ, there is a new creation: everything old has passed away; see, everything has become new!" (NRSV). The NRSV's "there is" is arguably correct, since in the Greek Paul simply says "behold, new things have come about" *(idou, gegonen kaina)*. Some texts are puzzling because they appear to disagree with other verses in the New Testament. But in this case Paul's declaration is quite clear; the difficulty is how this relates to everyday Christian life. Is it true that for every Christian who is in Christ "everything old has passed away"; and "everything has become new"? Most Christians feel that the old is very much present with us, and that to suggest that everything has become new appears to be an overstatement or an exaggeration.

Undoubtedly in this chapter Paul wishes to emphasize the newness of the new life when a person becomes a believing Christian. However, does it remain true that everything that relates to the old life has genuinely passed away? Even in this epistle Paul says that God has given us his Holy Spirit "as a first instalment" (2 Cor 1:22). He adds that he is writing to the Corinthian church "to test you and to know whether you are obedient in everything" (2:9). If chapters 10–13 are genuinely part of the same letter, Paul affirms that "we live as human beings" (10:3), and "we are ready to punish every disobedience" (10:6). In 11:3, Paul says, "I am afraid that, as the serpent deceived Eve by its cunning, your thoughts will be led astray from a sincere

III Paul and Salvation

and pure devotion to Christ." In another epistle, Paul says, "I am of the flesh, sold into slavery under sin" (Rom 7:14); "I do not do the good I want" (Rom 7:19); and "Wretched man that I am!" (Rom 7:24).

The best analogy that I know to the ambiguous situation of the Christian has been suggested by D. E. H. Whiteley. He writes as follows:

> It is usual to say that Christians were "living at the same time in each of two overlapping ages." This simply means that the Christians were subject to two sets of "forces," those of the old age of evil and those of the "new age," just as a man who has come out of the cold into a warm room is subject both to the cold which has numbed his hands and to the heat which is thawing them out. The cold is associated with the past, the warmth with the "new age" of the present and the future.[1]

If we try to apply this analogy, we may say that the decisive force that bears upon the Christian is the warm heat of the new age of the Holy Spirit. This is what Paul emphasizes in 2 Corinthians 5:17. But pockets of ice or cold, which stem from his or her being in the old age, still need to be fully thawed out. The heat is decisive; but fragments or pockets of cold still need attention.

The commentaries support this interpretation. Furnish writes: "In v. 17 the apostle emphasizes in a more comprehensive way the radical newness of the believer's eschatological existence."[2] Verse 16 shows that what is in mind is judgment according to worldly standards, which have been totally left behind. In this respect, Furnish argues, Paul invokes the apocalyptic tradition of a thoroughly new creation. Plummer had called this recreation and redirection of "old feelings, desires, and determinations of will . . . into a new channel."[3] But Furnish comments, "It is not just 're-creation,' but the institution of a wholly new creation."[4] The re-orientation of one's values is the "subjective" side; the "objective" side is newness under Christ's love. New attitudes are seen also in Galatians 3:27–28 and 6:15, where judgments according to race, gender, or social status are irrelevant. The Greek is without a subject: "[There is] a new creation" (*kainē ktisis*).

---

1. Whiteley, *Theology of Paul*, 126–27.
2. Furnish, *II Corinthians*, 332.
3. Plummer, *Second Epistle of Paul to the Corinthians*, 180.
4. Furnish, *II Corinthians*, 332.

Has everything old passed away and everything become new?

Everything old has passed away (*parerchesthai*). Yet there remains "a radical continuity between the new and the old."[5]

It is not surprising that Paul emphasizes the newness of the new creation. He captures the wonder and exultation of this concept in his cry, "Behold, [there is] a new creation," which "sounds an unmistakable note of spontaneous jubilation, . . . a sudden note of triumph, . . . delight, and wonderment."[6] Barrett calls this "a new act of creation."[7] God has fulfilled in and through Christ his purpose of sweeping aside the old, and bringing in the new. In Jesus Christ the wonder of restored creation is celebrated. The qualification that cold pockets of the old existence remain and still have to be thawed out is still true, but this is not the moment in the epistle to spell this out in full. As Bultmann observes, the eschatological triumph governs Paul's mind at this point.[8]

---

5. Furnish, *II Corinthians*, 316; and Hughes, *Paul's Second Epistle to the Corinthians*, 203–4.

6. Hughes, *Second Corinthians*, 203.

7. Barrett, *Second Epistle to the Corinthians*, 173.

8. Bultmann, *The Second Letter to the Corinthians*, 157.

Chapter 10

Baptism for the dead?
(1 Corinthians 15:29)

In 1 Corinthians 15:29 Paul appears to ask, "Otherwise, what will those people do who receive baptism on behalf of the dead? If the dead are not raised at all, why are people baptized on their behalf?" (NRSV). The critical Greek phrases may be *hoi baptizomenoi hyper tōn nekrōn;* and *ti kai baptizonti hyper autōn;* The Greek text alone, therefore, appears to shed no light on this verse beyond the usual English translation.

On the other hand, verse 29 begins: *epei ti poiēsousin hoi baptizomenoi hyper tōn nekrōn . . . .* The semantic range of *poieō* is vast. The verse may mean, "first": what are people *achieving*? Or, second, it may be the intransitive, "doing." Third, it could mean: what are they *fashioning*, perhaps in an indulgent, self-generating way? Or, fourth, it could mean "doing" in terms of what one *thinks* that one is doing. Hence, NJB translates: "What are people up to, who are baptized on behalf of the dead?" A. Schlatter also seems to imply such a view.[1]

We acknowledge that at least four commentators describe this passage as hopelessly ambiguous. Conzelmann calls this passage the most "hotly disputed" verse in this Epistle, and Dale Martin argues, "It is not clear precisely what this practice was."[2] Even Gordon Fee acknowledges, "Everything must be understood as tentative."[3] Raymond Collins argues that

---

1. Schlatter, *Die Korintherbriefe Ausgelegt für Bibelleser.*
2. Conzelmann, *1 Corinthians*, 275; Martin, *The Corinthian Body*, 107.
3. Fee, *First Epistle to the Corinthians*, 767.

the passage is "enigmatic."[4] Further, B. M. Foschini and Rudolf Schnackenburg allude to "more than forty" interpretations of this verse.[5]

Matthias Rissi devoted an entire book to this subject in 1962, in which he categorizes a mass of views in the history of interpretation, and eventually distinguishes between four main categories of interpretation.[6] One category identifies the dead with those who are being baptized; a second view understands baptism as the suffering and death of martyrdom; a third category interprets baptism broadly as washing; and a fourth understands the practice as vicarious baptism on behalf of people who are now dead. Rissi himself rejects the "sacramentalism" that is often implied in this "vicarious" view. C. K. Barrett agrees that the force of the verse is subjective: will not these people look fools?[7]

But can we suggest positive proposals, even if we test and assess them? (1) One fairly distinctive interpretation of the Greek preposition *hyper* is adopted by Martin Luther (1483–1546), followed in modern times partly by F. Grosheide, both of whom understand the Greek preposition in the *local* sense of *above* (i.e., above the graves of others). Grosheide argues that it is possible, although not certain, that some had themselves baptized literally above the graves of relatives who had died in Christ.[8] Luther speaks of "escorting the dead to their graves with honour" as part of the context of baptism as a sign of the hope of the resurrection.[9] Maybe some spiritual power was thought to be transferred from the deceased to the baptized person. In our day, Bethel Church in Redding, California provided examples of so-called "grave sucking"—an idea perhaps analogous to this proposal about baptism. The wife of Pastor Bill Johnson prostrated herself on the grave of C. S. Lewis to imbibe his spirit. This is not evidence for this interpretation but shows its popular plausibility. Most writers, however, regard this reading of the passage as, at best, speculative.

(2) Theodore Beza (d. 1605), Heinrich Bullinger (d. 1575), and Johannes Cocceius (1603–69), understood the reference to baptism as a metaphor for "washing." The Greek syntax forces it to mean those who

---

4. Collins, *First Corinthians*, 559.

5. Foschini, "Those Who Are Baptised for the Dead: 1 Cor. 15:29"; Schnackenburg, "Baptism for the Dead."

6. Rissi, *Die Taufe für die Toten: Ein Beitrag zur paulinischen Tauflehre*.

7. Barrett, *Commentary on the First Epistle to the Corinthians*, 362.

8. Grosheide, *Commentary on the First Epistle to the Corinthians*, 373

9. Luther, "1 Corinthians 15," 151–52.

III Paul and Salvation

wash their dead for burial (Beza), or who wash themselves from ceremonial defilement from touching a dead body (Cocceius). Perhaps these Protestant theologians sought alternatives to a "sacramentalist" view of the text. But neither the syntax nor the context seems to provide adequate support for this reading.

(3) Chrysostom, Theophylact, Photius, and Erasmus understand "for the dead" as meaning *soon-to-be-dead* bodies. Chrysostom firmly rejects the view of "baptizing *in place of* the departed" as a Marcionite heresy fit for people out of their mind.[10] He rightly understands the context as one of belief in the resurrection. But, in effect, he imports into the Greek an "elliptic" use of *tōn nekrōn* without evidence. Later patristic writers, however, perpetuated this tradition.

(4) W. E. Vine re-punctuates the verse to give it a different meaning. He reads: "Otherwise, what shall they do who are baptized? It is for dead persons, if the dead do not rise." This places a period or full-stop between "on behalf of the dead" and "those who are baptized." This is suggestive, but strains the syntax, and has no firm evidence for it.

(5) Much more widespread and influential is the tradition that this verse refers to vicarious baptism. Conzelmann declares, "the wording is in favour of the 'normal exposition in terms of vicarious baptism': in Corinth living people have themselves vicariously baptised for dead people."[11] Manfred Brauch argues that this would fit a time in the history of the church when those who professed faith in Christ went through an extended "probationary" period before they were baptized and became full members of the Christian fellowship.[12] Conzelmann, however, adopts a more "sacramentalist" view, arguing that Paul does not necessarily approve of the practice, but cites what is sometimes done in Corinth to support his argument for resurrection.

This notion of "vicarious baptism" has been supported by Walter Schmithals, Hans von Soden, Hans Lietzmann, Johannes Weiss, H-D. Wendland, R. St John Parry, Richard Hays, E-B. Allo, Raymond Collins, and many others. These approach this conclusion from different angles: Schmithals from a gnostic background in Corinth, von Soden from a sacramentalist background, and so on. A. J. M. Wedderburn, like Brauch, regards this as baptism as on behalf of Christians who had not yet been baptized,

---

10. Chrysostom, *Homilies on 1 Corinthians*, Hom. 40.2; Eng., *NPNF*, vol. 12, 245.
11. Conzelmann, *1 Corinthians*, 275
12. Brauch, *Hard Sayings of Paul*, 175.

whether or not it represents Paul's view.¹³ Similarly, R. Alistair Campbell advocates "vicarious baptism" at Corinth, independently of whether Paul approves of it.¹⁴ It seems most unlikely, however, that Paul would condone a practice that would be at odds with his baptismal theology. The practice appears nowhere else in the New Testament. Jerome Murphy-O'Connor urges that "Paul's understanding of the way the sacraments work would never have permitted him to condone [this] . . . in any of his churches."¹⁵

(6) In 1955, Maria Raeder, following G. G. Findlay, explicated more clearly than before a view that had been hinted at in earlier theories. She argued that baptism for the sake of the dead refers to the decision of a person or persons to ask for, and receive, baptism *as a result of the desire to be united with their believing relatives who have died*. Probably the believing relative would share the radiant confidence that they would meet again in and through Christ at the resurrection of the dead.¹⁶ This seems to be by far the most convincing reconstruction of the verse. J. K. Howard also argues that the motivation of baptism was to be united with loved ones at the resurrection.¹⁷

G. G. Findlay argues, surely correctly, "Paul is referring to . . . a normal experience, that the death of Christians leads to the conversion of survivors, when in the first instance 'for the sake of the dead' (their beloved dead) or in spiritual solidarity with the dead and in the hope of reunion, turn to Christ, e.g. when a dying mother wins her son by the appeal, 'Meet me in heaven!' Such appeals, and their frequent salutary effect, give strong and touching evidence of faith in the resurrection."¹⁸ This, I believe, is the solution of an otherwise puzzling passage. We need look no further.

---

13. Wedderburn, *Baptism and Resurrection*, 288–89.
14. Campbell, "Baptism and Resurrection (1 Cor. 15:29)."
15. Murphy-O'Connor, *1 Corinthians*, 178.
16. Raeder, "Vikariastaufe in 1 Cor. 15:29?"
17. Howard, "Baptism for the Dead."
18. Findlay, "St. Paul's First Epistle to the Corinthians," 931.

Chapter 11

Will all Israel be saved?
(Romans 11:26)

In Romans 11:26 Paul writes: "And so all Israel will be saved." He explains this with reference to Isaiah 59:20–21, possibly supplemented by Isaiah 27:9, "Out of Zion will come the Deliverer; he will banish ungodliness from Jacob." Jewett comments that "will be saved" (Greek, *sōthēsetai*) "refers to evangelical [i.e., Christian] conversion," but admits, with others, that the quotations from Isaiah 59 and 27 are not straightforward, but a probable conflation of substantial parts from both.[1] Yet if these words are taken at their face value, N. T. Wright observes, we have the implausible notion "that in the last minute massive numbers of Jews alive at the time will suddenly arrive at a Christian faith."[2] At first sight, Romans 11:26 constitutes a genuine puzzle.

The puzzle, however, runs deeper than this. Romans 9–11 present an agonizing personal problem for Paul. Paul refers to the Jews as his brothers and kinsmen by race (9:3); acknowledges their privileged position in human history governed by God's plan of salvation; and insists that the gospel must be preached to "the Jew first" (1:16; 2:9–10).[3] Israel's privilege is found in its election (11:5) which is irrevocable (11:29); and Jews thus remain "beloved of God because of the patriarchs" (11:28; and 15:7). God has heaped his covenant promises on Israel.

---

1. Jewett, *Romans*, 702 and 703.
2. Wright, "The Letter to the Romans," 692.
3. Fitzmyer, *Romans*, 129–30.

Will all Israel be saved?

Paul says, "I could wish that I myself were accursed and cut-off from Christ for the sake of my own people, my kindred according to the flesh," and expresses deep grief at Israel's general failure to believe the gospel. In the light of Romans 9:1–3, Wright comments that Paul's extreme grief seems to mean that "a huge hole has been ripped in the story of God and Israel."[4] Wright continues, "The problem of Israel's unbelief... is the obvious and major counterexample to Paul's thesis up to this point.... The question of Israel—of God's promises to Abraham and of how they have been fulfilled—has been central, not peripheral, to the letter all through."[5] Many commentators make this point. Does Israel's unbelief mean that God's promises have failed, after all?

Wright concludes that Romans 9–11 entail a retelling of the story of Israel from Abraham to Paul's present day. From 9:6 to 10:21 Paul retells the great narrative that every Jew knew. The question of *how, whether, and in what sense* "all Israel" will be saved has remained a poignant question during the second half of the twentieth century, following the tragic events of the Holocaust and Auschwitz. Paul clearly does not believe that God's promises and pledges through covenant have failed. But does Paul, in effect, *redefine* the meaning of "all Israel"?

Most commentators argue that in chapter 11 Paul unfolds a "mystery" in three-steps.[6] In 11:11–16 he explains, first, that the inclusion of the gentiles as equally honored members of the kingdom of God is expected to provoke the "jealous" conversion of Israel.[7] Munck writes, "What was Paul's conception of the way leading from the Jews' jealousy to their salvation?... As soon as the Jew can see and realize that the Gentiles are attaining what was promised to Israel, the possibility of jealousy exists."[8]

The second stage of the argument concerns "branches broken off from God's cultivated olive tree, while the Gentiles are like wild branches grafted in surprisingly" (11:17–24).[9]

The third stage is the mystery of God's dealings with Israel, stressing *God's faithfulness to his covenant promises*, and perhaps redefining "all Israel" (11:25–32, ending with a paean of praise in 11:33–36).

---

4. Wright, "The Letter to the Romans," 622.
5. Wright, "The Letter to the Romans," 622.
6. Jewett, *Romans*, 701; Thiselton, *Discovering Romans*, 211.
7. Bell, *Provoked to Jealousy*, 115–36.
8. Munck, *Paul and the Salvation of Mankind*, 45.
9. Thiselton, *Romans*, 211; Wright, "The Letter to the Romans," 680.

III Paul and Salvation

Almost every commentator interprets "all Israel" to mean "Israel as a whole" rather than simply "every single individual Jew." For one thing, "all" denotes in Greek not simply "all," but also "the whole." Jewett, Dunn, Cranfield, Fitzmyer, Ziesler, and Käsemann, all urge this.[10]

Second, Jewett, Cranfield, and almost all other commentators, suggest that four interpretations of "all Israel" have been proposed, but that only the fourth is entirely convincing.

(i) Some argue that "all Israel" (Greek, *pas Israēl*) denotes "*all* the elect, both Jews and gentiles." Calvin, Jeremias, and some others advocate this view.

(ii) Bengel and others argue that "all Israel" denotes "the elect of chosen Israel."

(iii) Thomas Aquinas suggested that "all Israel" denotes every single Israelite, at the fulfilment of time.

(iv) The overwhelming number of commentators argue that "all Israel" means "Israel as a whole," without necessarily implying every member of Israel will be saved. Cranfield, Dunn, Fitzmyer, Käsemann, and Wright urge this view.[11]

Many, including Cranfield, also cite the use of "all Israel" in the Mishnah tractate *Sanhedrin* 10, with the statement: "All Israel have a share in the world to come," but this is then followed by a considerable list of *exceptions*.[12] The exceptions are listed in Danby, *The Mishnah*.[13] In fact, the exceptions continue from 10:1 to 10:6, or even into 11. Jeroboam, Manasseh, Balaam, the generation of the flood, the men of Sodom, and members of "the apostate city" all feature among those who are excluded from "all Israel."[14] Cranfield also compares "all Israel" in 1 Samuel 7:5, 25:1, 1 Kings 12:1, 2 Chronicles 12:1, and Daniel 9:11. We should remember that the Greek *pas Israēl* reflects the Hebrew "*kol-Yisrāʾāl*."[15] It is unnecessary to

---

10. Cranfield, *Epistle to the Romans*, vol. 2, 573-77; Fitzmyer, *Romans*, 619-20; Jewett, *Romans*, 701-2, etc.

11. Cranfield, *Romans*, vol. 2, 576-77; Jewett, *Romans*, 701-3; Fitzmyer, *Romans*, 619-20, etc.

12. Cranfield, *Romans*, 577.

13. Danby, *The Mishnah*, 397-99.

14. *Mishnah* 10.2-4.

15. Fitzmyer, *Romans*, 623.

Will all Israel be saved?

postulate the entire conversion of the people of Israel, as some dispensationalists claim, even if "all Israel" has a positive future.[16]

In Romans 9–11, the sovereignty of God is a key outstanding feature. This shows itself in election (9:12–16), and in the analogy of the potter (9:19–24). God's sovereignty is shown in his faithfulness. Second, God's call is irrevocable: we cannot simply discount Israel, even though Jews and gentiles are co-equal in Christ. The whole epistle emphasizes this theme. To say that "all Israel" or "Israel as a whole" has been "redefined" is only partly true. Third, God's purpose will be fulfilled in God's way. Although the "mystery" of the gospel is primarily revealed in Christ, God does not lose all of his inscrutable nature because the gospel has come. We may have doubts about how God will fulfil his purposes, but most probably "all Israel" includes the co-equal Israel and gentile believers whom God purposed to be saved.

What is certain is that, after surveying God's plan and purpose, Paul bursts into praise: "God has imprisoned all people in disobedience that he might have mercy on all!" (v. 32, Fitzmyer's translation). Paul concludes, "O the depth of the riches and wisdom and knowledge of God! How unsearchable are his judgments and how inscrutable are his ways!" (v. 33).

---

16. Brauch, *Hard Sayings of Paul*, 63–72 also urges all these points.

IV

Paul, Women, and Men

Chapter 12

Should women not be permitted to speak?

(1 Corinthians 14:34; 1 Timothy 2:11–12)

In 1 Corinthians 14:34 Paul says, "Women should be silent in the churches. For they are not permitted to speak, but should be subordinate, as the law also says." 1 Timothy 2:11–14 raises perhaps more problems: "Let a woman learn in silence with full submission. I permit no woman to teach or to have authority over a man; she is to keep silent." These two passages constitute a genuine puzzle for modern readers, not least in the light of the following four factors.

First, Paul's statements in 1 Corinthians 11:3–16 presuppose that women will take a full speaking part in public worship and prayer. This at once suggests that his hesitation in 14:34 cannot be understood to be a universal prohibition for women not to speak in public worship. (The one problem of these verses is that Paul does appear to invoke the argument that "man was not made from woman, but woman from man" in 11:9. We shall try to address this later.)

Second, in Paul's epistles at least *half a dozen women do have leadership positions* that would probably involve *teaching, preaching, and leading in prayer*. These include Phoebe (Rom 16:1), Euodia and Syntache (Phil 4:2), Priscilla (Rom 16:3; 1 Cor 16:19; 2 Tim 4:19; cf. Acts 18:2, 18, 26), Junia (Rom 16:7), and (in Acts 16:14, 40, not the Epistles) Lydia.

Priscilla and Junia call for special comment. Priscilla is part of a husband-and-wife couple, whom Paul describes as his co-workers in Romans

IV Paul, Women, and Men

16:3-5. They were probably freedpersons of Jewish origin, who left Rome in A.D. 49 when Claudius closed a Jewish synagogue because of disturbances surrounding the figure of Christ. They probably became converted in Rome, but then came directly to the Roman colony of Corinth. There they set up their small shop in which to sell leathercraft among commercial developments on the Lechaeum road. When Paul came to Corinth, they were, as we noted, already Christian believers, and Paul would have been delighted to meet them and share with them. They even hosted him. Jerome Murphy-O'Connor suggests that they had a loft over their shop "while Paul slept below amid the tool-strewn work-benches and the rolls of leather and canvas. The workshop was perfect for initial contacts, particularly with women. While Paul worked on a cloak or sandal, he had the opportunity for conversation."[1] Aquila and Priscilla eventually left Corinth for Ephesus, and also hosted Paul there in 52. They joined him in sending warm greetings to the church in Corinth.[2] Contrary to convention, Paul always mentioned Priscilla before Aquila, presumably as the more forceful or influential of the couple.

Junia is still more significant. In Romans 16:7 Paul greeted Junia and Adronicus as "prominent among the apostles," and as "in Christ before I was." This provides firm evidence that Junia was *a female apostle*. However, her female name was obscured by earlier English translations of the Bible. William Tyndale (1526/1534), the KJB/AV (1611), and recently the NAB (1970) translated the feminine name *Junia* as the masculine name *Junias*. Yet Eldon Jay Epp, a foremost world-ranking textual critic, judges all of the various masculine forms to be implausible.[3] He argues that in all the existing literature from the Greco-Roman world of this time, no examples of the name *Junias* occur, while there are 250 instances of the female name *Junia*. Nor are there males called Junias as a shortened form of Junianus, as some have proposed. In a book of 138 pages and a substantial bibliography, Epp declares, "The conclusion to this investigation is simple . . . there was an apostle Junia. For me this conclusion is indisputable."[4]

Third, Paul's alleged reputation for viewing women as somehow inferior to men has been convincingly criticized by F. F. Bruce, among others. Bruce writes, "The most incredible feature in the Paul of popular mythology

---

1. Murphy-O'Connor, *Paul: A Critical Life*, 263.
2. Murphy-O'Connor, *Paul*, 171-72
3. Epp, *Junia the First Woman Apostle*, 23-31.
4. Epp, *Junia the First Woman Apostle*, 80; cf. also Bauckham, *Gospel Women*.

is his alleged misogyny. . . . We recall his commendation of Phoebe, the deacon of the church at Cenchreae, who had shown herself a helper to him as to many others. . . . In his friends he was able to call forth a devotion which knew no limits. Priscilla and Aquila risked their lives for him in a dangerous situation."[5] Priscilla, he suggests, would hardly have risked her neck for an incorrigible misogynist.

Fourth, Paul provides many examples of *declarations of the equal status* of men and women in Christ. Of these examples Galatians 3:28 is constantly given pride of place, even, some might think, quoted with disproportionate frequency. This verse reads: "There is no longer Jew or Greek, there is no longer slave or free, there is no longer male and female; for all of you are one in Christ Jesus" (NRSV). Probably the most radical commentator is Hans Dieter Betz. He comments, "The strongest of the three statements occurs in verse 28c: 'There is no male and female.'"[6] So far, so good. But he then suggests that because Paul uses the neuter for the names of the sexes [Greek, *arsen kai thēlu*], this "indicates that not only the *social* differences between man and woman ('roles') are involved, but the *biological* distinctions."[7] He speaks of "the metaphysical removal of the biological gender distinctions as a result of the salvation in Christ."[8] This appears to go much further than other commentaries on this verse. E. W. Burton, for example, regards the issue as "the basis of acceptance with God," and Donald Guthrie makes a similar comment.[9] John Bligh reminds us that in the context of Paul's contrast with Judaism, "In our day Jewish morning service still includes a series of blessings, for example: 'Blessed art thou, O Lord, King of the universe, who hast not made me a woman.'"[10]

This equality of status and probably ministry is reflected in some Old Testament eschatological traditions, for example in Joel 2:28-29: "Afterward I will pour out my spirit on all flesh; your sons and your daughters shall prophesy, your old men shall dream dreams, and your young men see visions. Even on the male and female slaves, in those days, I will pour out my Spirit." Peter quoted this passage from Joel in his sermon in Acts

---

5. Bruce, *Paul: Apostle of the Free Spirit*, 457.
6. Betz, *Galatians*, 195.
7. Betz, *Galatians*, 195 (his italics).
8. Betz, *Galatians*, 196.
9. Burton, *Epistle to the Galatians*, 206.
10. Bligh, *Galatians*, 322.

2:17–18. It is likely, then, that this was an element within the pre-Pauline gospel tradition.

In the light of these four convincing factors, it is likely that the puzzles to which 1 Corinthians 14:34 and 1 Timothy 2:11–12 give rise must be seen as "correctives" to tendencies in local situations, rather than as universal guidelines. In broad terms, the vast majority of commentators suggest this, and Manfred Grauch proposed the term *correctives* in his comment on these passages.[11] But can we take this further?

First, one alternative which a minority of commentators adopts is to suggest that 1 Corinthians 14:34–35 is a *non-Pauline interpolation* into the text. But the evidence for this is relatively weak. The United Bible Society's 4th edition of the Greek New Testament classifies the text of verse 33 as "B," i.e., "the text is almost certain." The only very slim evidence for any uncertainty is that the Western text (D, E, F, and G, and fourth-century Ambrosiaster) displace verses 34–35 to after verse 40. However, the very early $\mathfrak{p}^{46}$ (Chester Beatty papyri, c. A.D. 200) together with Sinaiticus, Vaticanus, Alexandrinus, 33, Old Syriac, and most other MSS all read the normal, straightforward text. Bruce Metzger finds it entirely understandable that a copyist should move verses 34–35 to the end of the chapter for several plausible reasons.[12] Recent debate has revived the issue, in which Philip Payne and Curt Niccum adopt opposite approaches. But Witherington concludes: "Displacement is no argument for interpolation."[13]

Second, if we set aside improbable theories of interpolation, a further alternative is to suggest that what is prohibited is "chatter" (Greek, *laleō*). A number have suggested this. Gaston Deluz writes: "Paul, then, is not forbidding women to undertake 'ministry of the word'; he is forbidding them to indulge in feminine chatter which was becoming a considerable nuisance."[14] James Moffatt goes further. He asserts, "*Keep quiet* means even more than a prohibition of chattering. Worship is not to be turned into discussion groups."[15] The notion that "speaking," in effect, means *chattering* seems to have gained currency from Heinrici, who, together with Héring,

---

11. Brauch, *Hard Sayings of Paul*, 168.
12. Metzger, *A Textual Commentary on the Greek New Testament*, 499–500.
13. Witherington, *Conflict and Community in Corinth*, 91–92.
14. Deluz, *A Companion to 1 Corinthians*, 215.
15. Moffatt, *First Epistle of Paul to the Corinthians*, 233.

cannot imagine Paul silencing inspired speech.[16] C. and R. Kroeger argue that Paul forbids either "chatter" or "frenzied shouting."[17]

Against this view, C. K. Barrett soundly dismisses the faulty lexicography to which such interpretations often appeal. The meaning *to chatter* does not occur in classical Greek of earlier centuries, "but in the New Testament and even in Paul the verb normally does not have this meaning, and is used throughout chapter 14 . . . in the sense of inspired speech."[18] The standard Greek Lexicon BDAG (3rd ed., 2000) has a lengthy consideration of the verb *laleō* and the noun *lalia*. The book gives the main meaning as "to utter words, talk, speak," with no lexical evidence for "chatter."[19] Danker's lexicographical evidence is decisive for excluding the notion of "chatter."

Third, many understand the argument as referring to controlled speech, and referring to "order" in worship. The use of *hypotassō* in the middle voice has the significance in this context of "imposing order," or of "controlled speech." REB well conveys the sense of *hypotassesthōsan* as "they should keep their place (as the law directs)." This is far preferable to the NRSV's "should be subordinate," and worse, the NIV's "must be in submission." Admittedly Chrysostom, Bengel, Godet, and Robertson and Plummer anticipate the NRSV and NIV meaning.[20] Nevertheless, Bruce and others convincingly argue that the context primarily concerns the maintenance of order.[21] The pattern of order has been demonstrated in God's pattern of creation through differentiation and order, as Leviticus and Deuteronomy declare. The Spirit creatively transforms chaos into order. As Stephen Barton argues, the theme includes "the social importance of boundaries."[22]

Fourth, as an extension of this, the best alternative of all is to understand "speaking" in the context of prophecy with particular reference to the *sifting or discernment of prophecy*. Ben Witherington expounds and defends this view. He comments, "Paul would be turning from a more

---

16. Heinrici, *Das erste Sendschreiben des Apostel Paulus an die Korinther*, 456-61; and Héring, *First Epistle*, 154.

17. Kroeger and Kroeger, "Strange Tongues or Plain Talk," 10-13.

18. Barrett, *A Commentary on the First Epistle to the Corinthians*, 332.

19. BDAG, 582-83.

20. Chrysostom, *1 Corinthians*, Homily 37:1; Bengel, *Gnomon Novi Tetamenti*, 661; Godet, *First Epistle to the Corinthians*, vol. 2, 311.

21. Bruce, *1 and 2 Corinthians*, 156.

22. Barton, "Paul's Sense of Place," 229.

general exhortation to orderly procedure in regard to weighing prophecy (vv. 32–33) to the more specific case of women weighing or questioning prophecy."[23] This would become especially sensitive and problematic if wives were cross-examining their husbands about their speech and conduct, and whether this supported or undermined their authenticity of claim to utter a prophetic message.

This would also readily introduce Paul's allusion to reserving questions of a certain kind for the home. The women would in this case be acting as judges over their husbands *in public life,* and risk turning worship into a discussion of private interests in the home. It would also militate against the ethics of controlled and restrained speech in the context in which the congregation should be silently listening to God rather than being eager to address one another. Such public "sifting" would also disrupt the sense of respect for the orderliness of God's agency in creation in the world, as against the confusion which pre-existed the creative activity of God's Spirit. The notion of the sifting of prophetic speech takes thorough account of the earlier context of verses 32–33, and of that to which these verses lead in verse 37: "Anyone who claims to be a prophet, or to have spiritual powers, must acknowledge that what I am writing to you is a command of the Lord."

We conclude that there is no contradiction between 1 Corinthians 14:34 and the numerous Pauline passages that cut across 14:34, if verse 34 is understood within its proper Corinthian context, and within the context of prophetic speech. We have no need to resort to theories of interpolation or of exceptional meanings of the Greek word *laleō.*

We have finally to consider briefly whether any special difficulty arises from 1 Timothy 2:11–12. 1 Timothy 1:3 makes it clear that this epistle is directed to a specific situation in Ephesus and concerns especially the danger of false or non-apostolic doctrine. Paul (or, some argue, a disciple or representative of Paul) declares, "I urge you . . . to remain in Ephesus, so that you may instruct certain people not to teach any different doctrine." William Mounce, who has written probably the most comprehensive commentary on the Pastoral Epistles in modern times, writes: "It [this verse] must be understood against the backdrop of the situation of the Ephesian women. . . . Some of these women are characterized as learning to be idlers, gadding about from house, gossiping (or talking foolishly), and in general being busybodies (1 Tim. 5:13). They were anything but quiet."[24]

---

23. Witherington, *Women in the Earliest Churches,* 102.
24. Mounce, *Pastoral Epistles,* 118.

Should women not be permitted to speak?

Not surprisingly, Mounce compares these women with those to whom 1 Corinthians alludes. The noun *hēsychios*, "quiet," he says, occurs twice, and the verb *hēsychazein* "to be quiet," four times. He continues, "Paul is attempting to correct the Ephesian situation in which the women are characterized as *argai manthanousin*, 'learning to be idlers.'"[25] The verb *hypotassō*, usually translated "submit," describes the relationship of people to authorities. Technically the verb *hypotassein* has no direct grammatical object. All the same, Mounce identifies those to whom submission is required as the bishops or overseers whom Paul introduces in the beginning of the next chapter. He concluded that this verse is context-relative, but insists that it is not entirely egalitarian. Schreiner agrees that not all men in the church had teaching authority.[26] If this is correct, in the next verse, verse 12, "I do not permit a woman to teach or exercise authority over a man" probably refers not to any and every man, but to male *leaders, bishops, or overseers*.

Commentators vary in how they interpret these verses. Anthony T. Hanson makes little attempt to smooth away supposed anti-feminine attitudes in these verses, asserting that "the author held [a] completely un-Pauline and sub-Christian a doctrine."[27] But even if perhaps the majority of biblical scholars have doubts about Paul's personal authorship, many respected scholars do not have such doubts, and 1 Timothy remains within the biblical canon and thus Christians need to give some account of this text.[28] C. K. Barrett insists, "Men and women are called equally to the service of God; but they are not called to precisely the same service."[29] The basis for this is the doctrine of creation. He continues, "Women also will pray, but with care not to draw attention to themselves. . . . Adornment consists of *good deeds*."[30] The reference to "not domineer," he says, perhaps, refers to their husbands. The key point, however, is that "practice was not uniform." "Women were apt to do much talking, and that of the wrong kind."[31]

---

25. Mounce, *Pastoral Epistles*, 119.
26. Schreiner, "An Interpretation of 1 Timothy 2:9–15."
27. Hanson, *Pastoral Epistles*, 38.
28. These include Kelly, *The Pastoral Epistles*, 30–34; Barrett, *The Pastoral Epistles*, 4–12; Guthrie, *Pastoral Epistles*, 11–52 and 212–28; cf. Guthrie, *New Testament Introduction*; Mounce, *Pastoral Epistles*, xli–cxxix; and Wall, *1 and 2 Timothy and Titus*, 4–27, and Wall, "Pauline Authorship and the Pastoral Epistles: A Response to Stanley Porter."
29. Barrett, *Pastoral Epistles*, 53.
30. Barrett, *Pastoral Epistles*, 55 (Barrett's italics).
31. Barrett, *Pastoral Epistles*, 55.

IV Paul, Women, and Men

Guthrie also insists on the equal status of men and women in Christ, but adds: "Woman's dress is a mirror of her mind. Outward ostentation is not in keeping with a prayerful and devout approach."[32] Today some balancing comment may be needed which would apply to both genders. Sometimes, he points out, plaits of the hair could be festooned with ribbons and bows, implying levity and frivolity in contrast to modesty and self-control. This alludes to the so-called Ephesian heresy, which expressed "the tendencies of newly emancipated Christian women to abuse their new-found freedom by indecorously lording it over men."[33] In verse 12, he argues, the prohibition may well have applied to married women not acting in domineering ways towards their husbands.[34]

We cannot enter here into the detailed interpretations that we considered on 1 Corinthians 14:2. Theories about 1 Timothy are more speculative than those about 1 Corinthians as we have a firmer knowledge of Corinth. Mounce declares that in general "Women, at least in some way, are promulgating the heresy, even if they are not leaders of the opposition."[35] The key quality required is "quietness." The word *epitrepō*, "I permit," is understood by some to mean only I express the opinion.[36] But this is not widely accepted. Padgett restricts this prohibition to women deceived by the heresy.[37] But, again, this is not a widespread view. On the other hand, since "teach" has no direct object, this is hardly a blanket prohibition about teaching anyone. It is best taken in conjunction with chapter 3 concerning church leadership and order. Further information about the Ephesian "heresy" and interpretations of these verses can be consulted in P. H. Towner and Robert Wall.[38] It is helpful that Towner relates the "heresy" to 1 Corinthians, for I adopted a similar approach to Corinth in 1978.[39]

Clearly 1 Timothy 2:11–12 is in many ways more sensitive than 1 Corinthians 14:2 for many women. Wall calls this a difficult passage

---

32. Guthrie, *Pastoral Epistles*, 74–75.
33. Guthrie, *Pastoral Epistles*, 75.
34. Guthrie, *Pastoral Epistles*, 76–77.
35. Mounce, *Pastoral Epistles*, 120.
36. Payne, "The Interpretation of 1 Timothy 2:11–15," 96–115.
37. Padgett, "Wealthy Women at Ephesus."
38. Towner, "Gnosis and Realized Eschatology in Ephesus (of the Pastoral Epistles) and the Corinthian Enthusiasm"; and Wall, *1 and 2 Timothy and Titus*, 85–98.
39. Thiselton, "Realized Eschatology at Corinth."

Should women not be permitted to speak?

that provokes deep struggles among many of his female students.[40] Some compare these verses with what Phyllis Trible called "Texts of Terror" for women.[41] Mounce devoted fifty-six pages of his commentary to 2:8–15, with nine pages of packed bibliography. At all events, there is no more reason to find 1 Timothy a puzzle than 1 Corinthians 14:2. It clearly relates to those wealthy women in Ephesus whose self-worth was connected more closely with costly jewelry and flamboyant ornamentation than to serious prayer and propriety.

---

40. Wall, *1 and 2 Timothy*, 86.
41. Trible, *Texts of Terror*.

Chapter 13

Why should women choose their head-covering "because of the angels"?

(1 Corinthians 11:10)

Gordon Fee regards 1 Corinthians 11:10 as "one of the truly difficult texts in this letter."[1] Since the time of Tertullian (c. 200), "because of the angels" (Greek, *dia tous aggelous*) has invited much speculation. In addition to this, the meaning of "authority" is no less debated, for Paul writes, "A woman ought to have a symbol of authority on her head (Greek, *exousian echein epi tēs kephalēs*), because of the angels." Controversy has dogged this phrase until Morna Hooker proposed a solution in 1964, which for a while seemed temporally to dispel further discussion. She argues that "authority over her head" denotes *her own* active authority as an empowered woman. She writes, "The head-covering . . . also serves as the sign of the *exousia* which is given to the woman—authority in prayer and prophecy."[2] This was generally accepted for a time, but then fresh difficulties arose, and it did not seem to explain completely why Paul says, "because of the angels."

There are at least two distinct puzzles about this verse. One concerns why women should be invited to wear approved headgear. The other concerns why angels are involved in any way.

Much speculation surrounds the understanding of "because of the angels." (1) Ephrem of Syria (c. 306–73), Ambrosiaster (c. 380), and

---

1. Fee, *First Epistle to the Corinthians*, 518.
2. Hooker, "Authority on her Head: An Examination of 1 Cor. 11:10."

Why should women choose their head-covering "because of the angels"?

Pelagius, followed by Cajetan (1469–1534), regarded the angels as priests (*sacerdotes*) or bishops (*episcopi*), appealing to "the angels of the churches in Revelation 2:1, 8, 12. (2) Tertullian (c. 155–c. 240), followed by Dibelius, Lietzmann, and Weiss, regards the angels as fallen "sons of God" or the "watchers" of Genesis 6:1-2. These beings desired the daughters of men, and hence Tertullian saw the need for modest clothing to restrain their lustful desires.[3] (3) Augustine, Peter Lombard, Aquinas, Grotius, Estius, followed by Hays, Collins, and others regard the angels as holy angels, who share in the worship of the church. Augustine (354–430) pointed to the purity and propriety of the heavenly realm.[4] (4) Theodoret (393–458) alluded to the guardian angels of Matthew 18:10.[5] Here they might be regarded as guardian of the creation order. (5) Meyer and others cite the angels (seraphim) in Isaiah 6:2, who "cover" their faces and feet as an act of reverence, and implied example to others.

Many modern commentators tend to conflate the third and fourth suggestions in the sense of the ascription of glory to God by the heavenly host (Wire, and perhaps Schrage).[6] Joseph Fitzmyer refers to angelology of Qumran, especially to 1 QM 7.4-6 and 1 QS 2.3-11. In the former, angels participate in the heavenly armies; in the latter, angels participate in the worshipping congregation.[7] He compares this with Leviticus 21:17-23, which excludes people with "defects" from the worshipping congregation. This approach converges with that of Cadbury and Kistemaker. But Hurd and Héring reject this interpretation as implausible. It would be plausible, however, that in Paul's view individual freedoms, or certainly "my rights," should be constrained by cosmic worship: "as in heaven, so on earth."[8] Although the allusion to Qumran might be speculative, we conclude that either the "covering" of angels in Isaiah 6:2 may be an explanation, or more probably the reference to the reverential order of the heavenly realm as a model for earthly reverence in public worship.

This seems to be confirmed when we enquire into the second general problem of this verse, namely the issue of head-covering for women

---

3. Tertullian, *On the Veiling of Virgins*, 7.

4. Augustine, *On the Trinity*, 12. 7. 10.

5. Theodoret, in J-P. Migne, *PG*, 82, 312–13.

6. Fee, *First Epistle to the Corinthians*, 521; Wire, *The Corinthian Women Prophets*, 128.

7. Fitzmyer, "A Feature of Qumran Angelology and the Angels of 1 Cor. 11:10."

8. Cadbury, "A Qumran Parallel to Paul"; Kistemaker, *1 Corinthians*, 376–77.

in worship. 1 Corinthians 11:5–6 introduce the interpretation of "head" (Greek, *kephalē*), and the relationship between dress-code and cultural convention. "Head" in verse 5 seems to begin with the physiological meaning, but also has its metaphorical meaning. It can be synecdoche for, e.g., husband or guardian. Aline Rousselle and Dale Martin show convincingly that the references to shame and honor make this a definite allusion to respect and respectability.[9] Both writers urge that in first-century Roman society the wearing of such head-covering (Greek, *akatakalyptō*) as a hood would serve to signify that the wearer was a respectable woman, and not "available" to men. Roland Barthes has shown the importance of such "semiotic codes" as dress, portraiture, and furniture, to symbolize standards and aspirations in modern daily life.[10] Jerome Murphy O'Connor and Richard Oster share their view that semiotic codes are far from trivial in many ancient and modern societies.[11] The covering of the head excludes self-advertisement, and regarding women as objects of sexual attraction. It would be unthinkable to lead public worship while employing a dress-code that might imply the opposite.

Various speculative theories have been cited to add to this. Judith Gundry-Wolf alludes in her helpful article to "Corinthian pneumatics," who prophesy with unfeminine head-dress.[12] This may add further point to our argument, but this cannot be identified with utter certainty. More broadly, R. F. Collins suggests, "It is probable that the situation was one that resulted from the attitude that 'anything goes.'"[13] A third speculative theory is that the Greek word *akatakalyptō* meant "having flowing, loose hair." However, Aline Rousselle and Dale Martin explore this proposal against the background of first-century Roman customs and argue that it is unlikely. They have shown that headgear such as the hood was a mark of respectability in Roman society, and Paul is advocating that Christian women would do well to conform to such practices. (Corinth, remember, was a Roman colony, as is further confirmed by the research of Lefkowitz and Fant.)[14] This critique

---

9. Rousselle, "Body Politics in Ancient Rome"; 296–337; and Martin, *The Corinthian Body*, 129–49.

10. Barthes, *Mythologies*, throughout.

11. Murphy-O'Connor, "Sex and Logic in 1 Cor. 11:2–16"; and "1 Cor. 11:2–16, Once Again"; and Oster, "When Men Wore Veils to Worship."

12. Gundry-Wolf, "Gender and Creation in 1 Cor. 11:2–16."

13. Collins, *First Corinthians*, 400 and 402.

14. Lefkowitz and Fant, *Women's Life in Greece and Rome*, 157–60.

Why should women choose their head-covering "because of the angels"?

also applies to Elizabeth Schüssler Fiorenza's suggestion of "disheveled hair" on the basis of the Hebrew of Leviticus 13:45.[15] After reviewing the evidence, Fitzmyer responded, "It has nothing to do with 'disheveled hair' or unbound hair."[16]

In the end, Morna Hooker's theory does not seem directly to address the two questions that most concern us here, namely about the angels and choice of head-gear. It concerns, rather, the specific meaning of "authority." The interpretations that we have found most convincing appear to have resolved the two points that have been most puzzling about 1 Corinthians 11:10.

---

15. Fiorenza, *In Memory of Her*, 227.
16. Fitzmyer, *First Corinthians*, 406.

Chapter 14

Should wives be expected "to be subject" to their husbands?

(Ephesians 5:22)

There are two relatively simple alternative ways of dissolving thinking of this verse as a puzzle. One is simply to dismiss it today as reflecting a "patriarchal" and ancient view of society that cannot be applied to today's world. The other is simply to read the passage in the Greek. This will show that that there is no verb in verse 22 ("wives to your own husbands"), but that this verse depends for its meaning on "Be subject *to one another*" (Greek, *hypotassomenoi allēlois*) in verse 21. "Be subject" is a participle which applies to all the groups mentioned in the following verses. The command to wives is merely one example of relationships that come under this general rule. As Mitton urges, these "rules for members of a household" (German, *Haustafeln*) are not borrowed from Jewish or Stoic *Haustafeln*; this constitutes three two-way Christian relations (six in all) between wives and husbands, children and fathers, and slaves and masters.[1] All relationships are qualified by acceptance of Christ as Lord and may be compared with Colossians 3:18—4:1, 1 Peter 2:18—3:7, and 5:1–5.

The verb "to be subject" (*hypotassō*) is used in Romans 13:1 of attitudes to rulers and shows that "The glad life of the Christian community is a life of duly constituted order. The Apostle of liberty is the Apostle of order and subordination. This is strikingly illustrated by the fact that the

---

1. Mitton, *Ephesians*, 194.

Should wives be expected "to be subject" to their husbands?

verb 'to submit oneself' (often rendered 'to be subject') is used twenty-three times by St. Paul."[2] In the Divine ordering of life, Robinson continues, "One is subject to another."[3] Westcott comments, "the Apostle deals . . . with the relation which is the foundation of ordered human life."[4] F. W. Beare comments, "Certainly the wife's submission to her husband is not unconditional, as is her subjection to the Lord; it is conditioned by the fact that he, unlike Christ, is a sinful and fallible human being like herself."[5]

However, it would be irresponsible to fail to address the issue of patriarchy in the ancient world. For example, it was said that the two happiest days in a woman's life in the ancient Greco-Roman world were when someone married her and when her husband carried her dead body to the grave. In Judaism, women were not counted in the quorum needed for a synagogue and were ritually unclean during menstruation. One rabbi advised, "Do not talk much with a woman," and a second rabbi added, "Not even with one's wife."[6]

One of the most extensive and comprehensive discussions of the relationship between the ancient and modern world on this subject has been provided by Klyne Snodgrass.[7] He points out, "Verse 23 is surely one of the most abused and debated texts in the New Testament. Its focus is not on the privilege and dominance of the husband, and Paul never intended to suggest that wives were servants, compelled to follow any and every desire of the husband. . . . Ephesians 5:23 does not focus on authority, but on the self-giving love of both Christ and the husband. 'Head' in this context suggests 'responsibility for.'"[8]

Several factors, Snodgrass says, point to the difficulty of bringing this passage into our modern world.[9] He cites the very existence of "house codes" with their stereotypical focus on the conventional three pairs (wives-husbands, children-parents, slaves-masters) points to the distance between the text and modern society. Other biblical texts, he continues,

---

2. J. Armitage Robinson, *St. Paul's Epistle to the Ephesians*, 123.
3. J. Armitage Robinson, *St. Paul's Epistle to the Ephesians*, 123.
4. Westcott, *Saint Paul's Epistle to the Ephesians*, 83.
5. Beare, "The Epistle to the Ephesians," 719.
6. Pomeroy, Goddesses, *Whores, Wives, and Slaves*; Swidler, *Women in Judaism*; Lefkowitz and Flint, *Women's Life in Greece and Rome*.
7. Snodgrass, *Ephesians*, 293–318.
8. Snodgrass, *Ephesians*, 294 and 295.
9. Snodgrass, *Ephesians*, 30.

IV Paul, Women, and Men

indicate that advice in the house codes was addressed to a specific cultural situation—the fear of some that Christianity was subversive. He cites Titus 2:5 in support of this, where the purpose of the household code is that "no one will malign the word of God." He adds, "Any movement in the ancient world that threatened the social order was viewed as dangerous."[10] Snodgrass continues:

> Such apologetic motivation must be considered in applying these texts in a society that views family relations differently.... Women are viewed differently in modern Western civilization than in ancient Judaism and the Greco-Roman world.... We must take into account both this devaluation of women in the ancient world and the problems caused in the early church by the new freedom and valuation women found in the Christian faith.... All statements are culturally and historically conditioned, some only more so than others.[11]

He concludes this section on "Bridging Contexts" by observing, "Another question we must face is whether the statement that the husband is head of the wife is descriptive or prescriptive.... Paul is only describing life in a sinful world when he compares the husband's headship to that of Christ.... Our society is also patriarchal. If it were not, discussions about 'glass ceilings,' unequal pay, abuse of wives, and rape of women, would not be so prevalent."[12] He concludes, "This text is not about all women being submissive to all. It is about mutual submission of all Christians to each other and of the submission of wives to their own husbands. It has nothing to do with the inferiority of women nor does it imply that women cannot function in leadership roles."[13]

In his section entitled "Contemporary Significance," Snodgrass writes, "Our society emphasizes equality, but mutual submission is a much stronger idea. With equality, you still have a battle of rights. Equality can exist without love, but it will not create a Christian community."[14] He adds that with mutual submission, we give up rights and support each other. Mutual submission is love in action. It brings equal valuing and is the power by which the *Christian* community establishes itself. He continues, "These

---

10. Snodgrass, *Ephesians*, 30.
11. Snodgrass, *Ephesians*, 302 and 303.
12. Snodgrass, *Ephesians*, 304.
13. Snodgrass, *Ephesians*, 305.
14. Snodgrass, *Ephesians*, 311.

statements have been misinterpreted to mean that wives always have a subservient role and that husbands always make the decisions. Women have been viewed as property that husbands may treat as they wish. Even abusive behavior by husbands has been justified on the basis of Ephesians 5:22–24. . . . Such misuse of Ephesians 5 is scandalous and cannot be tolerated."[15]

Snodgrass emphasizes that the real head of the Christian marriage is always Christ, and both partners are to live in mutual submission to each other to promote each other within the purposes of Christ. He concludes, "When a woman enters into a marriage relationship today she does so in a far different way from in the ancient world."[16] Nevertheless, the emphasis on mutuality in Christian marriage promoted by Snodgrass must be held in balance with the emphasis on the ordered and structured nature of society emphasized by Westcott, Robinson, and Mitton. In these passages the *apologetic motif* remains important, and sometimes the husband must represent the family responsibly. However, as Snodgrass emphasizes, "headship" must also involve love, care, and responsibility. A wife should not "submit" to any husband in matters where he is not directly under the authority of Christ as Lord.

---

15. Snodgrass, *Ephesians*, 313.
16. Snodgrass, *Ephesians*, 315.

Chapter 15

Can childbearing ever relate to salvation?
(1 Timothy 2:15)

In 1 Timothy 2:15, Paul says, "Yet she will be saved through childbearing, provided they [sic] continue in faith and love and holiness, with modesty" (NRSV). The writer appears to base his teaching on the previous verses: "For Adam was formed first, then Eve, and Adam was not deceived but the woman was deceived and became a transgressor" (vv. 13–14). Understandably Barrett calls verse 15 "very obscure," and verse 14, "not clear."[1] But it is not only a puzzle; many find it unpalatable. The Greek does not specify a subject or nominative for the verb "will be saved" (*sōthēsetai*, although singular). The number then shifts from singular to plural in "provided *they* continue" (*ean meinousin*), which anticipates the change from "she" to "they" in the NRSV. Susan Foh calls this verse "a puzzle and a sort of *non sequitur*."[2] A huge amount of material has been written on 1 Timothy 2:13–15. Yet many may regard the following discussion as one of the least satisfactory in this book. A "solution" to the conundrum is not clear.

In brief, New Testament specialists have proposed four broad types of explanation of this puzzle to their own satisfaction. (1) Some, for example Anthony T. Hanson, simply insist that this teaching is "completely unPauline and sub-Christian," and reaffirm their view that Paul is not the direct author of the Pastoral Epistles as a whole.[3] (Others allow that some parts

---

1. Barrett, *The Pastoral Epistles*, 56.
2. Foh, *Women and Word of God*, 118.
3. Hanson, *The Pastoral Letters*, 38.

of the epistle were probably written by a disciple of Paul. The vocabulary and grammar could easily reflect a secretary, and the concern for church order might readily be expected from Paul as a second generation of Christians was coming into dominance.)

(2) Some retain a belief in the Pauline authorship of this epistle, but regard this apparent emphasis on "male headship" in these verses as reflecting a divine ordering of creation. For example, Stephen B. Clark seems to advocate this, although he distinguishes between *ontological* difference and a *functional* difference of specific roles.[4] A host of writers follow this approach, arguing that the creation order is not irrelevant to Christians, who live in a now-but-not-yet situation of an eschatology in process of realization.

(3) Many writers see a special, even unique, problem raised by the culture of many women specifically at Ephesus. Gordon Fee writes: "It is hard to deny that this text prohibits women teaching men in the Ephesian church" (vv. 11 and 12). But he continues, "*It is a unique text in the New Testament*, and as we have seen, its reason for being is *not* to correct the rest of the New Testament, but to correct a very *ad hoc* problem in Ephesus."[5] Certainly both Ephesus and Corinth offer signs of an over-realized eschatology (e.g., by emphasizing that the new creation has come, with *no* qualification about the old being still in *process* of passing away). This may have been exploited to promote a relation between male and female that regards Christians as belonging exclusively to the new creation, rather than also recognizing the order of creation and the continuing influence of the former age, which is fading but still influential.

(4) Robert Wall advocates a fourth explanation. As we noted, there is no explicit subject or nominative governing the verb "will be saved." Most writers refer the clause to *women in general*, as Marshall does, and a few to Mary, although without convincing arguments. However, Wall argues that "childbearing" refers primarily to Eve.[6] If the "fall" and Eve's deception by the snake marked her downfall, Eve's rise and redemption were marked by her giving birth to a new generation of humankind. Wall writes, "The reader is naturally drawn to LXX Gen. 4:1–2, which picks up Eve's post-Eden existence as a woman in the act of childbearing. 1 Tim. 2:15a takes up Gen. 4:1–2 to complete Eve's biblical story with its third and most crucial

---

4. Clark, *Man and Woman in Christ*, 199.
5. Fee, "Issues in Evangelical Hermeneutics, III: The Great Watershed."
6. Wall, *1 and 2 Timothy and Titus*, 95–96.

step: her redemption."⁷ The third proposal (above) makes the situation at *Ephesus* a special case; the fourth makes *Eve's* situation a special case.

Within these four broad categories a number of finer distinctions and overlappings have been proposed. One especially thorough consideration (at times perhaps over-thorough) has been offered by Köstenberger and Schreiner.⁸ First, S. M. Baugh (one of the contributors to their volume) considers the special relevance of Ephesus.⁹ He first traces the ups and downs of the economic prosperity of Ephesus to show its importance, and its relation to the authority and influence of the cult of Artemis. He also addresses the place of women in antiquity, noting the relatively young age implied by the Greek term *gynē, woman,* in comparison with modern assumptions. Often girls would have been mothers at fifteen, and grandmothers at thirty to thirty-five. In Ephesus, the classical world valued and expected modesty or prudence (Greek, *sōphrosyne,* 1 Tim 2:15).¹⁰ More to the point, Baugh stresses that "young women faced significant dangers in childbirth, particularly where diet, health problems, and the rudimentary medical skills of the time made pregnancy and childbirth a very real threat to the lives of both mother and baby."¹¹ He quotes classical sources in support of his claim. He adds that young Christian mothers could rely on older women in the congregation for help and advice which would have come as a godsend during such times. This is what "being saved through childbirth" refers to. (A similar defense of "kept safe through childbearing" has also been well argued by Moyer Hubbard.¹²)

Nevertheless, we must ask whether the use of the Greek *sōzō* (*save*) has the meaning of physical health or spiritual salvation in the context of 1 Timothy 2:9–15. Most commentators undoubtedly argue for the immediate meaning of eschatological salvation, although, classical writers do speak of "escaping" (Greek, *ekpheugō*) the dangers of childbirth. So we should not dismiss Baugh's proposal out of hand.¹³

7. Wall, *1 and 2 Timothy and Titus,* 95.
8. Köstenberger and Schreiner (eds.) *Women in the Church.*
9. Baugh, "A Foreign World: Ephesus in the First Century."
10. Baugh, "A Foreign World: Ephesus in the First Century," 28–45; cf. Kearsley, "Women in Public Life in the Roman East."
11. Baugh, "A Foreign World: Ephesus in the First Century," 53.
12. Moyer Hubbard, "Kept Safe through Childbearing: Maternal Mortality, Justification by Faith, and the Social Setting of 1 Timothy 2:15," *Journal of the Evangelical Society* 55 (2012) 743–62.
13. Perhaps no less important is the contrast that Baugh draws between an emphasis

Thomas Schreiner also discusses the meaning of "will be saved" (*sōthēsetai*), considering the two meanings of "shall be physically preserved" and "will be spiritually eschatological saved," and agrees with the majority of commentators that Paul intends the latter.[14] He criticizes Craig Keener, who prefers the "shall be physically preserved" interpretation, for giving too much attention to the use of the term in extra biblical writings, in contrast to the Pauline texts. Paul's use of the terminology elsewhere would suggest a "spiritual salvation" interpretation here.[15] Schreiner also emphatically rejects the notion that "childbearing" could refer to the birth of Christ, as some have proposed.[16] Hanson and Guthrie likewise dismiss this interpretation as "romantic" or as utterly "obscure."[17] Schreiner also rejects the proposal that the allusion could refer to Eve.[18]

The debate becomes extraordinarily complex, in part because verse 15 is interconnected with a number of other controversial interpretative issues in verses 9–15. Schreiner alone includes nearly three hundred footnotes in his essay; Baugh, over one hundred on Ephesus; Al Wolters, nearly two hundred on the meaning of the Greek word *authenteō*, "to have authority" (over men), from verse 12; and Robert Yarbrough over 150 on translations of 1 Timothy 2:8–15. The bibliography on 1 Timothy 2:9–15 is massive, running to some thirty pages. Since the place of women's ministry is such a special concern for some conservative evangelicals, numerous discussions appear in such periodicals as *The Journal of the Evangelical Theological Society*. Some are extremely polemical. In sum, therefore, it is difficult to reject any proposed interpretation out of hand.

Yet there are still some loose ends to be addressed. We begin with a moderate approach that probably commands majority support among those who accept a broadly Pauline authorship. In his article on 1 Timothy 2:15, Stanley Porter rightly points out that we must take account of the subject of the verb "will be saved," the exact meaning of "childbearing," the function of the preposition *dia* (*by* or *through*) with the genitive case, and

---

on clothing, style, and finally with the simplicity of a quiet and modest life. "Braided hair and gold or pearls" (1 Tim 2:9, ESV) or the flaunting of exceptionally stylish dress would cause offence to many in Ephesus, and the church would wish to avoid doing that.

14. Schreiner, "An Interpretation of 1 Timothy 2:9–15."
15. Keener, *Paul, Women, and Wives*, 118.
16. Schreiner, "Dialogue" in *Women in the Church*, 219.
17. Hanson, *Pastoral Epistles*, 74; and Guthrie, *Pastoral Epistles*, 78.
18. Schreiner, "An Interpretation of 1 Timothy 2:9–15," 220.

the shift from singular to plural. He concludes that in the light of the ascetic and disruptive practices of the false teachers in the church in Ephesus (i.e., prohibiting marriage), the author endorsed the resumption of normal practices between men and women, including sexual relations that result in giving birth to children.[19]

Moo likewise suggests that false teachers in Ephesus encouraged women to "discard traditional female roles in favor of a more egalitarian approach" (i.e. equal functions without any qualification about a creation ordinance).[20] Paul is thus rejecting the "spiritual" teaching that undermines the goodness of marriage and childbearing in the believing community.[21]

Schreiner too considers the possibility that 1 Timothy 2:9–15 may presuppose that the false teachers in Ephesus are teaching an over-realized eschatology that "prohibited marriage and certain foods."[22] This would harmonize with 1 Timothy 4:1–5, where some explicitly "forbid marriage and demand abstinence from foods." Paul responds that "Everything created by God is good" (4:4). In view of parallels with 1 Corinthians, where over-realized eschatology was also a problem, this proposal should not be dismissed.

Yet this cannot be the last word on such a complex subject. We should not dismiss Wall's insistence that the reference to childbearing primarily concerned Eve, even if the majority of writers do not accept this. Nor should we discount Fee's suggestion that the situation in Ephesus made this text an untypically unique verse. The huge and complex literature on these verses make any judgment provisional. We conclude that several options of interpretation may point to ways in which 1 Timothy 2:15 may come to be

---

19. Porter, "What Does It Mean to be 'Saved by Childbirth' (1 Tim. 2:15)?"

20. Moo, "What Does It Mean Not to Teach or to Have Authority Over Men? (1 Tim. 2:11–15)" 181.

21. Perhaps related to this is the contrast that Baugh draws between an emphasis on clothing, style, and finally with the simplicity of a quiet and modest life. "Braided hair and gold or pearls" (1 Tim 2:9, ESV) or the flaunting of exceptionally stylish dress would cause offence to many in Ephesus, and the church would wish to avoid doing that. Schreiner too argues that "modesty" in dress and conduct would have been expected in Ephesian culture, and Mounce provides this kind of interpretation in his detailed commentary (*Pastoral Epistles*, 109). Mounce comments that seductive dress and excessive ornamentation with an accompanying lack of emphasis on character and doing good deeds find expression elsewhere in the New Testament, as Keener has also emphasized (*Paul, Women, and Wives*, 103–5).

22. Schreiner, "An Interpretation of 1 Timothy 2:9–15," 321.

seen as less unpalatable than might at first appear, although it is difficult to be certain about any. We should recall that the word "saved" in Paul refers to rescue from a past state, to the present process of being saved, and to the future goal of becoming finally saved in the culmination of God's purpose. All three aspects reverse the fall of Genesis 3, which had involved the pain of childbearing as well as other evils.

Chapter 16

Is it really "well for a man not to touch a woman"?

(1 Corinthians 7:1)

In 1 Corinthians 7:1 it appears that Paul writes, "It is well for a man not to touch a woman" (NRSV, and broadly the NJB). The Good News Bible (GNB) has: "It is good for a man not to marry." The NIV has the meaning: "It is good for a man not to have sexual relations with a woman," which is the *effective* meaning of the Greek. The NRSV reflects the *literal* wording of the Greek text: *kalon anthrōpō gynaikos mē haptesthai*. These versions might seem difficult enough. But the difficulty seems to be compounded when we also look at verses 5, 7–8, 9, and 26. When we put together these passages, it seems as if Paul is teaching that singleness and celibacy are somehow "higher" callings for the Christian than married life.

We may consider these passages one by one. In some ways, 1 Corinthians 7:1 is perhaps the easiest to explain. There was no such thing as quotation marks in the Greek of Paul's day. The opening words of the chapter provide a clue to the genuine meaning: "Now concerning the matters about which you wrote." This suggests that the words "It is well for a man not to touch a woman" constituted a *quotation from the previous Corinthians' letter* to Paul. They are not Paul's words at all. At least three reasons argue for this. First, an increasing consensus of specialist New Testament scholars today argue for it. These include Wolfgang Schrage, Raymond Collins, Dale Martin, John C. Hurd, F. F. Bruce, Gordon Fee, and an overwhelming host of others.[1] Second, the introduction "Now concerning" (Greek, *peri de*) often signifies a reply to a letter or report. Third, in the same epistle Paul gives positive advice about physical intimacy within marriage. In 7:3 Paul advises, "The husband should give to his wife her conjugal rights, and likewise the wife to her husband." In 7:5 he says, "Do not deprive one another except perhaps by agreement for a set time, to devote yourselves for prayer, and then come together again." Again, in 7:8, "To the married I give this command—not I, but the Lord—that the wife should not separate from the husband . . . and that the husband should not divorce his wife." In 7:17, 20, he says, "Let each of you lead the life that the Lord has assigned. . . . Let each of you remain in the condition in which you were called." In 7:28 he addresses the unmarried, "If you marry, you do not sin, and if a virgin marries, she does not sin." Finally, in 7:36, he repeats, "Let him marry as he wishes; it is no sin."

These repeated exhortations sound more as if Paul is combatting some ascetic teaching on celibacy from ultra-conservatives in Corinth than expressing his own albeit guarded approval of marriage. This would help to explain why Paul feels the need not to criticize every single argument of those who had extolled celibacy or singleness. These people do have certain points, he concedes. This is so, especially in the light of possibly impending difficulties which may face Christians in Corinth.

This explains the seemingly grudging comment in 7:7: "I wish that all were as I myself am. But each has a particular gift from God." It also explains why Paul adds in 7:28, "Yet those who do marry will experience distress in this life." Part of Paul's balancing act is familiar to many married couples. In 7:33–34a, Paul acknowledges, "The married man is anxious about the affairs of the world, how to please his wife, and his interests are divided." This is a common dilemma for most married couples. But in 7:29 he follows such a warning with a more specific concern: "I mean, brothers and sisters, that the time has grown short; from now on, let even those who have wives be as though they had none."

Here we encounter a much more specific problem: how specific is keenly debated. Probably the majority of New Testament specialists regard this as Paul's view of the problem of eschatological imminence of the End. But many distinguish between theological imminence and chronological

---

1. Schrage, *Der erste Brief an die Korinther*, vol. 2, 59; Collins, *First Corinthians*, 252 and 258; Martin, *The Corinthian Body*, 205; Hurd, *The Origin of 1 Corinthians*, 120–23; Bruce, *1 and 2 Corinthians*, 66; Fee, *First Epistle to the Corinthians*, 272–77. W. Deming has listed interpretations up to 1995 in *Paul on Marriage and Celibacy*, 5–49.

imminence. *Theological imminence* implies that Christians should not complacently "dig in" to the securities and solidarities of life in this present world, as if the world was their only and permanent home. *Chronological imminence* implies that the End may come during the Christian's lifetime. George B. Caird, V. L. Wimbush, and Ben Witherington have strongly argued that Paul was speaking of theological, not chronological, imminence. Caird argues that Paul often used end-of-the world language in a metaphorical way. Wimbush regards this language as relativizing the present world-order. Witherington stresses the indefiniteness of Paul's language. "Shortened" does not mean "short."[2] On the other hand, the Greek phrase *ho kairos synestalmenos esti* (normally, *the time has been shortened*) has been intensely debated. Oscar Cullmann argued that *kairos* meant critical time of opportunity, but this has not met with widespread support.

Further to this, Bruce Winter, Bradley Blue, and others have strongly argued for a third alternative, namely that this passage may well refer to an impending famine. They appeal to 7:26, which refers to "the impending crisis" (Greek, *dia tēn enestōsan anagkēn*) or literally, the impending necessity or "event that pinches" (i.e., severe pressures). It is more than likely that this refers to shortages and hardships that loomed large in AD. 51.[3] This does not necessarily exclude a dimension of eschatological urgency.

On the whole, this third possibility has much to commend it, and it would certainly underline the situational factors that surround any possible hesitations that Paul might seem to have about the married state. Paul may indicate in 7:7 that the unmarried state has some advantages in the present situation in Corinth, but he concludes that "each has a particular gift (Greek, *charisma*) from God," adding, "one having one kind, and another having a different kind" (7:7b). Both the unmarried state and being married require God's particular gift of enabling for God's call.

---

2. Caird, *The Language and Imagery of the Bible*, 219–71; Wimbush, *Paul the Worldly Ascetic*, 23–48; and Witherington, *Jesus, Paul, and the End of the World*, 27–30.

3. Winter, "Secular and Christian Responses to Corinthian Famines"; and Blue "The House Church at Corinth and the Lord's Supper: Famine, Food Supply, and the Present Distress."

Chapter 17

What is the "appointed time" that suggests people should live as if they had no spouse?

(1 Corinthians 7:29)

The NRSV translates the Greek phrase *ho kairos synestalmenos* by the vague English phrase "the appointed time has grown short" (1 Corinthians 7:29). Because this appointed time has grown short, Paul says, "From now on, let even those who have wives be as though they had none." The KJV/AV has "The time is short," following the Greek literally. Other English versions attempt more idiomatic renderings. The REB has "The time we live in will not last long"; the NJB has, "The time has become limited"; the NEB has "The time we live in will not last long"; while the NIV has "The time is short," returning to the KJV/AV. This variety of translations witnesses to the difficulty of translating Greek into plain English. The clause has been much debated. Caird, Wimbush, Witherington, Winter, Blue, Schrage, Deming, and many others all have a variety of suggestions about its meaning. The verbal participle *synestalmenos,* the perfect passive participle of *systellō* (which occurs in the New Testament only in Acts 5:6) means *shortened.* Wimbush and others are emphatic on this.[1] Danker suggests that the word means "to draw together so as to be less extended,

---

1. Wimbush, *Paul, the Worldly Ascetic,* 50; cf. Cullmann, *Christ and Time,* 39–45 and 121.

IV Paul, Women, and Men

limit, shorten."[2] Most writers in the twentieth century, including Albert Schweitzer, understood that this refers to the time before the parousia or the End.

The following four scholars have their own versions of this proposal. Deming urges that parallels with the "Stoic-Cynic marriage debate" suggest that marriage involved such weighty responsibilities that Paul regarded marriage as incompatible with a Christian life-style.[3] But Paul has such a positive view of marriage in 1 Corinthians 7 that such a theory is unconvincing. Delling argues that Paul's position on marriage and celibacy is so confused and inconsistent as to offer no clear guidance.[4] Larry Yarbrough takes account not only of the Stoic background, but also of rabbinic Judaism. He notes the divisiveness of a two-tier morality in which an "elite" claim a "higher" life-style. Paul's plea is essentially for unity among Christians.[5] Antoinette Wire reaches the conclusion that unity is Paul's aim, though by a different route.[6]

Caird, Wimbush, Withington, Winter, and Blue, however, offer a very different explanation of the use of the term. Caird asks, referring to the Roman Empire, "Does Paul mean that world history is about to come to an end, or simply that, in a period when the old regime is cracking up, Christians must expect to live under harsh social pressure?"[7] He insists that Paul is half-hearted about his so-called asceticism; "the one governing principle is 'I want you to be free from anxiety'" (7:32). In a crucially important statement, Caird writes, "[Paul] regularly used end-of-the-world language metaphorically to refer to that which they [readers] well knew was not the end of the world."[8] Caird, in informal consultation with Ullmann, Oxford colleague and Professor of Semantics, offered this as a *linguistic* critique on much work in New Testament. Other examples come from the Gospels. There is a key difference, Caird maintains, between *chronological imminence* and *theological imminence*. This was one of the confusions of

---

2. Danker, BDAG, 978.
3. Deming, *Paul on Marriage and Celibacy*.
4. Delling, *Paulus' Stellung zu Frau und Ehe*.
5. Yarbrough, *Not Like the Gentiles*.
6. Wire, *The Corinthian Women Prophets*, 14.
7. Caird, *The Language and Imagery of the Bible*, 270.
8. Caird, *The Language and Imagery of the Bible*, 236.

the Thessalonian believers in 1 Thessalonians 5:1–3 and 2 Thessalonians 2:1–8.[9] They understood Paul's eschatology too literally.[10]

Caird's work paved the way for Wimbush, who, similarly, regards 7:29–35 as relativizing the everyday world-order without entailing some chronological prediction, though he is less skeptical than Caird about its time-relation to the parousia of Christ or End. The NRSV translated the Greek, *to loipon*, as "from now on," but Wimbush interprets it as referring to the remaining time before the End, and translates it as "the remaining time," and with Moule regards it as having an imperative force. Yet he says, "The eschatological affirmation is not developed," but the emphasis falls on "the relativizing of worldly things, which comes to expression in the *hōs mē* ('as though . . . none') exhortations."[11] This includes "marrying, weeping, rejoicing, doing business," which are "typical of human worldly activities or responses to stimuli in the world."[12] Wimbush concludes, "The imminence of the End is no longer in focus: the concern seems to be to describe the *perennial* state of affairs in the present order."[13] A question mark is placed against all ordinary or "everyday" things. Wimbush and Caird both hold a "stereoscopic view of the whole situation." Schrage regards Wimbush's perspective as middle position between world-denying asceticism and a positive view of everyday life.[14] His phrase "Paul, the worldly ascetic" sums this up.

Witherington argues that the word *synestalmenos* adds a dimension of indefiniteness to Paul's view, but "Paul is not speaking of some future apocalyptic event, but of an eschatological process already begun."[15] He is not advocating withdrawal from, or renunciation of, the world. Schrage, Wimbush, and Witherington conclude that the world is the sphere where the believer is called to obey God's will.[16]

Bruce W. Winter and B. B. Blue have a radically different approach to the problem. In place of proposals about eschatological imminence, they argue that the threat of famine and food shortages constitute the crisis

---

9. Caird, *The Language and Imagery of the Bible*, 121.
10. Caird, *The Language and Imagery of the Bible*, 184.
11. Wimbush, *Paul, the Worldly Ascetic*, 33.
12. Caird, *The Language and Imagery of the Bible*, 30.
13. Caird, *The Language and Imagery of the Bible*, 34 (his italics).
14. Schrage, *The Ethics of the New Testament*, 226.
15. Witherington, *Jesus, Paul, and the End of the World*, 27–30.
16. Witherington, *Jesus, Paul, and the End of the World*, 29.

(*ho kairos*) that threatens the Christian church in Corinth. They perceive this as a particular threat to those who experience poverty and the fragility of everyday life, which constitutes a pressure.[17] Winter builds a careful case about the "distress" associated with famines in Greece in the reign of Claudius, one of which can be dated around A.D. 51.[18] He cites Tacitus as calling A.D. 51 an "ominous year."[19] Even the commercial prosperity of Corinth may have encouraged inflated prices for grain, putting food out of reach of the poor.

Without doubt Caird has made a breakthrough in the debate about the imminence of the End. The proviso that Paul places on "the world," including marriage, is *theological, not chronological*. In addition to this, there were other reasons that might explain why Paul urges that "those who have wives be as though they had none" (7:29). The exceptional pressures caused by food shortages place a question mark against entering married responsibilities. Winter and Blue have built up a careful argument that suggests that we should not dismiss their case for the circumstantial case for caution about marriage. Yet Caird, Witherington, and perhaps even Wimbush, make a reasonable case for caution about any "this-worldly" entanglements, provided that we do not understand them as chronological predictions. There are various ways in which 1 Corinthians 7:29 need not constitute a puzzle.

---

17. Winter, "Secular and Christian Responses to Corinthian Famines"; Blue, "The House Church at Corinth and the Lord's Supper."

18. Winter reaffirms this in his *Seek the Welfare of the City*, 55–57.

19. Tacitus, *Annals*, 12.43.

Chapter 18

Is an abandoned Christian spouse free to remarry?

(1 Corinthians 7:10–15)

In an article published in 2018 Brian Peterson has pointed out what a fraught issue divorce and remarriage have become today, even in our churches. He remarks, "No other issue has created more angst for pastors and church leaders than the issue of divorce and remarriage. Scarcely is a single family within most churches unscathed by the heartache experienced by a divorce."[1] This modern side of the issue would be bad enough, but when we explore Pauline scholarship and the text of 1 Corinthians 7, we find a wide plurality of interpretations among thinkers.

However, before we come to that, there is scholarly general agreement that a gulf exists between the seriousness with which Jesus and Paul regard the marriage bond, and the very relaxed attitude held by most Greco-Roman society at the time. Few, Seneca says, blush at divorce, and many "reckon their years not by the number of consuls, but by the number of their husbands. They leave home in order to marry and marry in order to divorce."[2] Tacitus also confirms the frequency of divorce in the Julio-Claudian period and time of Nero.[3] Among modern writers, Aline Rousselle points out how seldom the same couple remained married in Roman

---

1. Peterson, "A Possible Precedent for Paul's Teaching on Divorce (and Remarriage?) in 1 Corinthians 7:10–15," 43.

2. Seneca, *De Beneficiis* 3.16.2.

3. Tacitus, *Agricola* 6.1; cf. Musonius, *Fragment* 14.94.2–19.

society, not least because marriage could begin when women were as young as twelve.[4]

By contrast, in 1 Corinthians 7:10 Paul appears to quote the words of Jesus: "The wife should not separate (Greek, *chōristhēnai*) from her husband (Greek, *gynaika apo andros*). In verse 11 he adds, "(But if she does separate, let her remain unmarried or else be reconciled to her husband), and that the husband should not divorce his wife (Greek, *kai andra gynaika mē aphienai*). Most Greek MSS, including ℘11, B, and C, read *chōristhēnai*, aorist passive infinitive, while A, D, F, and G read the present infinitive *chōrizesthai*. To compound the problem of interpretation, ℘46 reads the present imperative *chōrizesthe*, which would imply a change from indirect to direct speech. The aorist may imply *initiating* the separation, while the present stresses the state of being separated. The two verses, when taken together emphasize the mutuality of the separation. The parenthesis (brackets in the UBS Greek Testament, or dashes in the UBS 4th edition) aims to avoid confusing the reader. On top of this, D. L. Dungan insists that in 1 Corinthians 7:10 Paul is directly quoting the words of Jesus.[5] He adds that between the two statements of verse 10 and verse 11 there is a parenthesis. The specific addressees are "those who remarried" (Greek, *gegamēkosin*, dative plural of perfect participle active).

In spite of Dungan's arguments, Collins regards this "charge" as a command of the risen Lord Christ (Greek, *paraggellō*), with accusative and infinitive of indirect speech.[6] The title "Lord" (*Kyrios*) is often used in contexts that require obedience.[7] In most contexts *chorizo* means "to separate," while *aphienai* means "to divorce," as in a legal context, although Wolfgang Schrage argues, "There is scarcely a differentiation."[8] However, W. D. Davies, supported by Bruce and Allison, like Dungan, asserts, "It was the words of Jesus himself that formed Paul's primary source in his work as ethical *didaskalos* (or teacher)."[9] Most writers refer the saying to Mark

---

4. Rousselle, "Body Politics and in Ancient Rome."

5. Dungan, *The Sayings of Jesus in the Churches of Paul*, 82; cf. 83–99.

6. Collins, *First Corinthians*, 264–65; similarly, Witherington, *Women in Earliest Churches*, 31–32.

7. Kramer, *Christ, Lord, and Son of God*, 65–83 and 169–73.

8. Schrage, *Der erste Brief an die Korinther*, vol. 2, 99.

9. Davies, *Paul and Rabbinic Judaism*, 138–39; Allison, "The Pauline Epistles and the Synoptic Gospels."

10:11–12, and also to the Decalogue. Paul is here referring to the alienation between a Christian husband and Christian wife.

In verse 10, Paul insists that if divorce occurs, the couple must not remarry, or else be reconciled with each other. Murphy-O'Connor argues that a man had initiated the separation, whereas Schrage, Hurd, and Wire argue that feminists in Corinth may have encouraged women to separate. The truth is that we cannot be certain.

In 7:12–16 Paul turns to a different, but related, subject. What happens if the Christian partner is abandoned by the unbelieving spouse? Here Paul gives his own apostolic view (whether advice or command), which does not rely on a specific saying of Jesus. The Christian partner is to remain with his or her spouse, *subject to their agreement*. If the unbelieving spouse consents to live with the Christian partner, marriage is better than divorce (NRSV, REB, NIV, NJB, and Collins all translate *aphietō* [from *aphiēmi*] as *divorce*, rather than *separation*). Some hundred years later, Justin illustrates the relevance of Paul's comment when he explains how a woman's lifestyle becomes different when she converts to Christian faith. In spite of her deep desire to go her own way, she is no longer "loose" or "unbridled" (Greek, *akolastainonti*) to please herself, but must stay to try to win her husband to Christian faith.[10]

The phrase "made holy" in verse 14 (Greek, the perfect passive indicative, *hēgiastai*) is controversial, but implies the dynamic influence of the Christian spouse, even on the children. The clause reflects the genuine anxiety of a Christian spouse about whether the new creation and lifestyle could be compromised by intimate living with an unbeliever. Will this relationship somehow damage the new life, if this is a "limb of Christ"? (1 Cor 6:12–20). Paul's reply is that, on the contrary, the unbeliever may be influenced by the new life of the Christian. Collins even argues that the non-Christian husband "participates in God's covenanted people . . . through her."[11] Holiness, as O. R. Jones argues, is not a static quality, but a *disposition* that depends for its manifestation on variable circumstances to which it responds.[12] If the unbeliever is willing to remain in the married relationship, the lifestyle of the Christian cannot but affect the ethos of the home, including prayer, witness, example, and the living out of the gospel.

---

10. Justin, *Apology*, 2.2.
11. Collins, *First Corinthians*, 271
12. Jones, *The Concept of Holiness*, throughout.

IV Paul, Women, and Men

Murphy-O'Connor, Robertson and Plummer, Lightfoot, and others, regard the reference to children as an *a fortiori* argument.[13]

Admittedly, the history of interpretation witnesses to diverse interpretations of these verses. Some vary according to their speculation about anticipations of "exceptions." Irenaeus, for example, cites the protection of the prostitute Rahab and the marriage of Hosea.[14] Tertullian carefully argues that these verses cannot apply to initiating a marriage with unbelievers, but only to Christians who find themselves in an existing marriage with an unbeliever.[15] Bullinger and Matthew Poole believe that Paul implies that the children have the status of members of the covenant.[16] But the most crucial words are "is not bound" (Greek, *ou dedoulōtai*; the perfect passive of *douloō*, "to enslave," "to bind," or "to remain in bondage"). If, as seems likely, Paul is allowing remarriage, this has become known as "the Pauline privilege."

Gordon Fee, among others, argues against this Pauline privilege. He points out that the chapter is in general against remarriage, that *douloō* would have to be used in an unusual way, and that 7:39 implies that only death can break the marriage bond.[17] Ben Witherington is more cautious, stating: "It is doubtful that there is a 'Pauline privilege.'"[18] Others, however take the opposite view. Conzelmann argues, "The Christian is not subjected to any constraint.... He [or she] can marry again."[19] Héring also says, "If the pagan leaves the Christian partner the marriage has been nullified, and the Christian can marry again ... with a member of the Christian Church (*en kyriō*, 7:39)."[20] It is important, he urges, for the Christian to live in peace. Further, R. H. Stein also interprets Paul as reflecting the words of Jesus in Mark 10:11, which soften the absoluteness of a harder approach.[21] Luther also adopts the view allowing remarriage.[22] Others explore the

---

13. Lightfoot, *Notes on the Epistles of St Paul*, 226; Robertson and Plummer, *First Epistle of St Paul to the Corinthians*, 142.

14. Irenaeus, *Against Heresies* 4.20.11.

15. Tertullian, *To his Wife* 2.2; and *Treatise on the Soul* 39.4.

16. Poole, *Commentary on the Bible*, vol. 3, 560.

17. Fee, *First Epistle to the Corinthians*, 303.

18. Witherington, *Women in the Earliest Churches*, 32.

19. Conzelmann, *1 Corinthians: A Commentary*, 123.

20. Héring, *First Epistle to the Corinthians*, 53.

21. Stein, "Is It Lawful for a Man to Divorce his Wife?"

22. Luther, *Luther's Works*, vol. 28, 36–38.

complexities of the debate with reference to the Greco-Roman background, often defending the *douloō* term.²³ All in all, the argument for remarriage in cases where the unbelieving partner is determined to break the bond has much to commend it.

This brings us to Brian Peterson's recent article on this subject, with which we began. He suggests a precedent for Paul's argument for remarriage when an unbelieving partner has abandoned the Christian spouse, which in many ways is no more speculative than precedents for "exceptions" suggestions offered by Irenaeus and others. He focuses mainly on 1 Corinthians 7:15, where Paul says that in certain circumstance the Christian is "free" (Greek, *eleutheros*) to remarry. He suggests that Paul appeals to the Torah for a precedent on remarriage, citing Ezra and Nehemiah, Judges, Hosea, but especially Exodus 4:24–26.²⁴ According to the Exodus account, Moses first married Zipporah, though apparently this was not sanctioned by God (Exod 2:21).

Peterson speculates that she was possibly a worshipper of Baal. Zipporah was by Moses' side in Egypt, but she left Moses when he introduced circumcision, "the sign of the Abrahamic covenant."²⁵ Apparently, Peterson continues, Zipporah had circumcised one son, but would not circumcise the second (Exod 4:26). She therefore abandoned Moses to return to her father in Midian. This is "in an equivalent manner to the unbeliever who abandons a Christian."²⁶ Peterson claims support for this proposal from the LXX of Exodus 28:2. Finally, he regards these events as providing a precedent for Paul's view of remarriage in 1 Corinthians 7:15.

Peterson's view cannot be certain, but it increases the probability that Paul is advocating permission for remarriage in cases where the Christian spouse has simply been abandoned.

---

23. E.g., Deming, *Paul on Marriage and Celibacy*.

24. Peterson, "A Possible Scriptural Precedent for Paul's Teaching on Divorce (and Remarriage?) in 1 Corinthians 7:10–15," 48–56.

25. Peterson, "A Possible Scriptural Precedent for Paul's Teaching on Divorce (and Remarriage?) in 1 Corinthians 7:10–15," 51.

26. Peterson, "A Possible Scriptural Precedent for Paul's Teaching on Divorce (and Remarriage?) in 1 Corinthians 7:10–15," 53.

Chapter 19

How can Christians be mismatched with unbelievers?

(2 Corinthians 6:14)

In 2 Corinthians 6:14 Paul urges, "Do not be mismatched with unbelievers. For what partnership is there between righteousness and lawlessness? Or what fellowship is there between light and darkness?" The AV/KJB has "Be ye not unequally yoked"; the RSV has "Do not be mismated with"; and Barrett translates, "You must not get into double harness with." As Barrett comments, "The metaphor looks back to the Old Testament prohibition of 'mixtures' (Lev. 19:19) where a related word for double harness is used."[1] In Deuteronomy 22:9–10 it is used of forbidding ploughing with an ox and ass yoked together.

Interpretations of to whom or to what "mismatching" applies have varied considerably. Some apply this to inappropriate or immoral sexual intimacy; some apply it to marriage; the most conservative and systematic are the Exclusive Brethren for whom the doctrine of separation, based largely on this verse in 2 Corinthians and Leviticus, has become a key doctrine. For them it includes not only marriage, but also business, education, family, and Holy Communion.[2]

---

1. Barrett, *Second Epistle to the Corinthians*, 195.

2. In 1848 they separated from the Open Brethren, who have held similar but less extreme views. This split originally also related to J. N. Darby's dispensationalist eschatology.

How can Christians be mismatched with unbelievers?

One initial question is whether this passage is part of an interpolation into 2 Corinthians, either a non-Pauline intrusion or an interpolation from another Pauline letter. Barrett sets out the arguments from both sides. One argument in favor of an interpolation is that if 6:14—7:1 is removed, 6:13 and 7:2 are found to connect admirably. Many who do hold that this passage is an intrusion suppose it to be drawn from another Pauline epistle such as the so-called "previous letter" (perhaps 2 Corinthians 10-13), in which case it is still a Pauline text. On the other side, Barrett points out that "Paul not infrequently allowed himself to wander from this point."[3] Two of the scholars most emphatic in arguing that this passage is an interpolation (and a non-Pauline one at that) are Rudolf Bultmann and W. Schmithals. Bultmann states that this section is "typically Jewish," especially offering parallels to the Testament of Levi 19; Schmithals proposes gnostic sources.[4] Fitzmyer and others also cite parallels with the Qumran literature.[5] H-D. Betz is another who disputes the Pauline authorship.[6]

On the other hand, Plummer argues forcefully that the material is genuinely Pauline, in spite of some unexpected vocabulary, which may betray the work of a secretary. He writes, "An interpolator would have chosen a more suitable place [to insert the material]."[7] Hughes, Furnish, Collange, Martin, Thrall, and (more tentatively) Filson, also maintain the Pauline authorship, especially in view of detailed applications of the principle in 1 Corinthians.[8] Furnish is among those who appeal to the similarity with specific cases in 1 Corinthians. Fee also cautions against placing too much emphasis on rare words in this passage.[9]

The other major problem is whether the principle of separation is a general one or whether it applies to more specific cases. Calvin argues, "Many think that here Paul is speaking of marriage, but the context shows

---

3. Barrett, *Second Epistle to the Corinthians*, 194.

4. Bultmann, *Second Letter to the Corinthians*, 175 and 180; cf. Schmithals, "Zwei Gnostishe Glossen."

5. Fitzmyer, "Qumran and the Interpolated Paragraph in 2 Cor. 6:14—7:1."

6. Betz, "2 Corinthians 6:14—7:1: An Anti-Pauline fragment?"

7. Plummer, *Second Epistle of All the Corinthians*, 205.

8. Collange, *Enigmes de la deuxième épître de Paul aux Corinthiens*; Hughes, *Paul's Second Epistle to the Corinthians*, 241-45; Furnish, *II Corinthians*, 372-73; Martin, *2 Corinthians*, 193-95; Thrall, "The Problem of II Corinthians 6:14—7:1 in Some Recent Discussion."

9. Fee, "II Corinthians 6:14—7:1 and Food Offered to Idols."

IV Paul, Women, and Men

clearly that they are mistaken."[10] He believes that the primary application of this is to "outward idolatry." Filson argues that "unlawful sex relations are included," while James Reid applies this passage especially to marriage.[11] But Filson also states, "Paul warns against close ties," so he does not restrict this to immoral relationships. Tasker reminds us that in the pagan city of Corinth Paul advised no permanent relationships with pagans.[12] Martin points out that the Greek present imperative (*mē ginesthe heterozygountes*) means "do not become mismated (or mismatched) with unbelievers." This may suggest that the Corinthians were engaged in the process of joining themselves to unbelievers.

Clearly, Martin continues, Paul is not asking the Corinthians to cease all contact with the gentile world. He recognized that this was an impossibility (e.g., 1 Cor. 5:10, "since then you would need to go out of the world") and he does exhort believers to be good witnesses. He is warning against compromising the integrity of the faith.[13] Martin includes marriage among the many other situations that Paul has in mind. This is underlined by Paul's use of the word "partnership" (Greek, *metochē*). The term may also include other relationships, but, as Hughes comments, "Marriages between Christians and non-Christians were discussed in 1 Corinthians 7:12–15, as well as eating meat that had been offered to idols in the home of an unbeliever (10:27–28), speaking in tongues when unbelievers were present at the service (14:24), and instituting legal proceedings against the Christian brother before unbelievers (6:5–8)."[14] Of all the possibilities, marriage is clearly the most sensitive of the relationships. To imagine two people pulling in different directions in such an intimate condition presents an extremely difficult and unattractive picture.

---

10. Calvin, *The Second Epistle of Paul the Apostle to the Corinthians*, 89.

11. Filson, "Second Corinthians: Exegesis," 352; and Reid, "Second Corinthians: Exposition."

12. Tasker, *Second Epistle of Paul to the Corinthians*, 98.

13. Martin, *2 Corinthians*, 197; Hughes, *Second Epistle*, 246.

14. Hughes, *Second Epistle*, 245.

V
Paul and Moral Concerns

Chapter 20

How can the God of love also reveal his wrath against all ungodliness and wickedness?

(Romans 1:18)

There are at least six considerations that show us that this verse does not present such a surprise or puzzle as we might otherwise imagine.

(1) One difference between God's love and his wrath is that whereas God *is* love through *all eternity*, God's wrath is a situation-related *disposition*. While love belongs *eternally* to God's *being*, wrath remains a *time-bound* manifestation of how he may choose to express himself. *Dispositions* are responses to hypothetical or actual situations. In Romans 1:18, God's wrath is revealed when humankind is ungodly or wicked.

(2) A second difference is that God's wrath is not the "opposite" of his love. The opposite of love is not wrath, but indifference. One analogy, even if partly imperfect, is a parent's love for a child. Lack of love is indifference; wrath can be a response to a dear child's determination to damage or to destroy himself of herself. Anders Nygren observes, "As long as God is God, He cannot behold with indifference that His creation is destroyed."[1]

(3) God is not only our loving heavenly Father, but also Sovereign Governor and Judge of the universe. Justice is entirely his domain. Anselm called attention to this point in his exposition of God's part in the atonement. The atonement, he insisted, is not only a manifestation of God's love,

---

1. Nygren, *Commentary on Romans*, 98.

V Paul and Moral Concerns

but also an expression of his righteous governance of the world.[2] We can hardly imagine a godly or righteous king in ancient Israel who would remain indifferent to flagrant injustice or oppression. We hear this also when the oppressed cry out for his salvation, and long for God's coming to put everything to rights. Perhaps surprisingly to some, the Psalms and Old Testament Writings suggest that believers look forward with gladness to the time when the Lord will come in judgement. For example, "God will judge the peoples with equity. Let the heavens be glad and let the earth rejoice. ... Then shall all the trees of the forest sing for joy before the LORD; for he is coming, for he is coming to judge the earth. He will judge the world with righteousness ... and truth" (Ps 96:10–13). Psalm 67 also exclaims, "Let the nations be glad and sing for joy, for you [God] judge the peoples with equity and guide the nations upon earth" (67:4).

(4) The fourth relates to whether liberalism embodies the whole Christian gospel. In his criticism of the liberal "social gospel," H. Richard Niebuhr (1894–1962) declared that liberalism taught that: "A God without wrath brought men without sin into a kingdom without judgment through the ministrations of a Christ without a cross."[3] The gospel is not to be confused with a liberal aspect of it.

(5) The frequent occurrences of references to God's wrath in the Old Testament remind us that this allusion to his wrath revealed against ungodliness and wickedness is not peculiar to Paul. It is a double liberal myth, first, that Paul stresses God's wrath more than Jesus, and, second, that whereas the Old Testament often stresses God's wrath, the New Testament normally stresses only his love. Jesus pronounces woes on Chorazin, Bethsaida, and Capernaum, and warns them of Hades and God's last judgment (Matt 11:20–24). He also drove out the traders in the temple in his anger (Matt 21:12–13). The book of Revelation likewise speaks of the winepress of the wine of God's wrath (19:15).

So divine wrath is a not uncommon theme in the Bible. In the Old Testament several words denote the wrath or anger of God, including *'aph* (Exod 22:24; Ps 2:2), which occurs at least two hundred times; *khēmā* (Deut 29:23, 18; Ps 2:5), which can mean fury; *'ebrā* (Ps 78:49; Prov 14:35); and *qetseph* (Num 16:46; Ps 38:1). Often God's anger was provoked by oppressors of Israel but it was also stirred up by Israel's own idolatry and sin.

---

2. Anselm, *Why God Became Man*, especially chapters 10–12, 156–62; cf. Vidu, *Atonement, Law, and Justice*, throughout.

3. Niebuhr, *The Kingdom of God in America*, 193.

How can the God of love also reveal his wrath?

Further, in the New Testament the Greek words *orgē* and *thymos* occur more than fifty times over a smaller span of writings. To remove wrath from the biblical portrait of God would require side-stepping a lot of texts.

(6) Romans 1:18 relates to a specific situation. In this chapter (1:18–32) Paul is specifically addressing the sins and wickedness of the gentile, pagan world. He will address Jews in chapter 2. His aim in verses 18–23 is to show that the wrath of God is revealed because the gentiles are without excuse when they sin. G. Stählin provides a full and detailed examination of the nature of the wrath of God, including its causes and effects.[4] The moral chaos of the pagan world is partly an effect of God's wrath as well as its cause. The cause of wrath becomes also its effect.[5] In other words, God's wrath involves his allowing the gentile world to sink even further into its own chosen sin. This pagan world has shown contempt for God, and rejected his love, "exchanging" (Greek, ēllaxan, vv. 23, 25, 26) implanted knowledge of God for idolatry, lies, and unnatural intercourse. Hence, God "gave them up" (Greek, *paredōken*, vv. 23, 25, 26). Later in Romans Paul will sum this up in the words "While we were enemies" (5:10); and "The mind that is set on the flesh is hostile to God" (8:7).

There is a grain of truth in Charles H. Dodd's insistence that God's wrath denotes here "an inevitable process of cause and effect in a moral universe."[6] The truth of this comment lies in the fact that the results of wrath may sometimes be "internal," i.e., bring their own penalty as a result of their causes of wrath. If someone refuses to learn at school, the time will come when needed qualifications for a job will be lacking. Numerous philosophers, biblical exegetes, and theologians endorse this principle. Nevertheless, many scholars, probably the majority, insist that Dodd has unintentionally depersonalized the notion of God's wrath, transforming it into an impersonal system. For this reason, many reject his interpretation as a whole. Paul explicitly states that God's wrath is revealed against all ungodliness and wickedness, i.e., against those who "suppress the truth" (v. 18). As we have noted, wrath against those who deliberately disjoint themselves and cause moral chaos to life constitutes an act of love, rather than the reverse. Some, including Schlatter, have suggested that ungodliness and wickedness correspond respectively to the two tables of the law, namely sin against God and sin against fellow humans.

---

4. Stählin, "*orgē, orgizimai*."
5. Stählin, "*orgē, orgizimai*," 444.
6. Dodd, *Epistle of Paul to the Romans*, 21.

V Paul and Moral Concerns

To conclude, six compelling reasons suggest why we should not be surprised that Paul speaks here of the wrath of God being revealed against ungodliness and wickedness. Indeed, it may well be an expression of his love that he has not been indifferent to the moral chaos that such godlessness and wickedness have brought about.

Chapter 21

What are a wounded conscience and a weak conscience?

(1 Corinthians 8:12)

In 1 Corinthians 8:12, Paul writes, "But when you thus sin against members of your family, and wound (Greek, *molynō*) their conscience when it is weak, you sin against Christ." What does Paul mean by a "wounded" conscience? And what does he mean by a "weak" conscience?

It is unfortunate that so many people wrongly assume that "conscience" is an absolute norm for distinguishing between right and wrong. There is nothing absolute about conscience. Whether our conscience provides a positive or negative verdict upon our conduct depends largely on how our conscience has been instructed and trained. One major interpreter on the subject of conscience, C. A. Pierce, writes that in the New Testament conscience denotes "the pain consequent upon the inception of an act *believed to be* wrong."[1] He argues that it has nothing to do with a "divine voice." (On the other hand, some may appeal to Romans 2:15 about "the law written on their hearts" for a contrary view.[2])

The Greek term for *conscience*, *syneidēsis*, is often translated as *self-awareness* in many biblical passages. In 1911, H. J. Holtzmann argued that New Testament uses of the term had been borrowed from Hellenistic sources. *Knowing* (*eidēsis*) was said to be *with* (*syn*) in the sense of scrutinizing

---

1. Pierce, *Conscience in the New Testament*, 22 (my italics).
2. Pierce, *Conscience in the New Testament*, 13–22.

V Paul and Moral Concerns

one's own conduct. Hence Spicq pointed out in 1938 that in 1 Corinthians 4:4 Paul says that he knows (Greek, *synoida*) nothing against himself (i.e., he does not have a bad conscience). In 1948, Bultmann and Dupont noted affinities between Paul's use of the term and Greek, especially Stoic, usage. But a new stage of New Testament research began with Pierce (1955) and with J. N. Sevenster's *Paul and Seneca* (1961).[3] Pierce argued that there was "insufficient evidence" of such dependence, and that a "weak" conscience in Paul meant an oversensitive one.[4] He linked those with a weak or oversensitive conscience with the "little ones" of Matthew 18:5-6, who can be easily hurt. To inflict hurt or pain is to "wound" someone's conscience.

Robert Jewett chronicled the history of research into conscience in Paul up to 1970.[5] A third stage began with an article by Margaret Thrall, and contributions from Horsley, Gooch, Eckstein, and others. Thrall argued in 1967 that although Pearce's approach was largely correct, he had failed to note positive uses of conscience in Paul, as well as even prospective functions of conscience, when conscience could act as a guide for the future.[6] Horsley (1978) and Gooch (1987) not only agree, but also consider whether "self-awareness" would promote a better translation of 1 Corinthians 8-10.[7] Research is further discussed by H-J. Eckstein and Paul Gardner.[8] The general outcome is that conscience may at times be fallible, and is relative to learned attitudes.

The Old Testament provides little help in the use of the word *syneidēsis*, since Hebrew has no special word for conscience, but normally speaks of the importance of the human heart in this connection. In certain classic passages, the text may point towards our notion of conscience.[9] For example, the narrator speaks of the hardening of Pharaoh's heart in Exodus 7:3, 13, 14, 22; 8:15, 19, 32. In 1 Samuel 24:5 "David was stricken to the

---

3. Sevenster, *Paul and Seneca*, 84-102.
4. Pierce, *Conscience in the New Testament*, 15; cf. 13-20 and 111-30
5. Jewett, *Paul's Anthropological Terms*, 402-46.
6. Thrall, "The Pauline Use of *Syneidēsis*."
7. Gooch, "Conscience in 1 Corinthians 8 and 10."
8. Eckstein, *Der Begriff Syneidēsis bei Paulus* and Gardner, *The Gifts of God and Authentification of the Christian*.
9. Though "our" notion is in fact a range of notions, for there is no agreed account of conscience. For instance, in the history of Christian theology, Franciscans regarded conscience as an expression of feeling and will, while Aquinas and the Dominicans regarded it as a cognitive and reflective capacity.

heart because he had cut of a corner of Saul's cloak." BDB lists various uses of "heart" of which one is *conscience*.

We conclude that a *weak* conscience in Paul is one that is exercised with little confidence and may be oversensitive. A *wounded* conscience is one that has suffered pain and perhaps even damage. In 1 Corinthians 8, those whom Paul ironically calls "the strong" (or overconfident and undersensitive) genuinely taint, pollute, stain, or defile the conscience of the "weaker" brothers and sisters. Moulton and Milligan illustrate the metaphorical force of *molynō*, to wound, from the Papyri. In Oxyrhynchus Papyrus 5:840:16 the word describes a polluted person who walks within a pure area; and BDAG place it within the semantic field of *defile, smear, make impure*, and *render unclean* or *dirty*.[10] The "weak" then react with alarm, disgust, or guilt.[11]

The "strong" think that they have more "knowledge," because Paul had said that an idol was not anything, it did not "really exist" (1 Cor 8:4), so they felt free to share in eating idolatrous temple feasts. In any case, temple feasts were part, they argue, of everyday life. But Paul replies, "It is not everyone who has this knowledge" (8:7a). Some have become accustomed to idols until now, and think of the food they eat as food offered to an actually existing idol, and "their conscience being weak is defiled" (8:7b). Habituation has made their conscience different from that of "the strong." We can imagine a confident Christian patron inviting a poorer Christian "client" to a festive dinner, only to cause damage to the Christian who had a "weaker" conscience. Once the terminology has been appreciated, the text becomes no longer a puzzle.

---

10. Moulton and Milligan, *The Vocabulary of the Greek New Testament Illustrated from the Papyri and Other Non-literary Sources*, 416; and BDAG, 657.

11. Thiselton, *The First Epistle to the Corinthians*, 640.

Chapter 22

Does love involve utter incredulity?
(1 Corinthians 13:7)

In 1 Corinthians 13:7 Paul writes that love "believes all things" (NRSV). This cannot be faulted for deviating from the Greek (*panta pisteuei*), which the English translation accurately reflects. It is usually translated by some equivalent, e.g., "believeth all things" (AV/KJV; RV; NKJV; and ESV), reflecting at least five English translations, including the NRSV. A recent commentator, R. F. Collins (1999), affirms the wording of these versions: "believes everything." The NIV's "always trusts" invites the same suspicion of credulity or gullibility. The New Living Translation (NLT) has "never loses faith," which seems slightly to ease the problem, and the NEB reading, "There is no limit to its faith," may be better. The NJB seems to avoid the problem by rendering: [Love] "is always ready to make allowances, to trust, to hope, and to endure whatever comes." But this is almost a paraphrase of the Greek, and, like the NIV's "always ready to trust," it does not entirely avoid credulity.

In the Greek text, however, the fourfold repetition of *panta* ("all") seems to convey what Jean Héring called "the absence of all limits."[1] The repetition of "all" excludes the limits of love rather than defining an all-inclusive content. The REB is one of the few major English versions to appreciate that this is best rendered in modern English by negating a series of negations: "There is nothing love cannot face; there is no limit to its faith, its hope, its endurance." Without such a careful protection of Paul's intended

---

1. Héring, *The First Epistle of St. Paul to the Corinthians*, 141.

meaning, this text may threaten to give credence to Friedrich Nietzsche's concept of Christianity as "servile mediocrity," or to Karl Marx's notion of Christianity as the opium of the people. Nietzsche wrote of Christianity that it "has sided with everything weak, low and botched; it has made an ideal out of antagonism towards . . . strong life."[2] If love literally believes everything, then Nietzsche might be pardoned for proclaiming that "truth has been turned topsy-turvy" and that Paul claims to be above the law.[3]

In my commentary on the Greek text, I suggested the translation, "Love never tires of support, never loses faith, never exhausts hope, never gives up."[4] The four occurrences of "never" correspond to Paul's fourfold "all." The REB offers a good precedent for this basic strategy. John Calvin, followed by F. Lang, commented that it is "not that a Christian . . . strips himself of wisdom and discernment, . . . not that he has forgotten how to distinguish black from white," but simply that he gets rid of "ill-founded suspicion."[5] C. Spicq says that love gives "a favourable interpretation of everything."[6] This coheres with suggestions from O. Wischmeyer and H. J. Blair.[7]

In the light of all these studies and commentaries, and in the light of the whole Greek text, it is clear that the translation "love believes all things" does not convey what is in Paul's mind. Literalistic translations of the Greek do not always convey the most accurate sense. The better translation may recall the words of Song of Solomon 8:6–7: "Many waters cannot quench love, neither can floods drown it. If one offered for love all the wealth of one's house, it would be utterly scorned." Thus C. F. G. Heinrici could speak of "the invincible power of good."[8]

---

2. Nietzsche, *The Antichrist*, 130.

3. Nietzsche, *The Dawn of Day*, 67–70.

4. Thiselton, *First Epistle to the Corinthians*, 1057.

5. Calvin, *First Epistle of Paul to the Corinthians*, 278; Lang, *Die Briefe an die Korinther*, 185.

6. Spicq, *Agapē in the New Testament*, vol. 2, 159. Cf. Augustine, on believing the best about people, in *Confessions* 10.3.

7. Blair, "First Corinthians 13 and the Disunity at Corinth."

8. Heinrici, *Das erste Sendschreiben des Apostel Paulus an der Korinther*, 421.

Chapter 23

Loveless brass and a flourish of cymbals?
(1 Corinthians 13:1)

The KJV/AV may have yielded a memorable translation of 1 Corinthians 13:1c ("I am become as sounding brass or a tinkling cymbal"), but for most modern readers it has become difficult to understand why these words have anything to do with "if I have not love" (13:1b). What is "sounding brass"? Further, today a crash of cymbals that "tinkles" sounds absurd! Cymbals may "crash" (NJB), make a "clanging" noise (NRSV), or sound a "flourish" or "reverberate" (my translation), but hardly make a "tinkle"![1]

Translations of "sounding brass" (KJB/AV) vary: NRSV, NASB, ESV, and Moffatt have "noisy gong"; NJB has "a gong booming"; NIV has "a resounding gong"; and J. B. Phillips has "blaring brass." In this particular case, the NIV comes probably nearest to some current research, while NJB and Phillips (followed by Raymond Collins) are tolerably near. However, both recent research on lexicology and musicology and the direction of Paul's argument point in the same direction. The most decisive research comes from W. W. Klein and W. V. Harris in specialist articles.[2] The Greek for "resounding gong" is *chalkos* ēchōn, and for "*reverberating cymbals*" is *kymbalon alalazon*. Harris discusses the phenomenon of acoustic resonance systems. He refers to Vitruvius' work, *On Architecture*, written around 30 B.C. Vitruvius records how the material of bronze (*chalkos*) was

---

1. Thiselton, *First Epistle to the Corinthians*, 1026.
2. Klein, "Noisy Gong or Acoustic Vase?"; and Harris, "'Sounding Brass' and Hellenistic Technology."

constructed in such a way as to amplify sound by functioning as an acoustic resonator, and a resonating acoustic jar. This was not a musical instrument, and would have had varying pitch.

The KJB/AV "sounding" is correct if it means "sound-producing," as if an ancient equivalent to a megaphone or amplifier, not a musical instrument. Likewise, the Greek ēcheō means, at least here, to transmit sound, not to pitch a note. The verb is often used in the context of the roar of the sea and a clap of thunder. Paul uses the continuous present participle, as in the LXX of Psalm 45:4 and Wisdom 17:18. The Greek *alalazon* underlines the continuing resonances which lack musical pitch. Harris adds that bronze vases or resonating jars would be placed in niches around the periphery of an auditorium, and that such a system operated in Corinth in the second century B.C. Later the Roman governor Lucius Mummius had them removed and sold to raise public funds. Paul's readers, he concludes, would have known of these bronze jars, which projected the voices of actors on stage.

Klein develops Harris's view. He notes that Lenski and Grosheide view it as a musical instrument, and that James Moffatt compares it with "gongs" used in pagan temples, especially those of Dionysius and Cybele. This last suggestion has been convincingly rejected by C. Forbes.[3] Klein concludes that we must reject the supposed temple context of pagan religious ecstasy, and understand that Paul compares tongues without love with "a reverberation, an empty sound coming out of a hollow, lifeless, vessel."[4]

On the other hand, Klein argues, *kymbalon alalazon* was probably a musical instrument. He rejects R. L. Laurin's view that it referred to metal castagnettes (modern castanets), but argues that *kymbē* denotes a hollow, shallow, metallic dish, which is struck against its partner to give a resounding note. The Greek LXX translates the Hebrew *metsilttaim* (from *tsalal*, to clash, crash, or clang, e.g., 1 Chr 13:8). In 1 Kings 18:6, however, it is just arguable, he says, that it might be derived from a three-cornered instrument like a triangle, which would make KJB/AV "tinkling" perhaps less ridiculous. Modern musicologists distinguish the *crotal*, which is of Turkish origin, and could be hit head-on by a club or hammer.[5] This is different from a modern cymbal.

---

3. Forbes, *Prophecy and Inspired Speech*, 135–39.
4. Klein, "Noisy Gong or Acoustic Vase?" 288.
5. Kruckenberg, *The Symphony Orchestra and its Instruments*, 193–95.

V Paul and Moral Concerns

The direction of Paul's argument confirms this lexicography. The combined Greek words imply a loud attention-seeking resonance and noise. The noise is unloving because it calls attention to the self, and is, in effect, self-glorying. J. Todd Sanders has since accepted Klein's argument in favor of the empty, noisy, negative character of the resonating jar, but understands the Greek ē to mean "than" rather than "or."[6] He interprets the verse to mean that without love, we should promote or hear a blaring, resonating, noise, rather than a pleasant, tuneful, sound. His argument deserves respect, but does not detract from our main point about acoustic resonators. Paul suggests that even if someone is speaking in tongues, if they do so without love, they are merely, like acoustic resonators, all show without any substance for others.

Since chapter 13 is so rhythmic and poetic, many have doubted whether Paul personally composed this chapter. Paul's style is usually argumentative and logically analytical. In 1 Corinthians 13, however, we have a poetic, rhythmic, reflective style, which is seldom apparent in Paul. Yet on the other hand, James Moffatt, C. T. Craig, and others suggest, in Craig's words, "On closer examination it is seen that almost every word in the chapter has been chosen with this particular situation at Corinth in mind. . . . The mood is instructive fully as much as it is lyrical."[7] And Paul, while normally argumentative in style, could be lyrical, as in his shout of triumph in Romans 8:31–39. It is plausible to suppose that Paul had long reflected on the situation in Corinth, and had begun to formulate a rhythmic expression of the problem, which he then interposed in 1 Corinthians. For example, "Love is not inflated with its own importance"; "love does not burn with envy" (13:4, my translation); "it does not behave with ill-mannered impropriety" (13:5). Ill-mannered impropriety occurred at the Lord's Supper (11:17–34); envy occurred in 3:1–4, and so on.

I first suggested this hypothesis in my early Tyndale Lecture on 1 Corinthians in the 1960s, and repeated it in my two commentaries in 2000 and 2006. And the hypothesis still seems to hold water.

---

6. J. Todd Sanders, "A New Approach to 1 Cor. 13:1."
7. Craig, "The First Epistle to the Corinthians," 165.

Chapter 24

Curses by Paul

(1 Corinthians 16:22; Galatians 1:8–9)

To many modern minds, declaring a "curse" (Greek, ētō *anathema*, let him be *anathema*) on those who do not love the Lord (1 Cor 16:22) seems even harsher and more intolerant than pronouncing a "curse" (Greek, *anathema estō*, let him be accursed) on those who "proclaim to you a gospel contrary to what we proclaimed to you" (Gal 1:8, repeated in Gal 1:9). In these days when "tolerance" seems to be prized as one of the highest virtues, to "curse" those who teach false doctrine may seem harsh enough, but to place all who do not love the Lord under the same condemnation seems to breach every plea to be patient and not judgmental. On the face of it, here is a true puzzle.

Manfred Brauch makes the case extremely well for the difficulty of Galatians 1:8–9. He argues that in Romans 2:1–4 Paul lays down the principle "that judgment passed on others is in some sense 'reflexive,' that is, when we pass judgement on others, we condemn ourselves at the same time."[1] We are all sinners (Rom 3:23). Paul repeats the warning not to judge others in Romans 14:1–13. Each disciple is responsible to the Lord (Rom 14:4, 10). Further, in Romans 12:14, Paul echoes the words of Jesus, "Bless those who persecute you; bless and do not curse." In Romans 12:21, Paul says, "Overcome evil with good."[2] Jesus himself, Brauch continues, said, "Do not judge, or you too will be judged. For in the same way you judge others,

---

1. Brauch, *Hard Sayings of Paul*, 192.
2. Brauch, *Hard Sayings of Paul*, 193.

V Paul and Moral Concerns

you will be judged" (Matt 7:1, 2; his translation). Jesus adds that our own vision is so impaired that it is sheer hypocrisy to try to remove the sawdust particle in the other's eye (7:3, 5). Jesus came into the world not to condemn it, but to save it (John 3:17). He wept over Jerusalem (Luke 19:41) and spoke forgiveness to the criminal on the cross (Luke 23:39-43).[3] Paul's words in Galatians 1:9 seem to conflict with all this.

Nevertheless, Brauch continues, Jesus also pronounces judgments. He calls the religious leaders of Israel "sons of the devil" (John 8:44), and those who oppose his ministry "an evil generation" (Luke 11:29), who will be condemned (Luke 11:31-32). He declares that there will be no forgiveness for those who oppose the Holy Spirit; they will be condemned eternally (Matt 12:31-32). Jesus calls teachers of the law and Pharisees "children of hell" (Matt 23:15), whitewashed tombs, and a brood of vipers (Matt 23:33).[4]

In Galatians 1:8-9 the issue at stake is life-giving doctrine. As we commented in our discussion of the wrath of God (Rom 1:18), the opposite of love is not wrath, but indifference, especially when someone is bent on self-destruction or the destruction of others. It is possible for today's fashion of prizing "tolerance" to go too far. If everything is permitted, no standards remain. In Galatians, Paul faces a life-and-death struggle for the gospel. Yet is it not extreme to "curse" those who seek to replace the true gospel by reliance on the law, even if Paul sees this as nullifying the work of Christ? Guthrie comments on Galatians 1:8: "Here was no outburst of personal anger because men were forsaking what Paul had preached. . . . The essence of the gospel itself was at stake."[5]

Betz describes this as a "self-curse," in which "The relationship between the two curses in vv. 8 and 9 is more subtle than a mere parallelism."[6] The second curse, he says applies the first curse to the present situation. Betz also cites parallels with "the magical concept according to which the curse . . . becomes automatically effective."[7] But Vernon Neufeld, Dieter Neufeld, and Anthony Thiselton regard the curse as a performative speech-act that has nothing to do with magic and is certainly not automatic.[8] In

---

3. Brauch, *Hard Sayings of Paul*, 193.
4. Brauch, *Hard Sayings of Paul*, 194 (his translations of texts).
5. Guthrie, *Galatians*, 64.
6. Betz, *Galatians*, 52.
7. Betz, *Galatians*, 53.
8. Thiselton, "The Supposed Power of Words in the Biblical Writings"; Thiselton, "Curse"; V. H. Neufeld, *The Earliest Christian Confessions*; D. Neufeld, *Re-conceiving Texts*

Curses by Paul

addition to this, Anders Eriksson insists that it is important to take full account of the rhetorical dimension of these "curse" pronouncements.[9] (Eriksson focuses on 1 Corinthians 16:21–24, not on Galatians 1:8–9).

In my survey of the meanings of "curse" in Scripture, I pointed out that it usually stands in opposition to *bless* (Hebrew, *bārakh*) in the Hebrew Bible, and is cognate with Hebrew *kherem* (or *kh-r-m*, disaster).[10] Both terms, bless and curse, occur in the Shechemite Decalogue of Deuteronomy 27:15–26, and in the blessing of Jacob (Gen 27:29). *Kh-r-m* occurs forty-eight times in the Hebrew mood called the *hiphil*, and twenty-nine times as a noun. The LXX translation of "curse" is *anathema*, which Paul uses in Galatians 1:8–9 and 1 Corinthians 16:22. Sometimes the word denotes abuse or disrespect, but it can also denote being outside the covenant.

The "word-magic" view originated with Hempel (1915) and Pedersen (1926), in which a curse was equivalent to an incantation, by analogy with the Balaam narrative (Num 22:6), where a curse cannot be recalled once it has been uttered.[11] In 1923, Mowinckel assimilated such a view, followed by Grether (1934), Dürr, Ringgren, and Zimmerli. But this view lost favor in the 1960s. Herbert Brichto undertook a more careful linguistic and exegetical study, exposing several fallacies in Hempel. Curses, he argued, could function as *prayers to God*. More important still, the *covenant* forms the primary background to them, as in Deuteronomy 27:15–26.[12] Brichto's approach, especially on "blessing," was endorsed by Wehmeier.[13] The final confirmation was provided by work on performative utterances and speech-act theory by Austin, Evans, Searle, and in biblical studies, by Thiselton and Briggs.[14]

Eriksson then showed the importance of the rhetorical and liturgical context of such utterances. Robert Gordon in 1996 underlined the view that much depends on the status of the speaker, and, again, *on the covenantal framework* of the utterance. Kuhn argues that the word *anathema* occurs only five times in Paul, although it is also found in a pagan table

---

as Speech-Acts; and Evans, *The Logic of Self-Involvement*; and several others.

9. Eriksson, *Traditions as Rhetorical Proof*, especially 290–313.

10. Thiselton, "Curse," 810–12.

11. Hempel, "Die Israelitischen Anschauungen von Segen und Fluch im Lichte altorientalscher Parallelen"; and Pedersen, *Israel: Its Life and Culture*.

12. Brichto, *The Problem of "Curse" in the Hebrew Bible*.

13. Wehmeier, *Der Segen im Alten Testament*.

14. Cf. also Thiselton, *Thiselton on Hermeneutics*, 51–150; Briggs, *Words in Action*.

of curses from Megara.[15] The meaning in Paul differs from pagan usage, and, as Gordon stresses, is covenantal.[16] Hence, in a covenant context, in comparing Christian faith with bondage to the law, he says that a person is either "in" or "out," in language that anticipates or reflects excommunication from the church in 1 Corinthians 5:5. Blessing and *anathema* represent two contrasting "ways" of living and status, akin to covenant loyalty or a rejection of it. The three lexica of Danker (BDAG), Grimm-Thayer, and Moulton-Milligan, do not comment in sufficient detail to help further, but they do not exclude our interpretation, and they confirm our lexicographical approach.[17]

To return to Eriksson's helpful comments on the rhetoric of 1 Corinthians 16:22, he observes, "It is not directly discernible how a prayer for the Lord's return can provide a reason for a conditional curse."[18] He answers, "Both the concept of 'loving the Lord' and the curse belong to covenantal terminology and point to the covenant as the context for the *enthymēme*."[19] (*Enthymēme* is used here in the sense defined by Aristotle in the context of the logic of deduction: it is where a syllogistic argument relies on an implicit, unexpressed premise.)[20] Moores comments, "Paul [is] being essentially reasonable where he treats his addressees as co-beneficiaries of good concrete evidence for their shared conviction ... Premises are constantly being taken for granted where it is far from easy to identify precisely what they are."[21] In the case of Paul's curses, the unstated premise is the underpinning covenantal context. Eriksson concludes, "The consequence of breaking the covenant is curses and for keeping the covenant, blessings."[22] This applies to both 1 Corinthians 16:22 and Galatians 1:8–9. It also removes those texts from outdated notions of word magic and enchantments.

---

15. Kuhn, "anathema," 81.

16. Admittedly some still focus on pagan parallels, and do not take sufficient note of the covenantal context.

17. BDAG, 63; Thayer, *A Greek-English Lexicon of the New Testament*, 37; and Moulton and Milligan, *The Vocabulary of the New Testament*, 33.

18. Eriksson, *Traditions as Rhetorical Proof*, 292.

19. Eriksson, *Traditions as Rhetorical Proof*, 292.

20. Moores, *Wrestling with Rationality in Paul*, 5–32.

21. Moores, *Wrestling with Rationality in Paul*, 28.

22. Eriksson, *Traditions as Rhetorical Proof*, 293.

Chapter 25

"Heaping burning coals on their heads"—Is this a Christian sentiment?

(Romans 12:20)

This phrase seems to contradict its context in Romans, where Paul is urging his readers precisely not to take revenge on people (v. 17), but to live peaceably with all (v. 18). We are to leave "vengeance" to God alone (v. 19). The NRSV translation reflects the Greek text accurately. The crucial phrase is Paul's quotation from the LXX of Proverbs 25:21–22. James Dunn calls the question of how the quotation from Proverbs is to be understood "a tricky issue."[1] The dispute, he adds, is ancient. Similarly, Fitzmyer writes, "The meaning of Prov. 25:22a is quite obscure."[2]

At least ten English versions (including the AV/KJB, NIV, NAS, NJB, and ESV) adopt virtually the same English translation. The odd one out is the "God's Word Translation," which replaces "heaps coals of fire on their heads" by "making them feel guilty and ashamed." This is an interpretation rather than a translation. However, Augustine and Jerome understood this to be the meaning of Proverbs 25:21–22 and Romans 12:20, and it is probably the majority view among modern interpreters. Robert Jewett comments:

> [It] has been explained as a mistaken metaphor due to ambiguities in the Hebrew text, [or] as a metaphor for "burning pangs of

---

1. Dunn, *Romans 9–16*, 750.
2. Fitzmyer, *Romans*, 657.

shame" felt by an adversary moved by the generosity of the persecuted, as a sophisticated form of revenge by increasing the guilt of the persecutor; and [also] . . . a reference to an Egyptian ritual of a sinner carrying a dish of hot coals on the head to symbolize repentance. None of these options is fully satisfactory.[3]

In the Hebrew, the participle *khōteh* means "remove" (i.e., *remove* coals from the head). But this would not reflect the meaning of the Greek LXX, which Paul quotes.

At the same time, Jewett considers that the Synoptic tradition about loving the enemy and overcoming evil with good is decisive for the meaning of Romans 12:20. Augustine, Jerome, and several of the church fathers, therefore, understand the verb in Proverbs, as we have noted, to mean "feel burning pangs of shame."[4] Ernst Käsemann similarly speaks of "the remorse and humiliation of the adversary (the majority view)."[5] The one difficulty, as Fitzmyer observes, is that this symbolic use of "coals of fire" is not otherwise attested. This, however, remains in line with N. T. Wright's comment, "Let your wrath smoulder away quietly. . . . Allow God to do justice. . . . Paul recommends a shockingly positive line of action."[6]

---

3. Jewett, *Romans*, 777.

4. Augustine, *Exposition of Paul's Epistle to the Romans*, 63.3-4, *On Christian Doctrine*, 3.56 (Eng. *NPNF*, series 1, vol. 1, 573), on figurative meaning; and Jerome, *Letters*, 120.1, on difficult passages.

5. Käsemann, *Commentary on Romans*, 349.

6. Wright, "The Letter to the Romans," 714.

Chapter 26

Death-penalty for immorality with no second chance?

(1 Corinthians 5:5)

In 1 Corinthians 5:4b–5, Paul writes: "When you are assembled, and my spirit is present with the power of our lord Jesus Christ, you are to hand this man over to Satan for the destruction of the flesh, so that his spirit may be saved in the day of the Lord." Almost all writers and commentators interpret this verse as a reference to a sentence of death for the immoral man whom Paul describes in v. 1. He writes, "It is actually reported that there is sexual immorality among you, and of a kind that is not found even among pagans; for a man is living with his father's wife. And you are arrogant! Should you not rather have mourned, so that he who has done this would have been removed from among you?" Ernst Käsemann represents the vast majority of commentators when he writes that this passage "obviously entails the death of the guilty."[1] The second alternative is that Paul consigns the immoral man to severe, painful, suffering.[2] A third group acknowledges that this is a very difficult verse.[3]

The difficulty for all these majority interpretations is the huge and variable semantic range of the Greek word *sarx* ("flesh") in Paul's usage. One major study of this term has been undertaken by Alexander Sand in a

---

1. Käsemann, *New Testament Questions of Today*, 71; also Schneider, "*olethros*."

2. Héring, *First Epistle to the Corinthians*, 35; Thrall, *1 and 2 Corinthians*, 40.

3. Barrett, *First Epistle to the Corinthians*; Lietzmann, *An die Korinther*, 29 and 173–74.

book devoted to the subject. He concludes that "flesh" and "spirit" in Pauline usage always denote "two different parts" of a man *as a whole*.[4] Either "flesh" or "spirit," he says, can denote the *whole* man. Now "the destruction of the flesh," according to Sand, does not necessarily denote death. Sand envisages that the immoral man may eventually reach a state of repentance that will enable him to begin again.

Where do we go from here? Several questions need to be addressed. For example, does Paul use *sarx* (flesh) for denotation and description, or might he use it for evaluation? Descriptive uses of language concern the state of affairs that is being described rather than attitudes or outlooks on the part of the speaker or writer. By contrast, evaluative uses of language express verdicts or attitudes, characteristically, for example, of praise or blame, or of commendation or disapproval. In practice, language is seldom used exclusively for pure description or pure evaluation, although this may sometimes occur. Usually two or more functions overlap. A term such as "murder" may both describe an act of bringing death, but may also serve to express an attitude of blame or disapproval at the same time. A descriptive content does not exclude the function of evaluation.

Paul, it has long been recognized, uses *sarx* both descriptively and evaluatively. Sometimes in its adjectival forms, *sarkinos* and *sarkikos* more characteristically express evaluation, as when the NEB signposts this by translating it as "unspiritual." This becomes clear in such passages as 1 Corinthians 3:1-3, where being "fleshly" stands in contrast to having a "spiritual" (i.e., non-bodily) or "Spiritual" (i.e., of the Holy Spirit) attitude. Similarly, in Romans 7:14 *sarkinos* expresses an evaluation (the law is "spiritual" but "I am fleshly"). This evaluation is negative, even though it may apply to a pious and zealous Jew, who delighted in God's law.

The heart of the issue comes to light when we examine Paul's frequent uses of *sarx* to express his evaluation of people as self-reliant or self-sufficient. Bultmann explicitly observes that, especially in Romans and Galatians, "flesh" in Paul's use may denote "the self-reliant attitude of the man who puts his trust in his own strength and in that which is controllable by him.... The attitude of self-reliance finds its extreme expression in man's 'boasting' (*kauchasthai*)."[5] J. A. T. Robinson adds: "The flesh ... represents

---

4. Sand, *Der Begriff 'Fleisch' in den Paulinischen Hauptbriefen*, 144.
5. Bultmann, *Theology of the New Testament*, vol. 1, 240 and 242; cf. 239-46.

human self-sufficiency," of the kind that is instanced in 1 Corinthians 3:21, "glorying in men," or 2 Corinthians 1:9, "trusting in ourselves."[6]

In relation to 1 Corinthians 5:5, the allusion to pride is unmistakable. Paul has just protested in 5:2: "And you are arrogant! Should you not rather have mourned, so that he who has done this may be removed from among you?" Long ago, A. D. Nock declared, "Many of the converts, convinced that they were on a new plane of life, felt that they could do anything; they were kings (4:8), they were in the Spirit, they were dead to the flesh and emancipated—so that their physical conduct might seem to them a matter of indifference; thus they were altogether different from the unchanged men around them."[7]

We may link this with the Corinthian slogan, "All things are lawful to me" (*panta moi exestin*, 6:12). They expected revision of more conservative attitudes towards moral issues (5:1—6:20). Hence Paul rebukes them: "Your boasting is not a good thing" (5:6); "Should you not rather have mourned?" (5:2). On the other hand, some in Corinth declared, "We have already become rich; we have become kings" (1 Cor 4:7). Such attitudes could suggest a version of proto-Gnosticism, as W. Schmithals suggests; or can be explained by an over-realized eschatology at Corinth, as I have argued; or simply be due to an exaggerated radicalization of Paul's message of freedom from the law.[8] Gaston Deluz comments:

> These Corinthians are lucky. Already they enjoy favours that the apostles could only hope for. They no longer "hunger and thirst after righteousness"; they are filled; in . . . the Spirit, they have eaten to satiety. . . . In short, the Messianic kingdom seems to have come to Corinth and these people have been given their thrones, while the apostles dance attendance and are placed with the servants.[9]

The wider context in 1 Corinthians, therefore, suggests that Paul's major concern about "the destruction of the flesh" is to use "the flesh" to mean not the physical body, but the disposition of pride, arrogance, self-reliance, self-sufficiency, and all that characterizes the community as just described. Clearly the immoral man had even surpassed the worst of the Corinthian community. Perhaps he had considered himself daringly bold

---

6. J. A. T. Robinson, *The Body*, 25–26.

7. Nock, *St Paul*, 174.

8. Schmithals, *Gnosticism in Corinth*; Schmithals, "The Corpus Paulinum and Gnosis"; Thiselton, "Realized Eschatology at Corinth."

9. Deluz, *A Companion to 1 Corinthians*, 46–47.

in ignoring the law and customary morality. Karl Barth is surely right when he concludes that the central nerve of 1 Corinthians lies in Paul's warning "Let no one glory in men" (3:21), and "He who glories, let him glory in the Lord" (1:31). These respectively represent the negative and positive thrust of the first four chapters.

What are we to make of Paul's purpose-clause, namely "so that his spirit may be saved in the day of the Lord" (5:5b)? The cessation of pride and arrogance suggests that the immoral man has undergone a period of genuine repentance. This cannot refer to some post-mortem transformation, for such a concept is entirely absent from Paul. A huge mass of Protestant scholarship has rejected any possible allusion to purgatory. Paul would hardly have presupposed an allusion to such an unknown concept, without carefully explaining what he had in mind. The clearest and most obvious explanation is that on this occasion Paul is using the term *flesh* in its *evaluative* sense, not in its *descriptive* sense as referring to the human body. Therefore, this passage does not imply that Paul expects the destruction of the immoral man. Paul hopes for the crushing of his fleshly pride and self-sufficiency. This will occur, Paul hopes, together with a new attitude on the part of the community in Corinth. It will bring about an end to the man's supposed privileged status as one of the boldest who were freed from the law; and, no longer shielded by his companions, his humbling will bring him fully to his senses.[10]

---

10. I have expanded this argument in greater detail in an article in the *Scottish Journal of Theology* in 1973. Thiselton, "The Meaning of *SARX* in 1 Corinthians 5:5: A Fresh Approach in the Light of Logical and Semantic Factors."

Chapter 27

Is the epistle to Titus incurably racist?
(Titus 1:12–13)

In Titus 1:12–13, we find apparently the most flagrant, stereotyped, generalizing, racially prejudiced saying in the New Testament. The Epistle says, "It was one of them, their very own prophet, who said: 'Cretans are always liars, vicious brutes, lazy gluttons.' That testimony is true" (NRSV). Astonishingly, since around 1900, at least twenty-four specific commentaries (the overwhelming majority) go to the trouble of trying to rescue the author from making tactless and racist truth-claims about Cretans, rather than discussing the function of a logical paradox. As I shall argue, this logical paradox implies truth-claims about the *language* used in the church of which Titus has oversight.

Even Calvin follows patristic interpreters in understanding the saying as a tradition about Cretan factual or empirical claims to possess the tomb of the supposedly immortal Jupiter. He comments on verse 13a, "Paul accepts the truth of what he has spoken, for there is no doubt that the Cretans ... were very wicked men. The apostle ... would not have spoken so harshly of the Cretans without the best of reasons."[1] This curious but uniform misinterpretation rests on a simple confusion between an *ordinary* descriptive proposition, which states *facts*, and a *logical* proposition, which expresses a *logical* paradox, though which has implications of a factual nature.

---

1. Calvin, *Second Epistle to the Corinthians and the Epistles to Timothy, Titus, and Philemon*, 363–64.

V Paul and Moral Concerns

In 1906, Rendle Harris argued that the accusation concerning Cretans being liars concerned only the religious claim that Zeus was buried in Crete.[2] In more recent years, Dibelius and Conzelmann, J. N. D. Kelly, and C. Spicq effectively argue for the *contingent, factual, or socio-historical* status of the proposition by looking beyond it to the empirical grounds which may seem to validate the declaration.[3] A. T. Robertson, E. F. Scott, C. K. Barrett, A. T. Hanson, Gordon Fee, Philip Towner, J. D. Quinn, and George Knight, feature among the twenty-four commentaries that we have cited above, even if a few partly begin to recognize aspects of logical paradox, alongside a merely factual or descriptive account of this puzzling proposition.[4]

The best-known version of the liar paradox was probably formulated by Eubulides of Miletus in the fourth century B.C.E. But earlier the liar paradox had been known since at least the exploration of Zeno of Elea, who flourished in the fifth century B.C.E., and was a pupil of Parmenides. In terms of purely formal logic, Parmenides pointed out, in opposition to the pluralism of Heraclitus of Ephesus and Pythagoras of Samos, only three logically alternative characterizations of reality remain logically possible. Either (1) Being or Reality *is*; or (2) Being or Reality *is not*; or (3) Being *both is and is not*. Of these options, the third excludes itself as self-contradictory; and the second is logically problematic. Only the first proposition, he argued, remains, and asserts the existence of one, unchanging, reality. Zeno formulated several paradoxes of motion. These include the Dichotomy, Achilles and the Tortoise, and the Arrow, all of which offer variants on the same theme.

The key point about these well-known logical paradoxes is that they are *not everyday, descriptive, propositions* about the world. They are not empirical and contingent. In each case, they are *metacritical* propositions about the *structure of language*. Ludwig Wittgenstein decisively observed this distinction. Logical tautologies say nothing about the world; only about logic and language. Most of his logical remarks in the *Tractatus* and the *Philosophical Investigations* serve the logic or grammar of *concepts*; they do not describe the world. For example, he compared the proposition, "He

---

2. In the *Expositor* 7 (1906) 305–11.

3. Dibelius and Conzelmann, *Die Patoralbriefe*, 101–3; Kelly, *Pastoral Epistles*, 233; and Spicq, *Les Épitres Pastorals*, 242.

4. The references are listed in an extended article in Thiselton, "The Logical Role of the Liar Paradox in Titus 1:12, 13."

believes it, but it is false"; with "I believe it, but it is false." The latter makes no sense. The point of the comparison is to show that "My own relation to my words is wholly different from other people's."[5] Similarly, Gilbert Ryle took up several of the long-standing logical paradoxes of the ancient world to show their genuine importance to life, under the book title *Dilemmas*.[6]

The importance of Zeno's logical paradox lay in the consequences to which it led, not least in the use of *language, logic, and communication*. In my article on Titus 1:12–13,[7] I aimed to show that this account of the function of logical paradoxes lasted from the ancient world to such modern examples as Cantor's paradox (1899) and the earlier Burali-Forti paradox, both in mathematics. *Is it, then, inconceivable that the use of the well-known paradox of the liar in the Pastoral Epistles should address meta-language, rather than function to describe Cretans?*

The paradox in Titus is clear: a Cretan is quoted as saying that Cretans are always liars. If he was telling the truth then his claim is false for as a Cretan himself he too is a liar and cannot be trusted. But if he was not telling the truth then his claim that Cretans are liars is a lie—in fact they speak truthfully. But then he too would be speaking truthfully. A paradox! What Paul is doing, I shall argue, is using this paradox to talk about right use of language.

Indeed, the context of Titus 1:12–13 also *concerns the use of language*. The writer observes, "There are also many rebellious people, idle talkers and deceivers. . . . They must be silenced, since they are upsetting whole families by teaching for sordid gain what it is not right to teach. It was one of them, their own prophets, who said, 'Cretans are always liars, vicious brutes, lazy gluttons.' This testimony is true. For this reason, rebuke them sharply" (Titus 1:10–13). These people, the passage continues, are paying attention to Jewish myths. They profess to know God, but they deny him by their *actions* (1:14, 16). Here the writer alludes to needless but endless conflicts in which practical actions deprive words of any practical currency. It is less surprising than it might seem that the relationship between my own words and my practical actions, to which Wittgenstein alludes, might be of vital relevance to the pastoral problems that Titus faced.

The aim of this passage is not to attack the morals or failures of Cretans, but to show the ineffectiveness of language and communication that

---

5. Wittgenstein, *Philosophical Investigations*, II. x, 190.
6. Ryle, *Dilemmas*; cf. "Achilles and the Tortoise," 36–53.
7. Thiselton, "The Logical Role of the Liar Paradox in Titus 1:12, 13."

V Paul and Moral Concerns

is not grounded in appropriate behavior and conduct. In certain circumstances, first-person utterances can become self-defeating. Verse 10 speaks of idle or empty talkers (Greek, *mataiologoi*). By contrast what is urged is "sound speech" (NRSV), or more strictly, "health-giving speech" (Greek, *logon hygiē*, 2:8).

However, why could such a crass misunderstanding arise? How could so many commentators be hoodwinked, from patristic until modern times? Clement of Alexandria, John Chrysostom, and Jerome ascribe the quotation to Epimenides of Crete. Clement listed seven wise men, and then commented, "Epimenides the Cretan, whom Paul knew as a Greek *prophet*, whom he mentions in the Epistle to Titus, where he speaks thus: 'One of themselves, a *prophet* of their own, said, *The Cretans are always liars, evil beasts, slow bellies*. And this witness is true.'"[8]

Here Epimenides is seen as a *prophet* attacking mythological claims about a tomb of Zeus in Crete, rather than as a philosopher exploring paradoxes. This view is then reflected in a debate between Origen and Celsus about the tomb of Jupiter on the Isle of Crete. Celsus attacked the Christian belief in the resurrection of Jesus Christ, alleging that such a belief is inconsistent with Christian skepticism about the Cretan claim concerning the tomb of Jupiter.[9] At very least, Celsus argued, this claim undermines the uniqueness of the Christian belief. Much earlier Aristotle referred to "Epimenides of Crete" as a "diviner."[10] Cicero also alluded to Epimenides as a prophet who claimed to predict the future.[11] In later years, in addition to Clement, Chrysostom and Jerome perpetuate this tradition about descriptive claims.[12] These writers give not the slightest hint of the status of paradoxes of logic, even though these paradoxes were familiar in the ancient world, and Jerome refers to Epimenides as a "poet."[13] The most decisive factor was the polemic in Origen about the truth of the resurrection of Jesus Christ.

The nearest that modern commentators come to recognising the paradoxical nature of the assertions in Titus is perhaps the work of Anthony

---

8. Clement of Alexandria, *Stromata*, 1.14 (Eng., *ANF*, vol. 2, 313 [my italics]).
9. Origen, *Against Celsus*, 3.44 (Eng. *ANF*, vol. 4, 481).
10. Aristotle, *Rhetoric*, 3.17.
11. Cicero, *De divinatione* 1.18.34.
12. Chrysostom, *Homilies on Timothy and Titus*, Hom. 3 (Eng., *NPNF*, ser. 1, vol. 13, 528-29).
13. Jerome, *Letters*, 70 (Eng., *NPNF*, ser. 2, vol. 6, 149).

Hanson and E. K. Simpson. Hanson regards the rhetorical purpose of the passage as "to impale the false teachers on the horns of a dilemma: either they accept the truth of the quotation and stand self-condemned: or else they deny it and condemn their own prophet."[14] But he still regards Epimenides as a prophet, not a logician, and also implies that the comment, "this is true," affirms a logically self-contradictory statement, which can have no logical validity. Simpson may go a little further by adding that the assertion is made "with a twinkle in his eye," but he does not really draw out the distinctive function of the logical paradox.[15] Clearly the patristic commentators laid down an iron track that modern commentators have become obliged to follow.

Was Epimenides a prophet who made descriptive truth-claims about Cretans, or a logician who used paradox to expose a problem about language and communication? In normal cases a logical paradox or *aporia* leads to what may be termed "a shift of frame," which involves something beyond and outside the original logical system. Wittgenstein, for example, appealed to the contrast between "saying" and "showing" as a possible means of reaching outside the single logical system. In the *Tractatus*, he observed, "Propositions can represent the whole of reality, but they cannot represent what they must have in common with reality in order to be able to represent its logical form. . . . Propositions *show* the logical form of reality."[16] In his *Philosophical Investigations* he draws out from a logical discussion the practical consequence: "If there were a verb meaning 'to believe falsely,' it would not have any significant first person present indicative."[17]

In Titus 1:12–13, the practical implication of the paradox concerns the logical asymmetry between first-person and third-person utterances, and calls for self-involvement in life on the part of bishops or elders. It is no more plausible to imagine that a Cretan might say, "we are always liars and evil beasts" than it is to imagine someone claiming to believe something falsely. The declaration, "what I say is a lie" gives rise to an endlessly fruitless escalation of self-defeating and purely verbal exchanges. This is entirely compatible with the instruction to Titus to "put in order" what has still be done in the church. Only those who possess the kind of qualities required of bishops, elders, or deacons can utter words that are grounded in honest

---

14. Hanson, *The Pastoral Letters*, 110–11.
15. Simpson, *The Pastoral Epistles*, 99–100.
16. Wittgenstein, *Tractatus Logico-Philosophicus*, 4.12 and 4.121.
17. Wittgenstein, *Philosophical Investigations*, II.X, 190.

conduct. The main target of rebuke is "idle talkers and deceivers.... They must be silenced" (vv. 10–11). Titus 1:12–13 has nothing to do with the character of Cretan people, and we should not suggest that the utterance could be understood to imply this.

Chapter 28

Is obedience to the state unconditional?
(Romans 13:1)

Paul's declaration, "Let every person be subject to the governing authorities; for there is no authority except from God" (Rom 13:1) has caused endless heart-searching over the centuries. Do we owe obedience to a government or state authority if it seems to overstep the mark, or even to promote anti-Christian or oppressive values? Is obedience unconditional? Or if it is not, does peeling away qualifications based on individual judgment ultimately lead to anarchy?

Through the centuries, emphases have changed. From the patristic era until the Reformation most writers tended to respond positively to Paul's emphasis on submission to the governing authorities. Paul continues, "For authorities have been instituted by God . . . as God's servants" (13:1 and 6). It was recognized that chapter 13, on public conduct, reflected Paul's emphasis on God's governance (Rom 9–11) and the implications of the new life (Rom 12). By contrast, in *modern* thought a more cautious exposition of Romans 13:1–11 has emerged. The state has been seen often to overstep its mark on many occasions. Further, is "the state" a suitable translation of the Greek *exousiais*? The NRSV prefers "governing authorities." O'Donovan argues that "the state" is not an appropriate translation. Its ancient equivalent would have been "political community."[1] Jewett comments, "The interpretation of this pericope has swung from abject subservience to political

---

1. O'Donovan, *The Desire of Nations*, 233.

V Paul and Moral Concerns

authorities viewed as virtually divine to critical submission on the basis of their advancement of justice."[2]

Nazism, totalitarianism, and state suppression of religion have colored the approach of a number of writers, notably Oscar Cullmann. He writes concerning Romans 13:1–7, "Few sayings in the New Testament have suffered as much as this one"; it has been used "as if . . . to abet the crimes of the totalitarian state."[3] He argues that the traditional interpretation contradicted themes in the teaching of Jesus and ought to be rejected. The work of Schlier, broadly of Caird, and of Walter Wink on "principalities and powers," together with Yoder on Mennonite theology, suggest the same negative or cautious approach.[4] Yoder writes, "The New Testament speaks in many ways about the problem of the state: Romans 13 is not the center of this teaching."[5] Instead, he appeals especially to the Gospels, where often secular government, he says, is the province of the sovereignty of Satan. He admits that this emphasis can be offensive to the modern mind, because it appears to stand in judgment on modern democratic humanism. He sees "the powers" as potentially hostile in the book of Revelation too.

In the patristic era, Origen wrote to Celsus, "We are not so mad as to stir up the wrath of kings and princes . . . for we read, 'Let every soul [person] be subject to the higher powers. There is no power but God . . .'" (Rom 13:1–2).[6] John Chrysostom devotes thought to this in his *Homilies on Romans*, pleading that, "All things should not just be carried on in confusion."[7] He further perceives that God who governs an ordered world does not encourage anarchy, writing, "Anarchy . . . is an evil."[8] Will God punish those who are doing well, he asks? The state is like a soldier, who keeps guard. Lactantius similarly declared, "Render to all [authorities] the fear that is due to them, offerings, or customs, or gifts, and taxes."[9] Eusebi-

---

2. Jewett, *Romans*, 785.

3. Cullmann, *The State in the New Testament*, 46.

4. Yoder, *The Politics of Jesus*, 104–7; Schlier, *Principalities and Powers in the New Testament*; Caird, *Principalities and Powers*; Wink, *Naming the Powers*; Wink, *Unmasking the Powers*; and Wink, *Engaging the Powers*, 195.

5. Yoder, *The Politics of Jesus*, 195.

6. Origen, *Against Celsus* 8.14 (Eng., ANF, vol. 4, 66).

7. John Chrysostom, *Homilies on Romans*, Homily 23 (NPNF, ser. 1, vol. 13, 511–14).

8. John Chrysostom, *Homilies on Romans*, Homily 23 (NPNF, ser. 1, vol. 13, 511–14).

9. Lactantius, *Constitutions of the Holy Apostles* 2.13 (Eng., ANF, vol.7, 436).

us quotes Polycarp as saying, "We have been taught to render to authorities ordained by God the honour that is due, so long as it does not injure us."[10]

We might suggest that Lactantius and Eusebius could be prejudiced since both were court theologians. But the same cannot be said of Athanasius, Basil, Ambrose, and Augustine. Athanasius writes, "Render to all their dues" on the basis of Romans 13:7.[11] Ambrose quotes Romans 13:7, and commented, "I will pay the deference due to authority, as it is written, 'Honor to whom honor is due, tribute to whom tribute.'"[12] Augustine writes that the Donatists should not "resist the ordinance of God."[13] During the mediaeval period, the church and state were often almost a single authority. Thomas Aquinas follows Augustine closely, comparing the state to a household: "it is ordained for the common good."[14] At the Reformation, Luther's "two kingdoms" theology owed much to the "two cities" of Augustine. He said that the state is "the institutionalized form of God's call to order," and a "remedy required by our corrupted nature."[15] It prevents self-destruction, he said. Both the state and the church have authority within respective narrow spheres. Calvin is also emphatically positive about civil authorities on the basis of Romans 13:1–7. He cites Romans 13:4 for the view that laws are just and "the strongest sinews of government."[16]

Calvin strongly dissented, however, from the Anabaptist and Radical Reformation tradition of Thomas Münster in its defense of pacifism, individualism, and egalitarianism. Münster and the Anabaptists arguably began a more modern tradition. Münster understood Romans 13:4 ("it is God's servant for your good") as referring to expelling evildoers from the *church* as a "protection for the pious" and "to wipe out the godless."[17] Another radical reformer, Obe Phillips, declared on the basis of Romans 13:1: "The higher power has received the sword from God, not that it just judges

---

10. Eusebius, *Ecclesiastical History* 4.22 (Eng., *NPNF*, ser. 2, vol. 1, 190).

11. Athanasius, *Letters* 6.5 and 10.11 (Eng., *NPNF*, ser. 2, vol. 4, 521).

12. Ambrose, *Letters*, 40.12 (Eng., *NPNF*, ser.2, vol. 10, 454).

13. Augustine, *The Letter of Petilian the Donatist*, 2.45 (Eng., *NPNF*, ser. 1, vol. 4, 540).

14. Aquinas, *Summa Theologiae*, I–II, qu.90, art.3, reply to obj.3.

15. Luther, *Luther's Works*, vol. 1, 104.

16. Calvin, *Institutes of the Christian Religion*.

17. Münster in G. H. Williams (ed.), *Spiritual and Anabaptist Writers*, 66, 68. Though this is a somewhat forced exegesis it is hard to imagine Paul envisaging the state playing the role of excommunicating the godless from the church.

V Paul and Moral Concerns

in spiritual matters ... but to protect the pious."[18] We have already noted the more radical interpretations of Paul in Cullmann, Schlier, broadly Caird, and Wink.

It would be a mistake, however, to assume that all modern writers adopt this approach. Helmut Thielicke writes, "The State is simply the institutionalized form of God's call to order ... a remedy required by our corrupted nature ... which puts a stop to the destruction of the fallen world."[19] O'Donovan also follows a more conservative approach, as we have seen from his definition of political communities. He writes in a later book: "The authority of government [is] essentially an act of judgment.... To reward the just and punish the evil."[20] Judgement, he writes, is an act of moral discrimination, which transcends the perspective of the individual.

Similarly, Emil Brunner insists that the institution of the state is a divine "ordinance" of God, which is part of his "preserving grace."[21] Reinhold Niebuhr also argues that the use of power is necessary to oppose abused power.[22] Pannenberg traces the biblical origins of the political order from the Davidic monarchy onwards and concludes, "something in law ... corresponds to the difference between church and state, for the political order is essentially a legal order."[23] Jewett remarks,

> The endless stream of studies has been marked by advocacy of various appraisals of the role of government shaped by nomination of traditions and by modern ethical considerations. The passage has been interpreted as a warning not to participate in Jewish zealotism, in revolutionary agitation, or, as seems even less likely, not to create unrest that would jeopardize "the already vulnerable situation of the beleaguered Jewish population in Rome."[24]

Jewett adds, "The quiet early years of the Nero regime are depicted as the background of this positive view of the state, and Paul wished to avoid any gesture of disloyalty that might jeopardize the peaceful extension of the

---

18. Phillips in G. H. Williams (ed.), *Spiritual and Anabaptist Writers*, 233.
19. Thielicke, *Theological Ethics*, vol. 2: *Politics*, 17.
20. O'Donovan, *The Ways of Judgment*, 4.
21. Brunner, *Natural Theology*.
22. Niebuhr, *The Nature and Destiny of Man*, vol. 1, 221-33, 288-94.
23. Pannenberg, *Systematic Theology*, vol. 3), 57; cf. 49-57.
24. Jewett, *Romans*, 785; cf. Elliott, "Romans 13:1-7 in the Context of Imperial Propaganda" 196.

Christian mission."[25] He stresses his belief that Paul was very concerned to gain support from Roman Christians for his projected visit to Spain, which he argues very convincingly.[26] He concludes, "Romans 13:1–7 was not intended to create the foundation of a political ethic for all times and places in succeeding generations—a task for which it is proving to be singularly ill suited."[27]

From a slightly different perspective Dunn offers the same conclusion. He observes that Romans 13:1–7 has often been taken to express the order of creation, and what Brunner calls "creation ordinances." Thereby, Dunn continues, Romans 13:1–7 is cited "to justify the use of state power in the suppression of Baptist and other radical groups." Nevertheless, "It should be clear . . . that the discussion in these verses is context-specific."[28] But whereas Jewett thinks that the context-specific issue is Paul's mission to Spain, Dunn alludes to the previous edict of Claudius that expelled some Jews from Rome, and refers to the need to refrain from bad "conduct in order to avoid a fresh edict."[29] Dunn concludes, "All that they [communities of Christ-followers] could do was to live within the structures which existed, accommodate to them—as everyone had to—and seek to benefit from rules or rights the governing authorities granted."[30]

Yet O'Donovan and Pannenberg appear to draw more from the order implied by the notion of God's creation ordinances than Jewett and Dunn. Cranfield tries to take a mediating view, stressing Paul's emphasis on obedience, but also commenting, "This will not mean an uncritical, blind obedience to the authorities' every command; for the final arbiter of what constitutes *hypotassesthai* (broadly, *obedience*) in a particular situation is not the civil authority but God."[31]

---

25. Jewett, *Romans*, 785–86.
26. Jewett, *Romans*, 84–91.
27. Jewett, *Romans*, 786.
28. Dunn, *Romans 9–16*, 768.
29. Dunn, *Romans 9–16*, 768.
30. Dunn, *Romans 9–16*, 770.
31. Cranfield, *Epistle to the Romans*, vol. 2, 662.

Chapter 29

Remaining in Slavery?
(1 Corinthians 7:17–24)

1 Corinthians 7:20 is the pivotal center of the roughly chiasmic structure that begins (v. 17) and ends (v. 24) with the injunction to remain in the situation in which one was called. The first half of this group of verses concerns circumcision; the second part, one's slave status. 7:21 finds opposite interpretations from a host of interpreters from ancient to modern times and constitutes a notorious controversy.

At least three commentators and three English versions translate the Greek: "the calling into which he/she was called" (*en tē klēsei hē eklēthē*), e.g., AV/KJB, RV, Conzelmann, Barrett, and Collins). But most interpreters avoid this rendering on the ground that Luther, rather than Paul, regarded "calling" as a professional or commercial vocation. In 1 Corinthians 1:26 "called" is decisive for Paul's meaning: called *to be Christians*; not to an occupational vocation. In this latter verse some versions or interpreters render the word as "state" (RSV, NJB), some as "condition" (NRSV, REB), some as "situation" (Fee), or "place" (NIV). In verses 17–24 Paul discusses marriage (being married, celibate, widowed, or separated) and slavery (slave, freeborn, or freedperson). Some have even interpreted these issues along the lines of F. H. Bradley's ethics as "knowing one's place."

Even then, verse 21 still remains difficult and controversial. Some take it to mean: *Were you a slave when called? Do not be concerned about it* (NRSV, virtually NIV, AV/KJB), i.e., do not worry about it. Others, notably S. Scott Bartchy, understand verse 21 to mean: *Were you a slave when called? Make use of (your opportunity)* (Greek, *mallon chrēsai*, aorist middle imperative of *chraomai*, "to use," "make use of").[1] The problem remains, however, that it is not entirely clear what it is that a slave can make use of. Is it his or her status as a slave, or the opportunity for freedom if it is offered? Bartchy rejects the notion that this is slavery, because the slave normally would have no option or choice. Certainly, the Greek releases those concerned from undue anxiety. Bartchy and Grosheide write: "Not slavery but vocation is the main thing. . . . [T]he first thing is to be a Christian, and that in all possible circumstances."[2]

However, after "make use of," Paul leaves the verb hanging without making it explicit what it is that is to be made use of. The force of *mallon* ("rather") is also unclear. Many supply "freedom," especially among patristic and Reformation writers. Chrysostom recognizes that this is an exegetical crux, but writes, "Have you been called, being a slave? Care not for it. Continue to be a slave."[3] He and Ambrosiaster are followed by Theodoret, Pelagius, Theophylact, and in the mediaeval period by Photius, Peter Lombard, and probably Thomas Aquinas. Among modern writers Allo, Barrett, Conzelmann, Senft, Deming, and Collins adopt this approach.

Several interpretations recommend remaining in slavery, but for different reasons. The main view suggests that a low social status is nothing in God's eyes, compared with being a Christian believer. The second finds the status of the slave may provide opportunities for Christian witness and service, which might otherwise not be available.

One important factor in seeking to understand Paul is recent research on Graeco-Roman slavery in the first century, especially by Dale Martin and Bruce Winter in *New Testament Studies* and Thomas Wiedemann in *Classics*.[4] Placing together the research of Wiedemann, Martin, Winter, and others, we establish the following conclusions. About a third of the slave population was born to women who were themselves slaves. A substantial further proportion actually sold themselves into slavery as an attempt to improve their chances, or what nowadays would be termed "eventual upward mobility." Sometimes this would provide an opportunity to pay off a

---

1.. Bartchy, *Mallon chrēsai*, throughout.

2. Grosheide, *Commentary on the First Epistle to the Corinthians*, 170; cf. Bartchy, *Mallon chrēsai*, 155–59.

3. Chrysostom, *Homilies on 1 Corinthians*, Hom. 19.5; (Eng. *NPNF*, vo. 12, 108).

4. Wiedemann, *Greek and Roman Slavery*; Wiedemann, *Slavery, Greece and Rome*, 1–46; Winter, "Social Mobility: 1 Cor. 7: 21–24"; and Winter, "St Paul as a Critic of Roman Slavery in 1 Cor. 7:21–23"; and Martin, *Slavery as Salvation*, 63–68, and throughout.

debt through small "earnings." Some slaves came from children who were stolen or kidnapped. Others had been captured as prisoners in war. This process reached its height in the late Republic.

The most important two points are, first, the fact that many people voluntarily considered it worth selling themselves into slavery, and, second, the huge variation in the role and status of different kinds of slaves. Admittedly some slaves were treated in a grossly oppressive way. Some slaves, especially manual laborers and women, were often subjected to torture and sexual exploitation and were regarded simply as their master's property, or literally as a "thing" (Latin, *res*), rather than as a human person.[5]

However, at the other end of the spectrum, many slave owners believed that it was a matter of honor and ethics to treat slaves well, especially those who gave good service. They often appointed "managerial" slaves as respected overseers of a household, or as managers or administrators of a country estate. Some slaves had more literary or financial/administrative ability than their masters had, and they could readily function as secretaries or as high-status members of a household. Martin lists a huge number of "slave jobs" from barbers, mirror-makers, goldsmiths, architects, to business managers, bureaucrats, and archivists, who would run country estates on behalf of their owners in Rome.[6]

References to the influence and numbers of *freed* persons are numerous. Relatively few spent their *entire* lives as slaves for two very different reasons. On one side, many owners felt it a matter of public honor to be known to treat their slaves fairly, and permitted their slaves manumission, either to reward loyal service, or to permit the slaves to redeem themselves using savings gathered from commercial sidelines. Suetonius and others give examples of this.[7] On the other side, many slave owners found the provision of shelter, clothes, and food relatively expensive when a slave had passed his or her prime.[8] Whichever the reason, it would not seem entirely surprising that Paul could regard slavery as an opportunity both for Christian witness and even for upward mobility.

We conclude that whether Paul urged Christian slaves to make use of their position as slaves, or whether he urged Christians slaves to take up

---

5. Wiedemann, *Greek and Roman Slavery*, 2–11 and 167–87.

6. Martin, *Slavery as Salvation*, 11–22.

7. Suetonius, *Claudius*, 25; cf. the extended note in Wiedemann, *Greek and Roman Slavery*.

8. Dio Cassius, 60.29; and Winter, "Social Mobility: 1 Cor. 7:17–24."

the opportunity of manumission, either option would be almost nothing compared with their privileged calling to live as Christian people.

Chapter 30

Who inherits the kingdom of God?
(1 Corinthians 6: 9–11)

In 1 Corinthians 6:9–11, Paul writes: "Do you not know that wrongdoers (Greek, *adikoi*) will not inherit the kingdom of God? Do not be deceived! Fornicators (*pornoi*), idolaters, adulterers (*moichoi*), male prostitutes (*malakoi*), sodomites (*arsenokoitai*), thieves, the greedy (*pleonektai*), drunkards, revilers (*loidoroi*), robbers—none of these will inherit the kingdom of God. And this is what some of you used to be. But you were washed, you were sanctified, you were justified in the name of the Lord Jesus Christ and in the Spirit of our God." The quotation is from the NRSV, but several of these words in Greek may be translated in more than one way.

"Who inherits the kingdom of God?" is the title given to this passage by Manfred Brauch in his book *Hard Sayings of Paul*.[1] He observes that many breathe a sigh of relief because their problems have not been included in this list of vices that disqualify people from membership of the kingdom of God. Others, however, read it with alarm if they "have misused the gift of sexual intimacy outside the boundaries of the covenant of marriage or find themselves overpowered by a homosexual orientation and its expression."[2] The investment of personal identity and the passions and emotions that this arouses today make this an exceptionally problematic passage in Paul.

---

1. Brauch, *Hard Sayings of Paul*, 103.
2. Brauch, *Hard Sayings of Paul*, 103–4.

Who inherits the kingdom of God?

The REB and NJB bring out the force of "Do you not know?" better than the NRSV. Paul uses this question when he is about to say what the readers ought to know already. The REB has "Surely you know that...?" and the NJB has "Do you not realize that...?" Collins translates "wrongdoers" (*adikoi*) as "unjust," although most translators keep the meaning broader, as "wicked" (NIV, Moffatt) or "unrighteous" (AV/KJV), or as "those who do evil" (NJB). It depicts a *habit or disposition*.

These qualities do not set out "disqualifications" for entry into God's kingdom, but express part of the contrast between two sets of habituated actions or states which correspond respectively with self-damage or with being put right with God which is the mark of the kingdom of God. The fact that these negative moral failures describe *habituated overt acts* suggests that Paul is silent about what today is often described as "a homosexual orientation," i.e., an innocent attraction to people of the same sex. "Inherit" (Greek, *klēronomeō*) is used in the sense of what corresponds logically rather than causally with two states. Roughly ten dispositions or habituated acts are listed. In the particular climate of today it is unfortunate that the issue of "gay rights" demands disproportionate attention in understanding these verses as a whole.

The detailed translation of the Greek for these dispositions is fiercely controversial. To be honest about the current debate on gay relations, there are several different ways in which some writers seek to distance these verses from any relation to same-sex intimacy. (1) One way is to dismiss Paul's "catalogue of vices" as simply replicating a conventional list of such vices in Greco-Roman thought. (2) It is possible to understand the Greek as referring to male prostitutes, as the NRSV translation does in part. (3) A third way is to stress that all moral values must be Christ-centered, and that all moral failures must be given equal weight as a whole. (4) Some appeal to "socio-critical hermeneutics" to expose biases or "pre-judgments" which most interpreters bring with them to the text. Jürgen Habermas constitutes one of many possible examples of this approach. These are all serious claims which both deserve and require careful scrutiny. We shall examine each of these four ways of approach in turn.

We must (1) examine claims that Paul lists a conventional "catalogue of vices" which he simply borrows from Greco-Roman and/or contemporary Jewish writers. It is true that Paul does use chains of habitual acts in more than one place. In 1 Corinthians 5:9–11, he listed more than a dozen specific moral failures, similarly lists such failures in Romans 1:29–31.

V Paul and Moral Concerns

These may perhaps be borrowed from Jewish synagogue homilies, in which the evils of idolatry and related evils which are frequently rehearsed. The Wisdom of Solomon 14:22–31 provides such examples. Because idols are human constructs, the Jewish preacher argues, there remains no secure basis for moral judgment. Johannes Weiss noted such lists of vices in 1910, and in 1932 B. S. Easton developed this idea further, arguing that these "catalogues" were derived from the Stoics. In 1936, A. Vögtle interpreted the lists in terms of an expansion of Plato's work on the virtues.[3]

Parallels with Stoics and Plato cannot be denied. Vögtle's work was followed in 1959 by Wibbing and in 1964 by Kamlah. These more recent studies constitute a turning point. Wibbing stressed a Jewish background, and Kamlah, a catechetical one.[4] Lietzmann, Conzelmann, and others have also shown the importance of catechetical backgrounds for ethical instruction for Christians, as witnessed in the later *Didachē*. Conzelmann declares that the lists have "to do with a realistic description of conditions at Corinth."[5] The scholarly climate has now settled from an over-readiness to consider parallels with Hellenistic sources involving theories of borrowings or dependence, to consider more convincingly the influence of catechism and ethical tradition from Dodd, Carrington, Selwyn, Cullmann, Verhey, and many others in more recent times.[6] All these moral failures stand together as examples of what characterizes the pre-Christian existence and falls below a Christian ideal.

A second issue is (2) whether Paul's Greek words point to "male prostitutes" or to "homosexuality," the latter being a concept that many deny was available in the world of Paul's day. Victor Furnish, Robin Scroggs, D. S. Bailey, and John Boswell are among the most widely-known advocates of the view that Paul would have known of male prostitution but would have had *no concept of "homosexuality."* Furnish asserts, "The word 'homosexuality,' as well as the very concept, is an anachronism when applied to the Bible, and to the ancient world. . . . There were no such concepts in the ancient world. . . . There is no applicable text about 'homosexuality' understood as a 'condition' or 'orientation.' 'Homosexuals' [in 1 Corinthians 6:9]

---

3. Vögtle, *Die Tugend- und Lasterkataloge im Neue Testament*.

4. Wibbing, *Die Tugend- und Lasterkataloge im Neue Testament und ihre Traditionsgeschichte*; Kamlah, *Die Form der katalogischen Paränese im Neue Testament*, especially 11–14 and 27–31.

5. Conzelmann, *First Corinthians*, 100–102.

6. Dodd, *Gospel and Law* provides one example; Verhey, *The Great Reversal* provides another of many examples.

is an anachronism."⁷ Scroggs says, "Not only is the New Testament church uninterested in the topic, . . . biblical judgments are not relevant to today's debate."⁸

Bailey insists that the biblical writers could have no concept of "homosexuality" because they did not possess the conceptual or psychological tools to distinguish between *inversion*, in which same-sex acts naturally express intimacy, and *perversion*, in which same-sex acts are not true to the nature of the self.⁹ The notion of whether ancient people have viable concepts, however, is fraught with peril. On the face of it, we had little concept of the "unconscious" before Freud. Yet Gerd Theissen has demonstrated that Paul certainly used the concept of the unconscious when he spoke of the self-deception of the human heart, and Bultmann briefly anticipated him in this respect.¹⁰

In Molièrre's play *Le Bourgeois Gentilhomme*, M. Jourdin exclaims, "My goodness! For more than forty years I have been speaking prose without knowing it."¹¹ M. Jourdin does not need the concept of prose to use it! James Barr attacks the notion that word and concept are equivalent.¹² David Wright insists that many of the arguments of Bailey, Scroggs, and Furnish "recall the pre-Barr era."¹³ Richard Hays, Robert Fyall, and Mark Bonnington similarly explicitly adopt a different approach from Scroggs, Boswell, and Bailey.¹⁴ The situation has become incredibly complex in the light of some postmodern writers. For example, it has become increasingly difficult to speak of anything as "natural" in the light of Michel Foucault's postmodern philosophy in his *History of Sexuality*. Michael Ruse concedes that whatever the pros and cons of the argument, it remains difficult to be certain about many definitions of terms.¹⁵

---

7. Furnish, "Homosexual Practices in Biblical Perspective," 253–66.

8. Scroggs, *The New Testament and Homosexuality*, 101 and 127.

9. Bailey, *Homosexuality and the Western Christian Tradition*, 29–41.

10. Theisssen, *Psychological Aspects of Pauline Theology*, 267–341; Bultmann, *Theology of the New Testament*, 224.

11. Molièrre, *Le Bourgeois Gentilhomme*, Act 2, scene.

12. Barr, *The Semantics of Biblical Language*, 209 and 244.

13. David Wright, "Homosexuality: The Relevance of the Bible," 292.

14. Hays, *Echoes of Scripture in the Letters of Paul*; and Hays, "Awaiting the Redemption of our Bodies."

15. Ruse, *Homosexuality*, 265–67.

V Paul and Moral Concerns

Admittedly some of the Greek words remain obscure. For example, *arsenokoitēs* is a rare word and has no lexicographical prehistory. But its component parts certainly indicate "sleeping with" or "having sexual relations with." Scroggs argues that while *malakos* denotes "unmanly" in general terms, it is used of "the youth who consciously imitated feminine styles and ways."[16] There is no doubt that the Greek word may include this. Few doubt Scroggs' research on the extent of "call boys" in the Greco-Roman world of Paul's day. But this does not define what else it may *include*. Barrett understands it to denote "the passive partner in male homosexual relations."[17]

We have already touched on (3), namely the need to avoid isolating words linked to discussions of homosexuality from the other ten or so moral failures itemized in 1 Corinthians 6:9–11, and further to insist that all suggestions of moral directive are placed in the framework of whatever *serves the cause of Christ*. This is the least contentious of the four considerations. The prohibitions against stealing and committing adultery occur in the Ten Commandments (Exod 20:13 and Deut 5:18, LXX). Kenneth Bailey points out that of the ten "vices" listed in 1 Corinthians 6:9–10 five allude to sexual issues (which replicate 5:1–13 and 6:1–12), while a further five relate to greed and grasping, and eating and being drunk.[18]

The second part of this third point concerns the hermeneutical principle emphasized by Martin Luther that we should interpret all the sacred books "to inculcate (*treiben*, "drive [home]") Christ."[19] Christ, he said, is the central point of the circle around which all Scripture revolves. Without Christ, Scripture is like the light of a candle; with Christ it is like the brilliance of the sun.[20] Furnish cites this approach to argue for the absence of any concern about homosexuality in the Jesus-traditions of the Gospels.[21] Adrian Thatcher states, "The Gospels are entirely silent about homosexuality."[22] Michael Vasey appeals to Jesus' sympathy for "the outsider."[23]

---

16. Scroggs, *The New Testament and Homosexuality*, 106.
17. Barrett, *First Epistle to the Corinthians*, 140.
18. Bailey, "Paul's Theological Foundation for Human Society."
19. Luther, *Luther's Works*, vol. 35, *Word and Sacrament*, 396.
20. Luther, *Luther's Works*, vol. 23: *Sermons on St John*, 279–80.
21. Furnish, "The Bible and Homosexuality," 23.
22. Thatcher, *Liberating Sex*, 18.
23. Vasey, *Strangers and Friends*, 249–90.

Yet this appeal may be taken to point differently. As Wolfhart Pannenberg insists, the Gospels on the face of it largely reflect the pre-resurrection teaching of Jesus, which should be supplemented from the Epistles and Acts.[24] However, the main problem with this claim is that, in the controversial debate, each side is as convinced as the other that it represents the mind of Christ.

(4) We come to appeals to socio-critical hermeneutics of the kind suggested by Habermas regarding the "pre-judgements" of the interpreter. At best this is a genuine appeal to discard anything that may prejudice the interpretation of the Pauline passages. This approach is not confined to Habermas. In softer form, it relates to Paul Ricoeur's "hermeneutic of suspicion." This originally suggested itself to him when he compared the difficulty encountered by Freud in interpreting dreams, when the dream as recounted by a patient differed radically from the actual dream itself. Freud needed to probe beneath the distortion, condensation, and "scrambling" that the dreamer had unconsciously erected to protect the self.[25]

Habermas is even clearer in attacking a merely positivist view of a value-neutral interpretation. He recognizes that "consciousness" is largely shaped by social life and its historical "givenness." Both Habermas and Ricoeur recognize that unconscious drives can "block" factors that the interpreter wants to suppress. Two of Habermas' most comprehensive books are his *Theory of Communicative Action* and his *Knowledge and Human Interests*.[26] Both writers build on insights of Hans Georg Gadamer on "pre-judgement" in his magisterial *Truth and Method*.[27]

This is not as fruitful as it sounds. Personally, I have participated in numerous seminars in which both sides in the debate are convinced that all prejudices and blindspots belong exclusively to the other side. It is no more capable of resolving the problem than general appeals to what serves the mind of Christ.

The upshot of examining the four sets of considerations above is in the first instance to recognize which issues cannot be settled decisively. The second step is to recognize that an ethical "two-ways" approach (i.e., clear specificity of right and wrong) is probably more convincing than theories

---

24. Cf. Thiselton, *Understanding Pannenberg*, chapter 4.

25. Ricoeur, *Freud and Philosophy*, throughout; and Ricoeur, *Interpretation Theory*.

26. Habermas, *The Theory of Communicative Action*; Habermas, *Knowledge and Human Interest*.

27. Gadamer, *Truth and Method*, especially 269–99.

about conventional "catalogues of vices" borrowed from Greco-Roman sources. A third step is to consider the weight or lack of weight in proposed retranslations of the Greek terms used by Paul. Personally, I do not find all the claims of Richard Furnish, Robin Scroggs, D. S. Bailey, and John Boswell wholly convincing, but I also regard their claims worthy of attention. I am hopeful that at least this consideration of 1 Corinthians 6:9–11 helps to point to possible ways forward. We must note the forward perspective of verse 11: "This is what some of you used to be. But you were washed, you were sanctified, you were justified in the name of the Lord Jesus Christ and in the Spirit of our God." The purpose of verses 9–11 is to underline the transformative nature of the contrast between two different mindsets.

VI

Paul and Christian Worship

Chapter 31

Self-examination before communion and "not discerning the Lord's body."

(1 Corinthians 11:28–30)

These two verses can be frightening in their seriousness. Paul writes, "Examine yourselves, and only then eat of the bread and drink of the cup. For all who eat and drink without discerning the body, eat and drink judgement against themselves. For this reason, many of you are weak and ill, and some have died." The previous verse, 11:27, is almost more challenging: "Whoever eats the bread or drinks the cup in an unworthy manner (Greek, *anaxiōs*) will be answerable (Greek, *enochos*) for the body and blood of the Lord." The Greek *anaxiōs* simply means "in an unworthy or careless manner."[1] The Greek word *enochos* means "liable, answerable, guilty," and in an additional comment, Danker observes, can relate to "sin against the body and blood, 1 Cor. 11:27."[2]

When we consider the thousands of Christians (some of them sometimes nominal Christians) who participate in the Lord's Supper or Eucharist every Sunday, often without very serious thought, Paul's words address us as very serious. Manfred Brauch recalls anxiously wondering: "What if I did not properly discern or recognize the body of the Lord? How would, or could, I make sure that in my eating the bread and drinking the cup I

---

1. Danker, BDAG, 68.
2. Danker, BDAG, 338–39.

would not sin 'against the body and blood of the Lord?'"[3] He adds, "'Sinning against' and 'not discerning' at times caused me to avoid participation in the Supper or to stay away from worship altogether when Communion was celebrated."[4]

Nevertheless, what does "not discerning the Lord's body" really mean in its first-century context? Fortunately, this particular puzzle is simpler than many others because there are really only three majority or mainline views of the verse among New Testament scholars. Complexity is due only to citing the holders of these views. The first concerns the Eucharistic elements. The second concerns "the body of Christ" in the sense of the true church. In 11:22 Paul speaks of "despising the church of God." Further, many of the earliest Greek MSS do not have the phrase "of the Lord" after "body" in verse 29 (Þ46, ℵ*, A, B, C*, 33, copsa bo). Still further, Paul often defines the church as "the body of Christ" or as "one body" (1 Cor 10:17; 12:12-13, 27; Eph 2:16; 3:6; 4:4; Col 1:18). The third main interpretation is serious involvement in, and commitment to, all that the cross of Jesus Christ and his passion means and implies for Christian believers without necessary allusion to the elements of bread and wine. We may now be specific, as follows.

(1) A strong tradition from Justin and Augustine through Thomas Aquinas, Peter Lombard, and even Beza, interprets Paul's words to mean distinguishing between the sacred Eucharistic elements of the Lord's body and ordinary bread from the table.[5] This interpretation has been supported by a number of modern writers, if mainly nineteenth-century ones, including Heinrich, Weiss, and in modified form Godet.[6] Godet believes that even Reformed theology can find room for the view that Paul is concerned for proper respect at the Lord's Table in contrast to merely social gatherings of Christians. Some more recent writers agree, including Allo and Lietzmann. The main problem for many more recent writers is whether such concern about the elements (especially about "consecrated" elements) would have arisen as early as Paul.

(2) A reaction, prompted by such writers as Bornkamm, Käsemann, Kümmel, and Schweizer, tends, in effect, to understand "discerning the

---

3. Brauch, *Hard Sayings of Paul*, 154-55.
4. Brauch, *Hard Sayings of Paul*, 155.
5. Justin, *Apology*, I, 66; Augustine, *Commentary on John*, sect. 62.
6. Heinrici, *Das erste Sendschreiben des Apostel Paulus an die Korinther*, 138-39; Weiss, *Der erste Korintherbrief*, 291.

body" as referring primarily to *respect for the congregation of believers as the body* of Christ.[7] Recently Witherington, Horrell, and Hays have defended this interpretation, although Collins seems to accept both (2) and (3).[8] Gordon Fee argues that this verse "makes sense of what is otherwise an unusual short digression in 10:17," where the "one loaf" is identified as the solidarity of the community of believers.[9]

(3) Neither the first nor the second interpretation entirely convince Barrett, Marshall, Hofius, Wolff, and Schrage, among others. In particular, Barrett argues that the second view "strains the meaning of *diakrinein* [to discern]."[10] Marshall argues that this verse is too far away from 10:16–17 to allow weight to be given to the argument that Fee uses.[11] Hofius and Wolff insist that in this verse "*to sōma* stands [as] *pars pro toto*" for the body and blood of Christ.[12] Schrage believes that "right judgment" extends to what it means to be identified with, and involved in, the cross of Christ.[13] Serious identification with Christ and his cross is what is at issue. The Lord's Supper must not be treated in some routine or nominal way as a mere ceremony. It is essentially transformative.

The accompanying reference to judgment should not surprise us in the light of such work as C. F. D. Moule's essay "The Judgment Theme in the Sacraments."[14] In this essay Moule compares baptism to "a pleading guilty," while in the Lord's Supper "The discerning, penitent communicant is alert to the meaning with which the bread and wine are charged both in regard to the incarnate Christ given for us and in regard to the fellow members of the Body which that surrender created."[15] This also means, incidentally, that Moule combines the second interpretation with the third. "Pleading

---

7. Bornkamm, "Lord's Supper and Church in Paul"; Käsemann, "The Pauline Doctrine of the Lord's Supper"; Schweizer, "*sōma.*"

8. Witherington, *Conflict and Community in Corinth*, 241–52; Horrell, "The Lord's Supper at Corinth and in the Church Today"; Hays, *First Corinthians*, 200; and Collins, *First Corinthians*, 446.

9. Fee, *First Epistle to the Corinthians*, 564.

10. Barrett, *A Commentary on the First Epistle to the Corinthians*, 279.

11. I. Howard Marshall, *Last Supper and Lord's Supper* (Grand Rapids: Eerdmans, 1980) 114.

12. Hofius, "The Lord's Supper and the Lord's Supper Tradition," 114 and n.224; Wolff, *Der erste Brief des Paulus an die Korinther*, 279.

13. Schrage, *Der erste Brief an die Korinther*, vol. 3, 51–52.

14. Moule, "The Judgment Theme in the Sacraments."

15. Moule, "The Judgment Theme in the Sacraments," 465 and 473.

guilty" means to pass through divine judgment, and avoiding "fundamental blindness." This passage, then, demands both serious commitment to the message and implications of the cross, and also respect for the unity and solidarity with other believers in that commitment.

Chapter 32

Should all Christians speak in tongues?
(1 Corinthians 14:5)

In 1 Corinthians 14:5, Paul declares "Now I would like all of you to speak in tongues (Greek, *thelō de pantas hymās lalein glōssais*), but even more to prophesy (Greek, *hina prophēteuēte*). One who prophesies is greater than one who speaks in tongues, unless someone interprets (Greek, *ektos ei mē diermēneuē*) so that the church may be built up" (NRSV).

Does Paul here urge that all Christians should speak in tongues? What does he mean by "speaking in tongues" and by "prophesy"? Every Greek word is significant, and their meanings in English are often fiercely debated. In my commentary on the Greek text of 1 Corinthians, I have discussed at least six possible meanings of "speaking in tongues" and comparatively a similar number of meanings of "prophecy."[1]

To anticipate the meaning of "speaking in tongues" the following six meanings are supported by reputable writers: (i) the notion of tongues as angelic speech (Ellis and Dautzenberg); (ii) tongues as the miraculous power to speak other human languages (Chrysostom, Theodore, Thomas Aquinas, J. G. Davies, Robert Gundry); (iii) tongues as using liturgical, archaic, or rhythmic phrases (Bleek and Heinrici); (iv) tongues as "ecstatic" speech (NEB, Tertullian, Kleinknecht, Currie); (v) unconscious cries of release from the subconscious mind (Theissen); (vi) unconscious or uninhibited

---

1. Thiselton, *First Epistle to the Corinthians*, 1087–94, 972–89; cf. 957–89, 1062–64, and 1094–1130.

cries to God from the heart, as in Romans 8:26, or subconscious mind (Macchia, probably Käsemann).

Before we review these six interpretations in detail, however, we must first address (1) the issue of how we translate *thelō*. The verb translated, "I would like" (NRSV; Greek, *thelō*) encounters debate. The NJB translates "I would much rather" in a concessive sense. The REB translates, "I am happy for . . . but happier still for . . ." in a conciliatory sense. Conzelmann adopts this approach when he comments, "Paul allows them their speaking in tongues."[2] Héring goes further. He writes, "'*Thelō*' does not express an order, but a concession in the form of a wish unlikely to be fulfilled (cf. 7:7)."[3] Likewise, F. F. Bruce comments, "He goes as far as he can with those whom he criticizes before imposing a caveat."[4] As we might expect, those in the Pentecostal tradition reject this interpretation. Gordon Fee translates *thelō* as "I wish."[5]

Moreover, it is not only Pentecostal writers who reject the view of Conzelmann, Héring, and Bruce. Schrage argues that *thelō* is usually more purposive than *boulomai* ("I wish").[6] S. J. Kistemaker also understands "wish" to govern the entire clause, partly as a fulfilment of God's promise to Moses in Numbers 11:29.[7] Finally, the standard Greek-English Lexicon (3rd ed., 2000), BDAG, translates *thelō* as "to have a desire for something, wish to have, desire, want" as the first meaning, with scores of New Testament passages. The second meaning in BDAG is "to have something in mind for oneself" or to resolve, and the third "to take pleasure in." So, although the view of Conzelmann, Héring, and Bruce, matches the context, we cannot regard this issue as closed.

(2) Our second task is to enquire into the meaning of "speaking in tongues." Many describe this as *glossolalia* (speaking a "language" one has not learned) or even sometimes as *xenolalia* (speaking in foreign languages one has not learned). Probably the miraculous power to speak other languages is the most widespread view. But this does not prejudge what *kind* of language is implied. The least highly regarded is the theory of Bleek and

---

2. Conzelmann, *1 Corinthians*, 235.
3. Héring, *The First Epistle to the Corinthians*, 146.
4. Bruce, *1 and 2 Corinthians*, 130.
5. Fee, *The First Epistle to the Corinthians*, 658-59.
6. Schrage, *Der erste Brief an die Korinther*, vol. 3, 389, n.67.
7. Kistemaker, *1 Corinthians*, 481.

Heinrici that speaking in tongues constitutes using liturgical, archaic, or rhythmic phrases.

(i) F. Bleek noted that Greek grammarians often used *glōssa, tongue*, to denote archaic words or dialects, provincial idioms, or, as in the present context, probably a mixture of ancient, quasi-Semitic liturgical words and phrases, perhaps spoken in poetic or exalted rhythms.[8] He argues his case in detail, alluding to the work of J. G. Herder and J. A. Ernesti. C. F. G. Heinrici develops this view further.[9] He explicitly bases his approach on the lexicography of Bleek. He cites expressions of joy and praise in Dionysius of Halicarnassus and Plutarch. He argues that "speaking in tongues" denoted "unfamiliar" or "out-of-the-ordinary" sounds and phrases.[10]

The main reasons for rejecting this theory include, first, that it inevitably remains speculative and without firm evidence that Paul actually means what Bleek and Heinrich suggest. Second, the use of rhythmic and liturgical speech hardly fits Paul's context. Paul does not seem to be speaking of some contrived form of speech, but of something more spontaneous. We need to look at other theories.

(ii) In the reverse order to its likelihood and influence, the view expressed by Earle Ellis and Gerhard Dautzenberg (tongues as angelic speech) deserves respect, but is probably less plausible than the main three or four interpretations. Although they do not explicitly subscribe to this view, Witherington and Barrett express sympathy with it.

The main argument for this view arises from the role of angels in apocalyptic and in the Qumran writings. In the Testament of Job, probably written in the first century BC, we have enigmatic references to "rapture." In 48:1—50:3 Job's enraptured daughters "no longer mind the things of earth but utter a hymn of angelic language to God according to the angels' psalmody . . . speaking in the language of the heights . . . in the language of the cherubim."[11] Other similar passages include Jubilees 25:14; 1 Enoch 40; 71:11; and 4 Maccabees 10:21. Heinrich Weinel first floated this theory in 1899.[12]

8. Bleek, "Über die Gabe des glōssais lalein in der ersten christlichen Kirche."

9. Heinrici, *Das erste Sendschreiben des Apostel Paulus an die Korinther*, 376–94.

10. Heinrici, *Das erste Sendschreiben des Apostel Paulus an die Korinther*, 381–86; Plutarch, *Isis*, 375B.

11. Dautzenberg, "Zum religionsgeschichtlichen Hintergrund der DIAKRISEIS PNEUMATÔN (1 Kor. 12,10)"; cf. Dautzenberg, *Urchristliche Prophetie*; and Ellis, *Prophecy and Hermeneutic in Early Christianity*, 63–71.

12. Weinel, *Die Wirkungen des Geistes und der Geister im nachapostolichen Zeitalter*

E-B. Allo and Wayne Grudem are among those who criticize and reject this view.[13] Grudem rejects Ellis's understanding of the plural *pneumata* (spirits) as angelic powers, while Allo suspects that this theory can too readily slide into traditions of Montanism rather than of Paul. In general, this theory has less support than the remaining views.

(iii) For a time, the notion of speaking in tongues as "ecstatic speech" came into vogue, as is witnessed by the translation in the NEB. Exponents of this view begin with Tertullian, especially in his Montanist period. In the modern era, J. Behm, H. Kleinknecht, S. D. Currie, N. I. J. Engelsen, and (in modified form) M. E. Boring and L. T. Johnson, broadly hold this view. Behm, perhaps unfortunately, drew on supposed parallels between Hellenistic and Christian devotional phenomena. He wrote, "Paul is aware of a similarity between Hellenism and Christianity in respect of these mystical and ecstatic phenomena."[14] He also compares "the ecstatic fervor" of Hebrew Prophets. Kleinknecht shared his approach, also citing Plato's notion of "mantic" prophecy and oracular speech at Delphi.[15]

Currie and Engelsen develop this theme. Johnson goes further by comparing Paul's choice of words in 14:23.[16] If all speak in tongues, and "outsiders" (NRSV; Greek, *idiōtai, uninitiated*) or unbelievers enter (the Christian assembly), will they not say that you are out of your mind (Greek, *mainesthe*)? Johnson argues that the inference that they are "raving" assumes the phenomenon of "ecstatic" speech.[17]

In some ways, Johnson's argument seems persuasive or convincing. On the other hand, many writers, especially Forbes, object that the parallels with Hellenistic phenomena of inspiration cited by Behm, Kleinknecht, and others are seriously misleading when seeking to understand Paul and the Corinthian church. Indeed Dunn, Grudem, and Williams contend that any exclusive choice between "ecstatic" and "non-ecstatic" would not do justice to Paul or to Corinth. Cyril Williams attempts to hold two aspects together. On the one hand, he writes, "I discover no compelling reasons to abandon the widely held view that the Corinthian phenomenon is unintelligible glossolalia, which in this case was attended by excessive and

---

bis auf Irenaeus.

13. Allo, *Saint Paul*, 377 and 374–84; and Grudem, *The Gift of Prophecy*, 120–29.
14. Behm, "*glōssa*."
15. Kleinknecht, "*pneuma*."
16. Currie, "'Speaking in Tongues.'"
17. Johnson, "Tongues."

uncontrolled behaviour."[18] On the other hand he adds, "The interpretation of One Corinthians 14 is not a simple choice of regarding tongues as either ecstatic incoherent utterances or speaking in real languages. Ecstasy is much too vague a term to employ. There are many degrees of it ranging from mild disassociation to extreme uncontrollable rapture."[19] This accords with Paul's allusion to "various kinds tongues" in 12:10.

(iv) The traditional view, which still perhaps has widest popular support, is that the gift of speaking in tongues constitutes the miraculous power to speak unlearned foreign languages (xenolalia). This was the most widespread pre-modern view held among the church fathers, mediaeval writers, and the Reformers. Among the fathers, Origen, Chrysostom, Theodore, Theodoret, Cyril, and Jerome held this view.[20] In the Middle Ages, Aquinas, Photius, and Estius held the same view, and among the Reformers, Calvin took this approach. In the modern era, Charles Hodge, J. G. Davies, Robert Gundry, and Christopher Forbes are prominent advocates of it.[21]

Theodoret urges that the gift of tongues serves the proclamation of the gospel, even to the point of using unknown languages.[22] Erasmus speaks of this gift "given that one may speak in various languages (*variis linguis loquatur*)."[23] John Calvin comments that "the interpretation of tongues" (1 Cor 12:9) was given because "often [someone] did not know the language of the people with whom they had to have dealings."[24] Hodge calls this gift "the ability to speak in languages primarily unknown to the speakers."[25] More recent scholarship in this tradition includes J. G. Davies, Simon Tugwell, Robert Gundry, and Christopher Forbes. Forbes refers to the Cornelius episode in Acts 10:46 and the disciples of John the Baptist at Ephesus in Acts 19:6, although these are controversial passages.

18. Cyril G. Williams, *Tongues of the Spirit*, 30.

19. Cyril G. Williams, *Tongues of the Spirit*, 25–45.

20. Origen, *Against Celsus*, 7.11; Chrysostom, *Homilies on Acts*, Hom. 4; and *Homilies on 1 Corinthians*, Hom. 19.

21. Hodge, *First Epistle to the Corinthians*, 248: Gundry, "'Ecstatic Utterance' (NEB)?"; Forbes, *Prophecy and Inspired Speech in Early Christianity and Its Hellenistic Environment*, 51.

22. Theodoret, *Interpetatio Ep. 1 ad Cor.* 245A in J-P. Migne, *Patrologia Graeca* 82, 325.

23. Erasmus, *Opera Omnia: in Epist. Pauli ad 1 Cor.*, 898.

24. Calvin, *First Epistle of Paul to the Corinthians*, 263.

25. Hodge, *First Epistle to the Corinthians*, 248.

VI Paul and Christian Worship

Nevertheless, powerful objections to this interpretation come from T. C. Edwards, H. A. W. Meyer, and L. T. Johnson. Edwards writes, "It is evident that the Corinthians did not use their gift of tongues to evangelise the pagan world. They spoke with tongues in their Christian assemblies, and not once does the Apostle urged them to apply the power to the purpose for which it would be so eminently serviceable."[26] In Paul's view, this gift empowers a person to speak not to other people, but *to God* (14:2).

It is a difficult and sensitive question to ask how much modern experiences of speaking in tongues could or should be relevant to New Testament exegesis. Early on in the development of the Pentecostal movement Alfred G. Garr (1874–1944), had received "baptism in the Holy Spirit" in the Azusa Street Revival of 1906. He had entered Asbury College, Wilmore, to receive a call to missionary work in Calcutta. To his surprise, Garr discovered that his gift of tongues proved to have no significance for the learning of the Bengali language, just as his wife, Lillian, discovered that her gift of tongues had nothing to do with learning Tibetan or Mandarin. They both henceforth regarded speaking in tongues as an expression of praise and prayer, and possibly a sign of empowerment, but as having nothing to do with the miraculous ability to speak foreign languages.[27]

In recent times this issue has been regularly debated in such Pentecostal journals as *Pneuma*, *Journal of Pentecostal Theology*, and similar publications, and also online. Specialists in linguistics have also debated whether examples of so-called glossolalia are capable of analysis into intelligible linguistic units. Such linguistics specialists include W. J. Samarin, J. P. Kildahl, and Felicitas D. Goodman.[28] On all sides, therefore, this theory is by no means regarded with the confidence that it once was.

(v) and (vi) We discuss the fifth and sixth meanings of speaking in tongues since these two interpretations are very closely related to each other. Both depend on understanding this gift as relating to the unconscious or subconscious, especially in the light of a ground-breaking work by Gerd Theissen, as well as articles by Krister Stendahl and others.[29] Theissen argues that tongues are "the language of the unconscious which becomes

---

26. Edwards, *First Epistle to the Corinthians*, 319.
27. Cf. Thiselton, *A Shorter Guide to Holy Spirit*, 139–40.
28. Samarin, *Tongues of Men and Angels*; Goodman, *Speaking in Tongues*.
29. Theissen, *Psychological Aspects of Pauline Theology*, 59–114 and 176–341; and Stendahl, "Glossolalia—The N.T. Evidence."

capable of consciousness through interpretation."[30] He works with comparisons with Euripides, Virgil, Plato, and Philo, as well as with apocalyptic and Paul. In Euripides, *The Bacchae*, for example, "Unconscious aggressive impulses develop in the ecstatic state and overcome deeply rooted moral inhibitions."[31] In some writers, he argues, to be filled by God entails relinquishing one's own thought to make room for God (Plato, *Ion,* 534E). But comparisons with pagan writers do not constitute the only or main form of his argument. They simply expose the point that the articulation of what is otherwise unconscious is an important feature of this special kind of speech.

In Paul, the inarticulate groans of the heart become important, and it may be that there is a parallel with the cries to God that come forth from the heart in Romans 8:26, where REB translates "heart" by "inmost being." Many years ago Rudolf Bultmann observed that the yearnings of the heart "need not penetrate into the field of consciousness at all, but may designate the hidden tendency of the self."[32] Romans 8:26–27 concerns the work of the Holy Spirit in actualizing inarticulate yearnings directed towards God from the depths of the heart, and the context is similar to that of 1 Corinthians 12:10—14:20, as we specify in our discussion of the sixth view of speaking in tongues. The further work of Robert Jewett and Krister Stendahl confirms these conclusions.

Stendahl begins his essay on "Glossolalia" in the New Testament with an emphasis on unspeakable groaning from the heart or "Sighs Too Deep for Words."[33] Pentecostal scholar Frank D. Macchia accepts this identification.[34] Robert Jewett sympathetically discusses this identification in Romans 8:26, stressing the work of the Holy Spirit in contexts of human weakness.[35] He notes Käsemann's anti-enthusiasm polemic and his discussion of the intercession of the Holy Spirit in his "Cry for Liberty" essay.[36] Even believing Christians, he says, do not know what it is fitting to pray for by virtue of their human limitations. Stendahl declares that it is "wise

---

30. Theissen, *Psychological Aspects of Pauline Theology*, 79.
31. Theissen, *Psychological Aspects of Pauline Theology*, 277–78.
32. Bultmann, *Theology of the New Testament*, vol. 1, 223.
33. Stendahl, "Glossolalia—The N.T. Evidence" 111.
34. Macchia, "Sighs Too Deep for Words."
35. Jewett, *Romans*, 521–23.
36. Käsemann, "The Cry for Liberty in the Worship of the Church," especially 129–32.

to let glossolalia gush forth . . . so that those who are not professional in the shaping of words are free to express freely their overwhelmed praise to the Lord."[37] He also accepts Paul's proviso about not everyone speaking in tongues because he comments: "few human beings can live healthily with high-voltage religious experience over a long period of time."[38]

This brings us to our conclusion about the precise meaning of "I would like you all to speak in tongues," or more importantly, it's Greek equivalent. Paul understands speaking in tongues to be a genuine gift of the Holy Spirit, but not in all circumstances and for everyone. On certain occasions it may be a gift of the Holy Spirit in moments of release, especially for a gift to the individual. But Paul makes it clear in 1 Corinthians 14:4 that "one who speaks in tongues edifies *himself*," i.e. it is a gift of personal value for the individual. This gift may bring a sense of release, intimacy with God, or other positive consequences. But many may feel unease at the use of such a gift in the public assembly of worship. Hence it may become divisive. The context of 1 Corinthians 12:8-10 and of 14:5 concerns the welfare of the whole community. All these gifts, whatever their nature, are to serve the good of the whole church, not simply the individual recipients of the gifts.

(3) There are two more final points that require discussion and clarification before the case for our conclusion has fully been made. The first concerns the gift known as "the interpretation of tongues" (Greek, *hermēneia glōssōn*, 12:10); (the second will concern the gift known as "prophecy," *prophēteia*, 12:10.

I considered "the interpretation of tongues" at length in 1979 in "The 'Interpretation' of Tongues: A New Suggestion in the Light of Greek Usage in Philo and Josephus." Lexicographical evidence about *diermēneuō* and *hermēneia* from Philo and Josephus reflects Greek usage in the time of Paul. In 1 Corinthians 14:13 Paul writes, "One who speaks in a tongue should pray for the power to interpret" (NRSV; Greek, *diermēneuē*). However, in 14:5, the NRSV (and broadly the RSV) translates: "One who prophesies is greater than one who speaks in tongues, unless *someone* interprets, so that the church may be built up" (my italics).

However, is Paul discussing *two* people in 14:5 or simply *one person*? Traditionally many regard the interpreter of tongues as a second person other than the speaker in tongues. But there is no Greek for "someone" (*tis*) in the verse. Paul may indeed believe that both speaking in tongues and the

---

37. Stendahl, "Glossolalia," 122.
38. Stendahl, "Glossolalia," 123.

ability to articulate what is spoken constitute gifts of the Holy Spirit. But he does not exclude these two gifts being performed by the *same* person. Paul declares, in effect: *the person who speaks in a tongue should pray for the gift and ability to articulate what this tongues-speech means to convey*, whether to God (as is implied by 14:2) or in general.

The lexicography of Philo and Josephus appears to confirm this interpretation of the verse. Philo uses the noun *hermeneia* thirty times, and *hermeneus* thirty-eight times, while the verb *hermēneuō* occurs 153 times. The compound verb *diermēneuō* occurs eighteen times. In the compound form, three-quarters of uses refer to the *articulation* of thoughts or feelings in intelligible speech. Less than fifteen can mean "to interpret" or "to translate." In the absence of the *dia*-compound, the two meanings are almost evenly divided. Sixty-four uses express the articulation of speech. Over one hundred refer to translation or interpretation.

Philo often uses these forms to mean *to put into words*. One of many examples concerns Aaron's task of putting the words of Moses into articulate speech (Exod 4:10–16, LXX). Verbal expression may be like a "shadow" (Greek, *skia*) or "copy" (Greek, *mimēma*) of meaning or substance, but it expresses "the matters that have been articulated or *put into words* (Greek, *tōn diermēneuomenōn . . . pragmatōn*).[39] The Greek verb could not here be rendered "translated" or "interpreted." Philo also speaks of language "articulating" a content or message in *The Confusion of Tongues*.[40] In his book *Abraham, Joseph, Moses*, Philo explains that Benjamin, who is a competent speaker, "puts into words" what his brothers thought.[41] I included at least fifteen specific examples of this meaning of the compound form in my article, and also some twenty-six examples of *hermēneuō* without the compound.

Josephus uses the word *hermēneuō* and its compounds perhaps only a tenth as often as Philo. This is not surprising in view of the difference of subject matter. A striking example, however, occurs when Josephus faces the task of trying to describe the many wonders of Herod's palace. He states that these wonders are "beyond all words." He mentions the walls, towers, banqueting-halls, precious stones, cloisters, and gardens, and concludes that it is therefore impossible to *articulate* all this or *to put it into words* (*outh'*

---

39. Philo, *The Migration of Abraham*, 12 (Loeb Library, vol. 4).
40. Philo, *The Confusion of Tongues*, 53 (Loeb Library, also vol. 4).
41. Philo, *Abraham, Joseph, Moses*, 189 (Loeb Library, vol. 6).

hermēneusai dynaton axiōs ta basileia).[42] Josephus uses the same strategy when he reminds us of Zedekiah's resistance to Babylon, against the counsel of Jeremiah. He says, "It would be beyond me to put [their enormities] into words"; for Moses is "my [God's] mouthpiece" (*di' hermēneōs emou*).[43] I have provided other examples in my article. In sum, our verb often means "to put into words."

Paul, therefore, is urging the Corinthians that anyone who speaks in tongues should pray for the power to put what is felt in the heart into words, or into articulate speech. It can then benefit the whole community, rather than merely edifying the particular person who speaks in tongues. The use of the word "interpretation" is an unnecessary distraction or digression. This strengthens our argument that Paul does not suggest that all Christian believers should speak in tongues, even though he recognizes its value for the individual Christian.

---

42. Josephus, *Jewish War*, Bk. 5, 182; cf. 176 and 178.
43. Josephus, *Antiquities of the Jews*, Bk. 3, 86 and 87.

Chapter 33

What kind of thing is prophesying in Paul?

(1 Corinthians 14:1, 3, 29–40, and 1 Thessalonians 5:20)

In 1 Corinthians 14:1, Paul urges, "Pursue love and strive for spiritual gifts, and especially that you [plural] may prophesy" (Greek, *hina prophēteuēte*). In verse 3, he says, "Those who prophesy speak to other people." In verse 29, "Let two or three prophets speak, and let others weigh what is said." In verse 31, he continues, "You can all prophesy one by one." In verse 39, "Be eager to prophesy." Finally, in 1 Thessalonians 5:20, "Do not despise the words of the prophets" (NRSV), or "Do not . . . despise prophecy" (NJB), or "Do not despise prophetic utterances" (NEB), or "Do not treat prophecies with contempt" (NIV). The Greek is *prophēteias mē exoutheneite*.

Our aim is to understand the meaning of "prophecy" as it is used by Paul. There is universal agreement that prophecy in the New Testament is a declaration of truth revealed by God. However, constant debate occurs about whether, because prophetic utterance is inspired by God, it is necessarily spontaneous and unprepared, or whether *it amounts to applied pastoral preaching*. There are parallels with the debate about whether the gift of healing (12:10) is restricted to "supernatural" or "miraculous" non-medical healing, or whether it may also include healing by prayer and medical intervention.

In modern times, David Hill, Ulrich Müller, Jean Héring, and Thomas H. Gillespie have argued a convincing case that in Paul "prophecy" may constitute *practical, applied, pastoral preaching*. It is not restricted to some supposed "charismatic" utterance, even if it may sometimes or occasionally include this. On the other hand, if I have understood them correctly, Max Turner, James Dunn, and Christopher Forbes, lay the primary stress on more "spontaneous," unprepared utterances. Dunn asserts, "For Paul prophecy is a word of revelation. It does *not denote a previously prepared sermon*. . . . It is a spontaneous utterance (14:30)."[1] Max Turner writes, "For Paul prophecy is the reception and subsequent communication of spontaneous, divinely given *apokalypsis*."[2]

We need to examine the arguments of Héring, Hill, Müller, and Gillespie in detail. Héring observes that since we know that "the aim of prophecy is to edify, exhort, and encourage, it coincides therefore to a large extent with what we call a sermon today."[3] As David Hill observes, constraint by the Spirit does not imply spontaneity: Paul writes, "Necessity is laid upon me; Woe to me if I do not preach the gospel" (1 Cor 9:16).[4] Further, the utterances are required to be tested for their authenticity. Paul refers to people who "think they are prophets," and makes their testing explicit in 1 Thessalonians 5:19-21.[5] Hill concludes: "Christian prophets exercised the teaching ministry in the church which included pastoral preaching."[6]

Thomas Gillespie includes as "prophecy": (i) the interpretation of tradition; (ii) continuity with prophetic declaration and argument in the Old Testament; (iii) utterances of intelligibility in contrast to speaking in tongues; (iv) its function as edification, exhortation and encouragement, which all confirms that "the proclamation of the Prophet is pastoral preaching."[7] Further to the work of Gillespie, K. O. Sandnes underlines Paul's prophetic role, together with that of Philipp Vielhauer.[8] As Bornkamm and Pannenberg argue, Paul did not spare himself the trouble of argument, in spite of his reliance on the Holy Spirit.[9] Prophets preach God's grace and judg-

---

1. Dunn, *Jesus and the Spirit*, 228 (my italics).
2. Max Turner, "Spiritual Gifts Then and Now," 10.
3. Héring, *First Epistle*, 127; so also Friedrich, *TDNT*, vol. 6, 835.
4. Hill, *New Testament Prophecy*, 115; cf. 112.
5. Hill, *New Testament Prophecy*, 118-21.
6. Hill, *New Testament Prophecy*, 131; cf. 110-40.
7. Gillespie, *The First Theologians*, 130-50.
8. Sandnes, *Paul—One of the Prophets?*; and Vielhauer, *Oikodomē*.
9. Bornkamm, "Faith and Reason in Paul," 29-46; and Pannenberg, *Basic Questions in Theology*, vol. 2, 28-64.

ment, but, as Pannenberg convincingly shows, the Holy Spirit is no less at work in mental and rational processes and in the formulation of argument.

Gillespie understands that "the prophetic announcement of the promise is thus the equivalent of the pre-proclamation of the gospel. The merging of the promise and the gospel in the resurrection event ... indicates that the prophets of the Old Testament are distinguished from those who bear the same title [i.e., of prophet] in the church."[10] Both Hill and Gillespie emphasize the function of a prophet as "edification, and exhortation and comfort," which amounts to "pastoral preaching, which ... offers guidance and instruction to the community."[11]

What may seem surprising is that in the pre-modern era the view that prophecy in the New Testament included any revealed communication of the gospel, *including preaching*, was virtually taken for granted before the advent of the Pentecostal and Charismatic Movements. For example, in the patristic era, Ambrosiaster explained that prophecy could take the form of biblical exposition.[12] In the mediaeval era, Thomas Aquinas asserted that prophecy "may be understood as divine doctrine"; "Those who explain divine doctrine are called 'prophets.' ... Do not despise preachers."[13] At the Reformation, John Calvin is no less explicit. He declares, "'Prophecies' mean the art of interpreting Scripture properly applied to the people present."[14] He continues, "This remarkable statement commends preaching."[15]

Among the major Reformers Zwingli and Bullinger (in contrast to Müntzer and the so-called left-wing or Radical Reformers) also held that "prophecy" was broadly pastoral preaching. In the early eighteenth century, Matthew Henry wrote, "By prophesyings, here understand the preaching of the word, the interpreting and applying of the Scriptures."[16] Finally, John Wesley comments on "prophesyings": "That is preaching, for the apostle is not speaking of extraordinary gifts."[17] In the nineteenth century, James Denney wrote, "The prophet was a man who possessed the power of

---

10. Gillespie, *The First Theologians*, 135.
11. Gillespie, *The First Theologians*, 141.
12. Ambrosiaster, *Commentaries on Galatians-Philemon*, 232.
13. Aquinas, *First Letter to the Thessalonians and the Letter to the Philippians*, 52.
14. Calvin, *1 and 2 Thessalonians*, 60.
15. Calvin, *1 and 2 Thessalonians*, 61.
16. Henry, *Expositions of the Old and New Testaments*, vol. 6, 533.
17. Wesley, *Notes on the New Testament* (CD-ROM, Bible Truth Forum, 1754), 694.

speaking edification, exhortation and comfort. In other words, he was a Christian preacher, endued with wisdom, fervour, and tenderness."[18]

We should be extremely rash and unwise to dismiss these witnesses from Aquinas and Calvin to Wesley and Denney as simply wrong. This is certainly not to exclude the possibility that prophesying is sometimes used by Paul in a spontaneous, "charismatic" sense. But this is not the primary sense. Much harm has been done by solemn utterances of an authoritative nature by members of churches who rightly or wrongly believe that God has given them a "prophecy" for a congregation. Paul is emphatic that claims to prophesy must be tested. In 1 Thessalonians 5:20, the NRSV plays safe by applying the reference to prophesying to "the prophets," which may include the Old Testament canonical prophets.

Any temptation to be unduly reflective or rational is less injurious to the church than responses to untested claims to speak as "prophets" to other Christians. As Wolfhart Pannenberg has rightly reminded us, "An otherwise unconvincing message cannot attain the power to convince simply by appealing to the Holy Spirit."[19] Much more to the point, he adds, "The Holy Spirit becomes effective through words and arguments. Argumentation and the operation of the Spirit are not in competition with each other. In trusting in the Spirit, Paul in no way spared himself thinking and arguing."[20]

---

18. Denney, *Epistles to the Thessalonians*, 239.
19. Pannenberg, *Basic Questions in Theology*, vol. 2, 34.
20. Pannenberg, *Basic Questions in Theology*, vol. 2, 35.

VII

Paul's Power in Weakness

Chapter 34

Why boast about "being let down in a basket through a window in the wall"?

(2 Corinthians 11:33)

The absurdity of regarding "being let down in a basket through a window in the wall" as a ground of boasting, especially alongside danger from bandits, danger at sea, toil, and hardship, arouses the suspicion that personal report has given way to humor. Paul's list of genuine "boasts" begins with stating his Jewish credentials (2 Cor 11:22), and traces through his effective ministry (v. 23a), his imprisonments (v. 23b), floggings, near death, lashings, stoning, and shipwreck (vv. 24–25), dangers from five different sources (v. 26), to hunger and thirst, cold and inadequate clothing (v. 27), and the daily pressure and anxiety for all the churches (v. 28). This very long list culminates in the anti-climax of being "let down in a basket through a window in the wall" to escape from King Aretras and his governor in Damascus (vv. 32–33)![1] At first sight, this sudden switch constitutes a puzzle.

---

1. Among the commentaries, the work by Murray Harris provides the most helpful detail on this verse. He explains that "the window in the wall" would have been "a narrow vertical opening in the wall to admit light and air and to enable people to see out" (Harris, *Second Epistle to the Corinthians*, 823–24). He then offers a careful comparison between Luke's account in Acts 9:23–25 and Paul's account in 2 Corinthians 11:32–33 (824–26). The term translated "basket," he adds, in the combined accounts, translates three Greek terms: *kophinos* denotes a stiff wicker basket; *spuris* denotes a flexible basket made from such materials as rushes; and *sarganē* was a flexible woven basket. Together they denote a basket large enough to hold a person.

VII Paul's Power in Weakness

The clue to the resolution of the puzzle lies in v.30: "If I must boast, I will boast of the things that show my weakness." This direction of approach is confirmed by Paul's earlier provisos, "I am talking like a madman" (v. 23), and "I am saying not with the Lord's authority but as a fool" (v. 17). There may even be a hint of humor in the wordplay on fool in "You gladly put up with fools" (v. 19), and "accept me as a fool" (v. 16).

More is at issue than this, however. Specialist studies abound of "catalogues of [Paul's] afflictions or hardships," some of which apply to 1 Corinthians 3:18–20; 4:8–13, 18–21; and 2 Corinthians 11:21–33. J. T. Fitzgerald argues that such catalogues constitute the mark of the authentic sage or wise man.[2] M. S. Ferrari provides an extensive history of research on catalogues of sufferings.[3] K. A. Plank examines Paul's self-descriptions in terms of hardships, and argues that Paul offers a rhetorical poetic metaphor of fundamental irony.[4] As far as 1 Corinthians is concerned, Kleinknecht regards 1 Corinthians 4:8–13 as the highpoint of Paul's ironic self-description, seeing the Corinthian tendency "to boast in human people" (1:29–31). This explains their tendency to jealousy and strife (1:10–11), and their infantile attitude, which called forth Paul's critique of the cross. L. L. Welborn presses this point with reference to 1 Corinthians 1–4 and parts of 2 Corinthians.[5] He sees Paul in the tradition of comic mime, even speculating that his occupation or work was as "a maker of stage properties" or "prop maker" (Greek, *skēnopoios*, traditionally translated "tentmaker").

It is a very short step to interpret "being let down in a basket" as a special piece of Pauline humor. To be "first over the wall" was a singular mark of honor among warriors who sought to capture a besieged city. The hero who first scaled the city wall would risk every kind of retaliation poured down upon his head. He would receive the honor due to an exceptionally brave, courageous man. But Paul has said that the comparisons of strength are foolish. He boasts only in his *weakness!* What could be more impressive as a sign of weakness than to be *not* "first over the wall," but first to escape *in the opposite direction*? This is irony indeed!

---

2. Fitzgerald, *Cracks in an Earthen Vessel*, including 117–48.
3. Ferrari, *Die Sprache des Leids in den paulinischen Peristasenkatalogen*.
4. Plank, *Paul and the Irony of Affliction*, especially 33–70.
5. Welborn, *Paul, the Fool of Christ*, throughout and 86–90; and Welborn, "The Runaway Paul."

Why boast about "being let down in a basket through a window in the wall"?

It is, to say the least, surprising that Windisch and Héring think of this episode as a mere postscript to the catalogue of hardships.[6] E. A. Judge mentions the Roman soldier's reward for being the first to scale the wall of a besieged city.[7] In this light, Travis well sums up the situation as follows: "He [Paul] thus achieves a *reductio ad absurdum* of the self-glorying which is so precious to his critics. He can then come back to the only kind of boasting of which of he approves: boasting in the grace and power of Christ (12:9)."[8] In the incident to which Paul alludes, probably some critics would have accused him of cowardice. If there is to be boasting, Paul says, I will boast of being called a coward! Murray Harris similarly observes that it is now commonplace for commentators to cite the suggestion of Judge that Paul is parodying the Roman award given to the first soldier to scale a fortified city, noting that Paul turns "first up" into "first down."[9]

Wellborn writes, "Because Paul believes that, in the cross of Christ, God has affirmed nothings and nobodies, he is able to embrace the role of the fool as the authentic mode of his own existence. Paul's appropriation of the role of the fool is profound, but not unexpected, given the way in which Jesus was executed and the socially shameful experience of Jesus' early followers."[10] David Hall adds, "Paul talks about various kinds of weakness in his epistles," and he concludes on 2 Corinthians, "None of the arguments commonly used for separating chapters 10–13 from the rest of 2 Corinthians stands up to examination."[11]

---

6. Héring, *Second Epistle to the Corinthians*, 87.

7. Judge, "The Conflict of Educational Aims in New Testament Thought," 45; cf. 32–45; and Judge, "Paul's Posting in Relation to Contemporary Professional Practice."

8. Travis, *Christ and the Judgment of God*. 131.

9. Harris, *Second Epistle to the Corinthians*, 824.

10. Wellborn, *Paul the Fool of Christ*, 250.

11. Hall, *The Unity of the Corinthian Correspondence*, 61 and 106.

Chapter 35

Why not boast about visions and being caught up in the third heaven?

(2 Corinthians 12:1–2)

In 2 Corinthians 12:1–2 Paul speaks of "visions (Greek, *optasiai*) and revelations (Greek, *apokalypseis*) of the Lord," but then the next verse changes from the first person to a linguistic construction for the third person: "who fourteen years ago was caught up to the third heaven." He adds: "Whether in the body or out of the body I do not know; God knows." He then repeats the very same observation in verse 3, adding in verse 4, "was caught up into paradise and heard things that are not to be told, that no mortal person is permitted to repeat." In verse 5, Paul resumes his normal way of discourse in a letter, and in verse 7 admits that this third supposedly anonymous person was indeed Paul himself. Here, however, it is his humiliating "thorn in the flesh" that is the main point of his self-description, thereby showing that he "boasts" *only of his weakness*.

Tasker and others make two important comments. First, Tasker follows Plummer and anticipates Hughes in asserting that "of the Lord" is subjective genitive, i.e. visions that *the Lord gave*, not visions of the Lord like that of Paul's experience on the Damascus road. Second, Tasker continues, "The somewhat enigmatic reference to himself as a man in Christ is due partly to his reluctance to speak about the subject, and partly to a desire to give the impression that *any* Christian . . . might have been privileged to

Why not boast about visions and being caught up in the third heaven?

experience this vision."[1] 12:1 underlines Paul's reluctance to speak about his visions and revelations, in spite of different MS readings of the text. Indeed, Plummer comments, "The text of this verse is so confused that it is impossible to disentangle the original text with certainty."[2] Barrett translates: "I must boast; it is not expedient, but I will come to visions and revelations"; he does this on the basis of the most probable Greek text: *kauchasthai dei. ou sympheron men, eleusomai de* . . . . Some MSS place "if" before "boast," but 𝔓46, B, G, 33, and copsa, bo support the generally accepted reading.[3]

This first verse (12:1) underlines that Paul speaks of himself only because circumstances force this. These include the claims of opponents in Corinth. Personally, he finds this enforced need uncongenial, unprofitable, and embarrassing (Greek, *ou sympheron*, strictly, not profitable). His use of the third person shows his concern *not to draw attention to himself*. All the commentaries make this point, with Martin underlining that Paul's use of the third person is to hide his embarrassment.[4] Crafton has argued that the essence of true apostleship is to be like transparent windows through which we can see only Christ, not to be self-promoting, like the false "super-apostles" in Corinth.[5] These "super-apostles" sought to make themselves weighty and impressive, in a way that anticipates some self-styled "leaders" in parts of the church today.

Paul's reference to "fourteen years ago" may point to an experience in about A.D. 44, several years after his conversion and call. However, it cannot be identified clearly with any particular event in the Acts narrative. The purpose of this reference to fourteen years is to underline the truthfulness of what he is saying, not to pinpoint a chronological timing or setting. In the case of ecstatic experiences, many might judge that Paul was actually "crazy" or had "unrestrained imagination."[6]

With regard to Paul's language about "the third heaven" (12:2), Irenaeus described this as "something great and pre-eminent."[7] He therefore

---

1. Tasker, *Second Epistle of Paul to the Corinthians*, 170 (his italics).
2. Plummer, *Second Epistle of St Paul to the Corinthians*, 337.
3. Metzger, *A Textual Commentary on the Greek New Testament*, 516; Barrett, *Second Epistle to the Corinthians*, 305.
4. E.g., Hughes, *Paul's Second Epistle to the Corinthians*, 428–29; Martin, *2 Corinthians*, 390–92 and 398; Furnish, *II Corinthians*, 523–26 and 542–45.
5. Crafton, *The Agency of the Apostle*.
6. Plummer, *Second Corinthians*, 338; cf. Furnish, *II Corinthians*, 543.
7. Irenaeus, *Against Heresies*, 2.30.7(Eng., ANF, vol. 1, 405).

excludes the relevance of gnostic cosmology and speculations about a seventh heaven. In the same vein, most commentators exclude a reference to Rabbinic notions of seven heavens. Bengel distinguished between the first heaven of clouds and sky, the second heaven of the stars and planets, and the third heaven as spiritual and transcendent. This may not be farfetched in view of Deuteronomy 10:14, which distinguished between "heaven" and "the heaven of heavens," which is non-terrestrial. Psalm 68:33 uses the Hebraism "heaven of heavens" in the same way. Calvin called this the "three" of eminence, to denote what is highest. In verse 4, Paul appears to use "paradise" as a synonym. Here "things that must not be divulged" contrasts with other apocalyptic journeys. Apocalyptic literature of the time sometimes fails to be marked by Paul's reticence. Betz thinks of verses 2–4 as a *parody* of Jewish and other ascension narratives.[8] These abounded in the ancient world. In spite of this, Barrett insists that Paul's words are "essentially independent of the parallels."[9]

The next puzzle in these verses is Paul's aside: "whether in the body (Greek, *sōma*) or out of the body, I do not know; God knows" (v. 2). Does this imply that the self may exist without the body? It may, but Paul does not relish this prospect (cf. 2 Cor 5:1–10). Here he considers this question to be inapplicable.[10] Paul is answering a criticism of the false apostles that he produces no evidence of his apostleship, but he insists that only "boasting" of his weakness counts as a criterion.[11]

In this "third heaven" or "paradise," Paul "heard things that are not to be told, that no mortal is permitted to repeat" (12:34). Paradise (Greek, *paradeisos*) is derived from the Persian for a garden or nobleman's park. The word is used of the Garden of Eden and is identified with the third heaven in 2 Enoch 8 and The Apocalypse of Moses 37:5.[12] In this ecstatic or transcendent state he heard "unutterable" (Greek, *arrēta*) words (or utterances; Greek, *rhemata*). The self-contradiction in Greek, *arrēta rhemata*, "is probably another instance of playing upon words."[13] The Greek *arrēta* is a term used often in mystery religions.[14] But Barrett rightly says, "It would

---

8. Betz, *Der Apostel Paulus und die sokratische Tradition*, 84–92.
9. Barrett, *Second Epistle*, 307.
10. Barrett, *Second Epistle*, 308.
11. Lincoln, *Paradise Now and Not Yet*, 76–77.
12. Barrett, *Second Epistle*, 310–11.
13. Plummer, *Second Corinthians*, 345.
14. E.g., Apuleius, *Metamorphoses* 11:23.

Why not boast about visions and being caught up in the third heaven?

be wrong, however, to suppose that Paul was directly dependent on the mysteries."[15]

In verse 5, Paul clinches the matter: "On my own behalf I will not boast, except of my weakness." He has already introduced the climax of his ironic humor about being let down in a basket,[16] and will soon mention his "thorn in the flesh."[17] All three "puzzles" cohere together as a single picture of Paul's parodying his opponents to boast only in his "weakness." It is all sparked off by his opponents' claims about "proof" of legitimate apostleship.[18] From verse 7, Paul resumes his normal language.

---

15. Barrett, *Second Epistle*, 311.
16. See puzzling passage above.
17. See puzzling passage below.
18. Cf. Käsemann, "Die Legitimität des Apostels"; and the commentaries cited above

Chapter 36

What was Paul's "thorn in the flesh"?
(2 Corinthians 12:7)

Some may be disappointed that there seems to be no clear and definitive "solution" to the puzzle of what constitutes Paul's "thorn in the flesh." But can we know certain things about it. For example, it was certainly Paul's view that it was given to keep him from being unduly elated about his ecstatic visions and experiences. It functioned to keep him humble. The term "thorn in my/the flesh" occurs in the NRSV, AV/KJV, NIV, NJB, REB, ESV, NASB, RV, Weymouth, and NLT. The major exceptions are the NEB, which has "a sharp physical pain," and Phillips, "a physical handicap," although NEB gives as its marginal reading, "a painful wound to my pride." Numerous theories have been proposed concerning various physical illnesses that the term might imply, but even whether the thorn is physical or something else cannot be determined with certainty, as even the NEB, with its marginal reading, suggests. As Plummer commented some one hundred years ago, "These three words . . . have elicited a very large amount of discussion."[1]

If the reference is to a physical illness, H. Clavier has written that the list of suggestions reads like a medical dictionary.[2] The Greek term is *skolops*, which means thorn, splinter, a pointed stake, or injurious foreign body that causes serious annoyance.[3] In the passage in question it impales *sarx*, *flesh*. Elsewhere I have shown the variety of meanings that *sarx* can

---

1. Plummer, *Second Epistle of St Paul to the Corinthians*, 348.
2. Clavier, "La Sante de l'Apotre Paul," 66.
3. BDAG, 930–31; cf. Plummer, *Second Corinthians*, 349–51.

have, from purely physical to other meanings, and Danker confirms this.[4] The majority of commentators understand this to refer to the bodily or physical, but many do not wish to exclude a wider reference.

Hughes and Allo list the most influential theories from patristic times.[5] They note that J. B. Lightfoot's comment that interpreters in different periods of church history have tended to see in the apostle's trial a more or less perfect reflection of the trials that beset their own lives. We list nine of many possibilities from among others, some medical, others not. [NL 1–9]

(1) Tertullian proposed that the "thorn" was headache or earache.[6]

(2) Chrysostom, Pelagius, and Jerome associated it with Galatians 4:13, also interpreting "a messenger of Satan" (2 Cor 12:7) as an adversary. This could then apply to various adversaries such as Alexander the coppersmith or Hymenaeus and Philetas.

(3) Augustine, Theodore of Mopsuestia, and Theodoret cite persecutions, or perhaps some bodily pain.

(4) Modern commentators, including Plumptre, have often cited Galatians 4:15 (where the Galatians would willingly have given their eyes to Paul) as evidence of eye problems. But this reference may have been a metaphor for "doing anything" to help Paul.

(5) Many, including Lightfoot, Findlay, Bousset, and H.-J. Schoeps, argue that *epilepsy* was the thorn. Many leaders, including Julius Caesar, Oliver Cromwell, and Napoleon, are said to have suffered in this way.

(6) Sir William Ramsay has argued for malarial fever, which was known to be active in Pamphylia and the Eastern Mediterranean. This could have prostrating and distressing effects.

(7) Cambier points out that Paul must have had a robust constitution to withstand all the pressures of shipwrecks, bandits, and other dangers, but developed eye trouble and fatigue as his thorn in the flesh.

---

4. BDAG, 914–16; Thiselton, "The Meaning of Sarx in 1 Cor. 5:5."

5. Hughes, *Paul's Second Epistle to the Corinthians*, 442–48; Allo, *Saint Paul: Seconde Épître aux Corinthiens*, 313–23, "Excursus XVI, "La Maladie de Saint Paul."

6. Tertullian, *On Modesty* 13.16 (Eng. ANF vol. 4, 87).

(8) P. H. Menaud argues that Paul's great suffering was that he was largely unable to win Jews to faith in Christ, not physical illness, citing Acts 22:17-21. This was Paul's "great sorrow."[7]

(9) J. J. Thierry also excludes any reference to physical illness, but he argues that "a messenger of Satan" suggests no specific source of trial, but something that humiliated Paul's spirit.[8] [/NL]

Plummer concludes, "Any acute and recurrent malady will suit 2 Cor. 12:7."[9] The Greek for "messenger" is *aggelos*, which means *messenger* as much as *angel*. Martin declares, "Discussion of this verse will not lead the exegete to certainty regarding the identity of Paul's 'thorn in the flesh.' . . . The exact meaning remains elusive."[10] Hughes concludes: "While we do not wish to disparage sane speculation, we are convinced that the very anonymity of this particular affliction has been and is still productive of far wider blessing to the members of the Church . . . than would have been the case had it been possible to identify with accuracy the specific nature of the disability in question."[11] We endorse this conclusion. Paul was consciously reticent about the experience; so should we be.

---

7. Menaud, "L'Echarde et L'Angel Satanique."
8. Thierry, "Der Dorn im Fleische (2 Kor. XII 7-9)."
9. Plummer, *Second Corinthians*, 351.
10. Martin, *2 Corinthians*, 411 and 413.
11. Hughes, *Second Epistle*, 446.

VIII

Puzzling Passages in Paul

Chapter 37

Bland, progressive optimism about everything?

(Romans 8:28)

In Romans 8:28, Paul says, according to the NRSV and AV/KJB, "All things work together for good." This reading is supported by some of the oldest manuscripts, including C, D, and G, and 33. This seems to contradict the experience of many Christians, who would be reluctant to say that every single event in their lives works together for good. On the other hand, other manuscripts, including the ancient papyrus p46, A, B, and Origen include "God" (*ho theos*) as the subject of the sentence: "*God* works all things together for good for those who love God." N. T. Wright helpfully insists, "Verse 28 does not represent a completely new thought.... It is bound tightly to the sequence of the argument.... The train of thought is, 'God knows the mind of the Spirit'; but we know that God works all things together for good to those who love God."[1] In the light of this evidence, it is not surprising that the NJB, the Revised English Bible (REB), and the NIV adopt this interpretation.

Admittedly the textual criticism of the Greek manuscripts is finely balanced. Joseph Fitzmyer comments, "In view of the fluctuation in the text tradition, it is not easy to be certain about which interpretation is better. Any one of them would suit the context."[2] James Dunn also respects the

---

1. Wright, "The Letter to the Romans," 600.
2. Fitzmyer, *Romans*, 523.

support of both textual readings, although he suspects that the Alexandrian editor moves out of the text by adding "God" rather than "all" as the subject.³ Robert Jewett, however, regards understanding "all things" as the subject, as C. H. Dodd has done, as risking "a natural tendency towards progress," which is emphatically not Paul's view.⁴

Although Anders Nygren and Ernst Käsemann follow the NRSV's reading, omitting "God," Charles Cranfield, N. T. Wright, and Robert Jewett are decisive in following the reading "God works all things together for good," also together with the NJB, the REB, and the NIV.⁵

Cranfield discusses eight possible grammatical reconstructions of the text over seven or so pages, pointing out that the verses imply no change of subject from the earlier verses about God. He argues that "Dodd's objection seems to have no cogency."⁶ Furthermore, the term "all things" no doubt refers to "the sufferings of the present time" (v. 18), and to what Calvin calls "adversities" or "the cross." This is confirmed by verses 35–39. The Greek term *synergein* means not only "to work together with," but also "to assist," or "to help on." Cranfield observes, "Even those [events or experiences] which seem most adverse and hurtful, such as persecution or death itself, are profitable to those who truly love God."⁷ On top of all this, Cranfield further cites the acknowledged place of this saying in Jewish tradition.

We conclude that any notion of a "natural tendency towards progress" owes perhaps more to a secular evolutionary mindset than to Paul himself. The context makes it plain that God's purposes may embrace even hostile or discouraging situations, as serving his ultimate victory for Christian believers.⁸

---

3. Dunn, *Romans 1–8*, 466.
4. Jewett, *Romans*, 526.
5. Cranfield, *Epistle to the Romans*, vol. 1, 424–29.
6. Cranfield, *Epistle to the Romans*, vol. 1, 427.
7. Cranfield, *Romans*, 428.
8. Cf. Thiselton, *Discovering Romans*, 180–81.

Chapter 38

Who is the "god of this world"?
(2 Corinthians 4:4)

The vast majority of commentators believe that the reference to "the god of this world" in 2 Corinthians 4:4 refers to Satan. They follow Calvin, and likewise Bengel's comment, "*grandis sed horroribilis descriptio Satani.*"[1] Barrett says, "The god of this age is a bold expression for the devil (cf. 1 Cor. 2:8)."[2] 1 Corinthians 2:8, the cross-reference Barrett appeals to, refers to the rulers of this age. Similarly, Ephesians 2:2 speaks of "the ruler of the power of the air, the spirit who is now at work in those who are not obedient" and in Galatians 1:4, Paul speaks of being set free "from the present evil age." Thus, Plummer, Bultmann, Furnish, Tasker, Harris, and Thrall, also adopt this approach, and Hughes comments, "It is plain that by 'the god of this age' Satan is meant."[3] This identification is not surprising, since Paul immediately says, "The god of this world has blinded the minds of the unbelievers, to keep them from seeing the light of the gospel of the glory of Christ" (v. 4).

---

1. Calvin, *Second Epistle of Paul to the Corinthians*, 53–54; Bengel, *Gnomon Novi Testamenti*, 685.

2. Barrett, *Second Epistle to the Corinthians*, 130.

3. Plummer, *Second Epistle of Paul to the Corinthians*, 114; Bultmann, *Second Letter to the Corinthians*, 103; Hughes, *Paul's Second Epistle to the Corinthians*, 126; Furnish, *II Corinthians*, 247; Tasker, *Second Epistle of Paul to the Corinthians*, 70; Harris, *Second Epistle to the Corinthians*. 327.

VIII Puzzling Passages in Paul

Yet Plummer also comments, "The expression occurs nowhere else."[4] Furnish calls it "strange."[5] Paul's term "the god" is singular, while "the rulers of this age" is plural, although in John Jesus speaks of "the ruler of this world" (John 12:31; 14:30; 16:11; cf. Eph 2:2). Plummer further comments, "This does not mean that God abdicates or renders any portion of his dominion to Satan, but that those to whom he has granted free will place themselves under the power of darkness."[6] Furnish sees this as part of the dualism that Paul takes over from apocalyptic, in contrast to the new creation. Bultmann compares this dualism with Homer and Sophocles.[7] Yet such dualism is only partially characteristic of Paul. Paul does think in terms of the two ages, but God also exercises his governance over the whole world. Paul usually speaks of "Satan" by name, and then only rarely in his epistles (probably some eight times in all the epistles).

This fact leads us to consider Frederick Long's alternative explanation of this verse.[8] (1) Long begins by stressing that 2 Corinthians 4:4 presented more puzzles to ancient commentators than to writers today.[9] Tertullian, for example, considered three possibilities. He first rejected Marcion's hypothesis of "two gods."[10] Second, he proposed an interpretation suggested by Irenaeus, Origen, and Chrysostom.[11] These regarded *God*, not Satan, as "blinding the minds" of unbelievers. (Most Greek MSS would not distinguish between capitals and lower-case letters.) Third, Tertullian admitted the possibility of today's view that "the god of this age" might be Satan, alluding to Isaiah 14:14.[12]

(2) Long's second main point is that in the ancient world Mediterranean kings were readily praised as gods.[13] He cites evidence relating to Augustus, Tiberius, and Nero. This explicitly related to Roman Corinth,

---

4. Plummer, *Second Epistle of Paul to the Corinthians*, 114.

5. Furnish, *II Corinthians*, 247.

6. Plummer, *Second Epistle of Paul to the Corinthians*, 114.

7. Bultmann, *Second Letter to the Corinthians*, 104–5.

8. Long, "'The God of This Age' (2 Cor. 4:4) and Paul's Empire-Resisting Gospel at Corinth."

9. Long, "'The God of This Age' (2 Cor. 4:4)," 219

10. Tertullian, *Against Marcion* 5.11 (Eng., *ANF*, vol. 3, 454).

11. Irenaeus, *Against Heresies*, 4.49.1 (Eng. *ANF*, vol. 1, 502); Chrysostom, *Homilies on Second Corinthians*, Hom. 8 (Eng. *NPNF*, ser.1 vol. 12, 314).

12. Tertullian, *Against Marcion* 5.11 (Eng., *ANF*, vol. 3, 454).

13. Long, "God of the Age (2 Cor. 4:4)," 221–24.

because Corinth was a Roman province with Roman customs, laws, and ethos.

(3) His third section, which is closely linked to the above, relates to Imperial devotion at Corinth and Achaia. Here he quotes the maxim "Paul's greatest enemy in Corinth was the Imperial Cult," as Bruce Winter and others have argued.[14] In 2 Corinthians 2:14—7:2, he says, "Paul uses Roman triumphal processional themes and builds them climatically to address the Christ followers as Corinthians."[15]

Long then declares, "Paul presented a thoroughgoing counter triumphal and Imperial reality: God in Christ provides the ultimate triumph against all other competing religio-political claims, and this reality should affect how Christ-followers viewed and lived in the world, specifically in Corinth."[16] What made this triumphal imagery so attractive for Paul and Corinthian converts, Long continues, was the sheer number of triumphal processions observed in Vespasian's reign. With regards to 2 Corinthians 4:4, Ian Lambert argues that the god of this age is the defeated foe in God's triumphal procession in Christ. But Long rejects this for want of evidence. He sees the key in "the context of totalizing imperial claims."[17]

(4) The word "Lord," Long argues, is repeated four times in 2 Corinthians 3:16–18, in preparation for 4:5.[18] But the word is also used as a religious-political term for the reigning emperor. Long provides documentary and ostrica-related evidence for its application to Augustus, Tiberius, Claudius, and Nero. Hence, he concludes, "Within the interpretive context . . . for 2 Cor. 4:5, Paul would be countering the imperial claim to the status of emperor as lord."[19]

(5) The final stage of Long's argument hinges on the mutually exclusive polarities of "What fellowship has light with darkness? What harmony has Christ with Belial? What agreement has the temple of God with idols?"[20] He concludes, "By 'the god of this this age' in 2 Cor. 4:4 Paul did not specifically have as his referent Satan but the defiled emperor Augustus who everywhere in public, civic spaces was blinding and counter-shining

---

14. Long, "God of the Age (2 Cor. 4:4)," 225–27.
15. Long, "God of the Age (2 Cor. 4:4)," 227.
16. Long, "God of the Age (2 Cor. 4:4)," 229.
17. Long, "God of the Age (2 Cor. 4:4)," 242.
18. Long, "God of the Age (2 Cor. 4:4)," 245.
19. Long, "God of the Age (2 Cor. 4:4)," 247.
20. Long, "God of the Age (2 Cor. 4:4)," 255–58.

VIII Puzzling Passages in Paul

the glorious gospel of the Messiah Jesus."[21] Paul's later statement in 11:14 that Satan is disguised as an angel of light would have helped Corinthian Christians to understand how Satan worked through the reigning emperor Nero, and hence Augustus. "Paul was critiquing the age present at Corinth that was reflecting the broader Mediterranean world, which was enamored with (all-)powerful earthly rulers. This is idolatry."[22] In modern translation, he adds, "the god of this age" in 4:4 may be placed within "scare quotes."

The strongest part of Long's proposal is that the city of Corinth was a firmly *Roman city* as may be illustrated from Donald Engels' book, *Roman Corinth*, and from my longer commentary on the Greek text of First Corinthians.[23] Beyond this basic correct assumption, we must admit that Long's article seems convincing, especially with its huge fund of original evidence, but may not be quite decisive. The mass of commentaries understood the reference of 2 Corinthians 4:4 to be to Satan, but many of Long's comments are forceful. Further, they remind us today of the huge part played by secular (often anti-Christian) culture, which increasingly aspires to be totalizing. There is perhaps more than one possible way of understanding "the god of this world."

---

21. Long, "God of the Age (2 Cor. 4:4)," 259.

22. Long, "God of the Age (2 Cor. 4:4)," 260.

23. Engels, *Roman Corinth*, throughout; and Thiselton, *First Epistle to the Corinthians*, 1–54, and throughout.

Chapter 39

Who is "the lawless one" and what is "the mystery of lawlessness"?

(2 Thessalonians 2:3, 7)

In 2 Thessalonians 2:3 Paul writes, "Let no one deceive you in any way; for that day will not come unless the rebellion comes first and the lawless one (Greek, *ho anthrōpos tēs anomias*) is revealed, the one destined for destruction (*ho hyios tēs apōleias*)." In 2 Thessalonians 2:7, he continues: "For the mystery of lawlessness (Greek, *to mystērion tēs anomias*) is already at work, but only until the one who now restrains it (Greek, *ho katechōn*) is revealed." Who is "the lawless one" in verse 3? What is "the mystery of lawlessness" in verse 7? And further, who is "the one who now restrains," and from what does this person or thing restrain?

These verses have given rise to much debate and often puzzlement. One problem emerges from the different manuscript readings, which give rise to different translations of "lawless one" in 2:3. Most textual witnesses read "man of lawlessness, as ℵ, B, copsa bo, and Tertullian. However, other ancient MSS read "man of sin" (Greek, *hamartias*), namely the "Western" A, D, and G. The rebellion and revelation of "the lawless one" are often thought to refer to public events, perhaps to forces of evil that work behind the scenes. But whatever form these take, their identity may be revealed and exposed immediately before Christ's parousia. Some common features exist between 2 Thessalonians and Jubilees 23:14–27, 4 Ezra 5:1–2, and The Assumption of Moses 5, which are all in the Jewish Pseudepigrapha.

In verse 3, "the rebellion" (Greek, *apostasia*) is also difficult. It denotes either a political rebellion, as in Josephus, or a religious defection, as in Acts 21:21. Bruce comments, "Since the reference here is to a world-wide rebellion against divine authority at the end of the age, the ideas of political revolt and religious apostasy are combined."[1]

In verse 7, both "the mystery of lawlessness" and "the one who now restrains" are puzzling. Witherington refers to "scholarly uncertainty" about the referent.[2] Tertullian and Hippolytus had suggested that this refers to the Roman Empire or Emperor; Nicholl and others refer more widely to the principle of law and order.[3] Paul would have heard of the chaos experienced under the Emperor Gaius (Caligulla), which was then held back or restrained under Claudius. But many call these identifications only conjectures.

Beda Rigaux makes three helpful points. First, Paul shares with this Jewish literature a cosmic or world-wide perspective. Second, divine intervention and new creation are prominent. Third, these themes are apocalyptic ones, which appeal to other parts of revelation. Paul regularly speaks of tribulation alongside the day of redemption (Gal 4:30; Rom 9:22).[4] At all events, the church in Thessalonica was troubled and unsettled, and pastoral clarification was now urgent.

Some have tried to shelve or divert the problem by claiming that the emphasis on the imminence of the return of Christ in 1 Thessalonians is inconsistent with the emphasis in 2 Thessalonians that certain events must happen first. Therefore, some claim, the second epistle is not Pauline. This, however, is to ignore the fact that the whole of the New Testament witnesses to this double emphasis on the suddenness, surprise, and imminence of the parousia, and also that certain signs of its coming must take place first. The eschatological sayings of the Gospels witness to this double polarity. It is probable that Paul writes in 2 Thessalonians to correct an unduly exaggerated response to the theme of imminence in the first Epistle.

It may clarify this puzzling passage if we first look at its "reception" or post-history from the early church fathers. The patristic era witnesses to the puzzlement of the ancient church about Paul's words. In the history of exegesis Tertullian (c. 160–c. 225) was probably the first to discuss

---

1. Bruce, *1 & 2 Thessalonians*, 166.
2. Witherington, *1 and 2 Thessalonians*, 208.
3. Nicholl, *From Hope to Despair in Thessalonica*, 228.
4. Rigaux, *Saint Paul: Les Épitres aux Thessaloniciens*, 213–22.

Who is "the lawless one" and what is "the mystery of lawlessness"?

2 Thessalonians 2:1–10 in detail, declaring that Marcion had wrongly erased this epistle to serve his system of belief.[5] He then refers to "the one who restrains," as we noted, as the Roman state. Origen (c. 185–c. 254) quotes 2 Thessalonians 2:1–12 in full, and regards the "the lawless one" as one who sits in the temple of God.[6] Hippolytus (170–236) quotes 2 Thessalonians 2:1–11 among a cluster of apocalyptic material, including Mark 13.[7] Lactantius (c. 250–c. 325) speaks of both persecutions and cosmic signs, including earthquakes, diseases, falling stars, and prodigies, and quotes 2 Thessalonians 2, citing "the father of lies" who will turn people from God.[8]

In the post-Nicene era, Athanasius (296–373) considers 2 Thessalonians 2:1–12, arguing for the importance of an unknown date of the End.[9] Basil of Caesarea (c. 330–79) calls for endurance, and refers to "the son of perdition" who exalts himself and is worshipped.[10] Ambrosiaster (c. 380) comments closely on the text, warning against deception by the Antichrist, who is part of the failure (Latin, defection) in the Roman Empire: "Rome will falter, then the Antichrist will come," and take his seat in the House of the Lord.[11] Perhaps the first new break in routine comments comes with Tyconius (died c. 400), who saw the Antichrist or "lawless one" as a corporate reality *within* the church.[12] The "man of sin" is said to build a false temple. Tyconius's "Rule 4" concerns supernatural opposition to the church.

John Chrysostom (c. 347–407) is also explicit about the lawless one. He argues that 2 Thessalonians 2 refers to false prophecy. The "son of perdition" is not Satan, but "some man" in whom Satan works, and "a kind of opponent to God." He is not only in Jerusalem, but "in every church."[13] As for "the mystery of lawlessness," Chrysostom considers that this concerned

---

5. Tertullian, *Against Marcion*, 5.16 (Eng., ANF, vol. 3, 463–64).

6. Origen, *Against Celsus* 6.46.1–2, and 2.50 (Eng., ANF, vol. 4, 594 and 450–51).

7. Hippolytus, *Treatise on Christ and the Antichrist*, 64 (Eng., ANF, vol. 5, 218).

8. Lactantius, *Institutes* 17 (Eng., ANF, vol. 7, 214).

9. Athanasius, *Four Discourses against the Arians* 1.13.54 and 3.28.49 (Eng., NPNF, ser. 2, vol. 4, 338 and 420–21).

10. Basil of Caesarea, *Letter* 139 (Eng., NPNF, ser.2, vol. 8, 203).

11. Ambrosiaster, *Commentarius in Epistolas Paulinas*, 239–40.

12. Tyconius, *The Book of Rules*, 1.3, 10–14; 2.10; 4.88; 6.108–11; cf. Hughes, *Constructing Antichrist*, 84–94.

13. John Chrysostom, *Homily on Thessalonians*, Hom. 3 (Eng., NPNF, ser. 1, vol. 13, 386).

VIII Puzzling Passages in Paul

Nero, as a type of Antichrist, alluding to Daniel's language about Empires.[14] Theodore of Mopsuestia (c.350–428) argues that "the lawless one" is indeed human: "He will be a man, with a demon working everything in him."[15] He explains that the "lawless one" will "serve sin," and appear before many. Pelagius (c. 360–c. 430) sees the lawless one as part of a succession of false prophets, while the "man of sin" is Satan. He sees 2 Thessalonians 2 as a fulfilment of Daniel 7:24.[16] Jerome (c. 345–420) regards the lawless one as the son of the devil. Like Theodore, he sees him as trying to establish a restored temple either in Jerusalem or in the church. He tries to mimic Christ. In general Jerome resisted millennialism, but accepted the apocalyptic implications of 2 Thessalonians 2:1–12.[17] Augustine (354–430) regarded the method of Tyconius with respect. He discussed 2 Thessalonians 2:1–12 in *The City of God*, predicting the damnation of the devil, the new creation, and the glory of the church.[18]

In the mediaeval era, the majority of writers tend to repeat the speculations or conclusions of the patristic era. Haimo of Auxerre (died c. 865), for example, regarded the "lawless one" as "the Antichrist," and "the mystery of lawlessness" as the persecution of martyrs, most notably under Nero.[19] Ambiguities of interpretation did not cease at the Reformation. Almost predictably, Martin Luther (1483–1546) tends to identify forces of evil and deception with the papacy of the time. He explicitly identifies "the man of sin" with the papacy, and asserts that "Satan can make himself appear as if he were God."[20] John Calvin also understands 2 Thessalonians 2:1–12 as a warning against deception, when the devil "masquerades as an angel of light" as a "fickle adversary."[21] But he also combines a historical comment on the collapse of the Roman Empire with a contemporary illusion to "the claims of the Pope" and the "abomination" of popery.[22] Obbe Phillips

---

14. John Chrysostom, *Homily on Thessalonians*, Hom. 4 (Eng., NPNF, ser. 1, vol. 13, 388).
15. Theodore of Mopsuestia, *Epistolas B. Pauli Commentarii*, vol. 2, 50–51.
16. Pelagius, *Expositions of the Thirteen Epistles of St Paul*), 443–44.
17. Jerome, Letter 121.
18. Augustine, *City of God*, 20.1–19.
19. Haimo of Auxerre, *Two Mediaeval Apocalyptic Commentaries*, 25, 27.
20. Luther, *Selections from His Writings*, 307.
21. John Calvin, *1 and 2 Thessalonians* (Wheaton: Crossway, 1999) 83 and 84.
22. Calvin, Ibid, 86–87.

(c. 1560) speaks of the papacy as Sodom and Babylon, while Arminius says that the man of sin arises "out of the ruins of the Roman Empire."[23]

We should not be surprised if the interpretations are sometimes conflicting or mixed and imprecise. The apocalyptic imagery which Paul uses in 2 Thessalonians 2 draws perhaps on what Brevard Childs and George B. Caird term "broken myth," i.e., imagery that may be mythological *in origin*, but non-mythological *in function*.[24] Further, Marshall points out that one reason for the ambiguity of these terms is that the "lawless one" in 2:5–7 refers to the period before his appearance that is described in 2:3–4, and 2:9–12 go back to the period of his appearance before his destruction described in verse 8.[25]

In the nineteenth century, Hermann Olshausen (1796–1839) acknowledged that "the Restrainer" (2:6) is "extremely obscure," even if Paul clearly points to "the appointed time."[26] God has his purposes in history. He admits that "the phrase 'the mystery of lawlessness' here is peculiar."[27] It may refer to a universal unchristian spirit in the city of Rome. Paul *meant* to say: "The spirit of lawlessness is already at work; it is already in motion; nothing hinders its revelation but he *only* now keeps it back; until he shall have been removed it cannot come forth; . . . *then* the lawless one will reveal himself without delay."[28] He rejects any specific identification of "the lawless one" with Nero or another historical figure.

On the other hand, Benjamin Jowett (1817–93) suggested that "that which restrains" may be the prayers of Christians or the ministry of Paul. He reviewed specific historical allusions to Nero, Caligula, Titus, and Vitellius, and even beyond the Roman emperors to the pope, Muhammed, and the French revolution, and concluded, "Most of these . . . may be set aside."[29] The "man of sin," he urged, is a symbolic or figurative image of evil, which was "around and very near him [Paul]."[30] This kind of language,

---

23. Arminius, *The Works of James Arminius*, vol. 1, 330.

24. Childs, *Myth and Reality in the Old Testament*, 42; and Caird, *Language and Imagery of the Bible*, 226–28.

25. Marshall, *1 and 2 Thessalonians*, 185.

26. Olshausen, *Commentary on Galatians, . . . 1 and 2 Thessalonians*, 459.

27. Olshausen, *Commentary on Galatians, . . . 1 and 2 Thessalonians*, 459 460.

28. Olshausen, *Commentary on Galatians, . . . 1 and 2 Thessalonians*, 462, (Olshausen's italics).

29. Jowett, *The Epistles of St. Paul to the Thessalonians*, 179.

30. Jowett, *The Epistles of St. Paul to the Thessalonians*, 181.

VIII Puzzling Passages in Paul

he argued, was used by Ezekiel, Daniel, Matthew, Peter, and Revelation. These are not unreal abstractions, but living realities. The Jewish law and the Roman Empire may have had a role in sustaining them.[31]

J. B. Lightfoot (1828–89) acknowledged that such symbolic imagery had been applied to Antiochus Epiphanes in Daniel 11:36, and that "the man of sin" is a personification in analogy with the Hebraism "son of death."[32] The watershed in a more symbolic interpretation of apocalyptic thus began in the nineteenth century.

In the twentieth century, one of the early commentaries was that by W. F. Adeney in 1910. On verse 3, he accepts the MS reading "man of sin," which he regards as a Hebraism for *sinful man*.[33] On verse 7, he expounds the mystery of lawlessness as "the restrained power of wickedness, still hidden, but ultimately to be revealed."[34] Two years later J. E. Frame's International Critical Commentary appeared. The *anomos* (Greek for "lawless one"), he writes, must come before the parousia can take place, together with "the apostasy" or religious revolt.[35] As we observed from Bruce's comment, both meanings may be involved. Frame suggests that Paul is thinking of "the apostasy of non-Christians as a whole."[36] He adds that the function of the "restrainer" is not permanent, but is exercised for God's purpose that the lawless one may be revealed in his proper time, namely the time that it has been appointed by God. Frame has a long discussion of "man of lawlessness" and "the restrainer," tracing a modern history of interpretation, including Bousset, Charles, and others. He exposes the wildly different conjectures about the restrainer, from the Roman Empire to the Holy Spirit.[37]

G. G. Findlay wrote in 1925. The apostasy, he says, was predicted by Jesus in Matthew 24:10–13, 24, where Jesus speaks of false prophets, who will mislead many. Likewise, the Thessalonians must not be misled. The man of sin "concentrates into himself all that in human life and history is most hostile to God and rebellious to his law."[38]

---

31. Jowett, *The Epistles of St. Paul to the Thessalonians*, 183 and 192.
32. Lightfoot, *Notes on Epistles of St. Paul*, 111–13.
33. Adeney, *Thessalonians and Galatians*, 236.
34. Adeney, *Thessalonians and Galatians*, 239
35. Frame, *The Epistles of St Paul to the Thessalonians*, 250.
36. Frame, *The Epistles of St Paul to the Thessalonians*, 251.
37. Frame, *The Epistles of St Paul to the Thessalonians*, 259–62
38. Findlay, *The Epistles to the Thessalonians*, 168.

Who is "the lawless one" and what is "the mystery of lawlessness"?

By the middle of the century, the symbolic character of the lawless one has become established. Two commentaries that appeared in the 1950s are by William Neil and Leon Morris. Neil also refers to Matthew 24, concerning events that must precede the parousia. Paul uses a technical term from apocalyptic for "a widespread and violent defiance of the authority of God."[39] The lawless one is associated with the rebellion. He is, as most point out, hidden, until the time comes for him to be revealed. He will be "the incarnation of evil, as Jesus was the incarnation of goodness."[40] Neil paraphrases the mystery of lawlessness in verse 7 as "the secret force of lawlessness," which is at work already.[41] He adds, "The restraining power cannot be God or the Holy Spirit because of the closing words of v. 7" (i.e., "it is removed").[42] He then discusses the traditional view that the restrainer is the Roman Empire in the shape of concrete people such as Claudius and Nero. But 2 Thessalonians was written in A.D. 50, Nero would have been a boy of thirteen at the time! Neil rejects the identification with a historical person, rather than a symbolic force, as in most apocalyptic literature.[43]

In 1959, Leon Morris in effect retraces the same ground. He repeats, "All attempts to equate the Man of Lawlessness with historical personages break down."[44] "The mystery of lawlessness" denotes simply something that was hidden from humankind but will be made known. It alludes to the purposes of God and is "the spirit of the antichrist."[45]

Two English commentaries of note appeared in 1969 (Whiteley and Moore), and one in 1972 (Best). Whiteley cites parallels with Mark 13 about woes that precede the parousia. He then retraces the ground covered by Neil, including textual variants.[46] Arthur Moore had already published *The Parousia in the New Testament* in 1966. The man of lawlessness, he argues, is taken over from apocalyptic imagery. He is "the one in whom Satan's power is concentrated and in whom Satan is to be unmasked."[47]

---

39. Neil, *Thessalonians*, 160.
40. Neil, *Thessalonians*, 161.
41. Neil, *Thessalonians*, 165.
42. Neil, *Thessalonians*, 166.
43. Neil, *Thessalonians*, 168–71.
44. Morris, *First and Second Epistles to the Thessalonians*, 221.
45. Morris, *First and Second Epistles to the Thessalonians*, 228.
46. Whiteley, *Thessalonians*, 98–102.
47. Moore, *1 and 2 Thessalonians*, 101.

Ernest Best published his commentary three years later. He refers to intertestamental literature and the New Testament to explain the apostasy (1 En. 91:5ff.; Jub. 23:4ff., 2 Bar., etc.). This apostasy is not of Christians but is "to us unidentifiable."[48] The "man of rebellion" (Greek, *anomias*, "lawlessness") denotes a figure in whom the rebellion crystallizes. He is not Satan, but Satan's tool, often a false prophet, who exalts himself against everyone.[49] Best writes, "Many of the characteristics of the Rebel, e.g., his self-exaltation, his entry into the temple, are also seen in some of those who had oppressed the Jews in the immediate past, e.g., Antiochus Epiphanies, Pompey, Caligula; sometimes these features are also attached to non-historical figures . . . who may represent historical persons but who, once the historical period of their reference was passed, might become detached from an anchorage in history."[50]

On verse 7, Best produces eleven factors to determine the meaning of "he who restrains," including Oscar Cullmann's opinion that in the view of the early Christians the end was delayed until the gospel had been preached to the gentiles. But after lengthy discussion he rejects Cullmann's approach and defends the traditional view that the Roman Empire was in mind.[51] "The mystery of rebellion" (his phrase) denotes evil now at work in the present.

We have already considered some comments of F. F. Bruce (1982) on the rebellion, where he sees a reference to "a general abandonment of the basis of civil order."[52] The man of sin denotes the leader of this great rebellion, while the mystery of lawlessness is "already active."[53] Like Best, he rejects Cullmann's interpretation of the one who restrains.

Abraham Malherbe (1987 and 2000) rightly argues that in pastoral terms the purpose of 2 Thessalonians 2:1–12 is to build the confidence of the church.[54] The "man of lawlessness" is part of Paul's visual imagery.[55]

---

48. Best, *First and Second Epistles to the Thessalonians*, 282.

49. Best, *First and Second Epistles to the Thessalonians*, 284–85.

50. Best, *First and Second Epistles to the Thessalonians*, 289.

51. Best, *First and Second Epistles to the Thessalonians*, 297–301; cf. Cullmann, *Christ and Time*, 164–66; and Giblin, *The Threat to Faith*, 167.

52. Bruce, *1 and 2 Thessalonians*, 167.

53. Bruce, *1 and 2 Thessalonians*, 170.

54. Malherbe, *Paul and the Thessalonians*, 75.

55. Malherbe, *The Letters to the Thessalonians*, 419.

Who is "the lawless one" and what is "the mystery of lawlessness"?

Earle J. Richard (1995) builds on what his predecessors have argued about apocalyptic, and the need to counteract false understandings of the End. The "person of lawlessness" is "at the service of the power of lawlessness that is opposed to God."[56] The mystery of lawlessness means "the actual appearance of evil."[57]

Finally, we considered above the commentary of Ben Witherington III (2006), in which he endorses the apocalyptic background of this passage, and relates it to Paul's other work.[58]

Our survey of the history of interpretation has revealed that much ink was spilt before the nineteenth century on speculating about historical identities for "the lawless one" and even "the mystery of lawlessness." With an increasing awareness of the imagery of apocalyptic, however, the *symbolic* nature of these terms became increasingly established from the nineteenth to the twenty-first centuries. In this specific case, the history of exegesis has been a process of increasing enlightenment.

---

56. Richard, *First and Second Thessalonians*, 326–27.
57. Richard, *First and Second Thessalonians*, 330.
58. Witherington, *1 and 2 Thessalonians*, 214–18, 221–26.

Chapter 40

Bewitched? Or Rational and Logical?
(Galatians 3:1)

In Galatians 3:1 Paul says to the church in Galatia, "You foolish Galatians! Who has bewitched (Greek, *ebaskanen*) you? It was before your eyes that Jesus Christ was publicly exhibited as crucified!" Paul is using language that in another context might be thought "biting and aggressive," even "insulting."[1] Yet, Betz argues, in the diatribe (the language of debate) such language is not infrequent. Today, this verse might perhaps not seem so puzzling, but for the fact that so often it is suggested that Paul had a very low estimate of human reason. Many assume that reason, logic, and rationality do not feature among his positive priorities.

Burton comments that Paul's address signals "surprise touched with indignation that the Galatians are turning away from his [Paul's] gospel of Christ crucified."[2] The Galatians are addressed in the vocative case as "foolish" (Greek, *anoētoi*), the term that Jesus used in Luke 24:25 of the two disciples who were slow of heart or understanding to believe. F. F. Bruce rightly comments, "Paul uses the adjective here and in v. 3 to emphasize the *illogicality* of the Galatians' retrogression."[3] Bligh paraphrases verse 1 as "Can a Christian be so foolish as to imagine that Christ died for nothing?"[4]

---

1. Betz, *Galatians*, 130.
2. Burton, *Epistle to the Galatians*, 143.
3. Bruce, *The Epistle to the Galatians*, 148 (my italics).
4. Bligh, *Galatians*, 225.

Bewitched? Or Rational and Logical?

The word translated "bewitched" (Greek, *baskainō*) means to fascinate or bewitch, originally by means of the evil eye, i.e., to exert an evil influence through the eye.[5] Paul tells his readers that some malign influence must have overcome them for them to lose their sense of logic and rationality. Guthrie also argues that this *illogicality* seemed as if their good sense had been dissolved by magic.[6]

The path that the Galatians are now tempted to follow is utterly inconsistent with their experience of becoming Christians and learning the faith. Paul remonstrated that he had "placarded," or painted publicly, the gospel of Christ crucified before them. Lightfoot first suggested the term "placarded" for the Greek, *prographō*, and Burton, Bornkamm, and Bruce follow this suggestion.[7]

Many people assume that in Paul's eyes conviction through the Holy Spirit far outweighs any intellectual competence. Nevertheless, Pannenberg states, "One cannot run away . . . from the question of truth by appealing to the Holy Spirit, for instance . . . an otherwise unconvincing message cannot attain the power to convince simply by appealing to the Holy Spirit."[8] He continues, "Argumentation and the operation of the Spirit are not in competition with each other. In trusting in the Spirit, Paul in no way spared himself thinking and arguing."[9]

Pannenberg insists on the importance of argumentation and rationality for Paul and for the Christian faith: "The essence of faith must come to harm precisely if in the long run rational conviction about its basis fails to appear. Faith is then perverted into blind credulity."[10] It is precisely for the sake of the purity of faith that "the importance of rational knowledge of its basis has to be emphasised."[11] The knowledge of that which faith believes cannot, of course, displace the act of self-abandoning trust.[12] But neither can subjective trust displace the objective content and rationality of what is believed. Pannenberg believes in this so strongly that he argues: "The tendency towards a subjectivization and individualisation of piety . . . has

---

5. Danker, *BDAG*, 171.
6. Guthrie, *Galatians*, 95.
7. Bornkamm, *Paul*, 159; Bruce, *Galatians*, 148; Burton, *Galatians*, 143.
8. Pannenberg, "Insight and Faith," in *Basic Questions in Theology*, vol. 2, 34.
9. Pannenberg, "Insight and Faith," in *Basic Questions in Theology*, vol. 2, 35.
10. Pannenberg, "Insight and Faith," in *Basic Questions in Theology*, vol. 2, 28.
11. Pannenberg, "Insight and Faith," in *Basic Questions in Theology*, vol. 2, 28.
12. Pannenberg, "Insight and Faith," in *Basic Questions in Theology*, vol. 2, 37.

VIII Puzzling Passages in Paul

threatened the life of our churches and wrought its divisiveness for a long time."[13]

Pannenberg allows, however, that Paul's alleged disparagement of reason has a limited basis. Luther, he admits, called reason "a monster" and "the source of all evil," and never tired of stressing that the gospel is "against all reason."[14] But at Worms, Luther appealed to Scripture and also to clear evidence of reason (*ratio evidens*) as judges of his case. In the modern era, Pannenberg says, "the task of a rational account of the truth of faith has acquired ever more acute urgency."[15] In any case, he continues, upon closer inspection "reason" is by no means a uniform entity. There are differences between *a priori* reason, perceiving reason, and historical reason. Thomas Aquinas related faith and reason in a complementary way: the contents of Christian faith, he said, could not be derived from *a priori* reason, but reason, in the sense of rationality, always has a necessary place *alongside faith*. In philosophical thought since Hamaan, Herder, and Jacobi, the idea of "receiving reason" has to be distinguished from Kant's notion of reason. In Hegel, historical reason undergoes increasing importance. Pannenberg further concludes, "Reflection upon the historical nature of reason has led us into the horizon of eschatology."[16]

Reason takes on a much more positive profile in Paul than many assume or expect. We find positive evaluations of reason in virtually every epistle. In chronological sequence, (1) Paul writes to the Thessalonians that they should have a right mind (Greek, *nouthetein*; 1 Thess 5:12, 14; 2 Thess 3:15). (2) He pleads that the Christians of Galatia should not be seduced or bewitched by failing to use reason and logic (Gal 3:1-2). (3) To the Corinthians he says, "I will pray with the spirit, but I will pray with the mind also" (1 Cor 14:15); and he explains that the Holy Spirit brings "the mind of Christ" (1 Cor 2:16). (4) Paul prays that the church of Rome may experience "the renewing of your mind" (Rom 12:2; cf. Eph 4:23). (5) He prays that the Philippians will use their minds and think (Phil 4:7). Mind (Greek, *nous*) is the agent of rationality.[17]

---

13. Pannenberg, "Insight and Faith," in *Basic Questions in Theology*, vol. 2, 43.
14. Pannenberg, "Insight and Faith," in *Basic Questions in Theology*, vol. 2, 48; and Luther, *Luther's Works*, vol. 40, 175.
15. Pannenberg, "Insight and Faith," in *Basic Questions in Theology*, vol. 2, 53.
16. Pannenberg, "Insight and Faith," in *Basic Questions in Theology*, vol. 2, 62.
17. Cf. Thiselton, *Systematic Theology*, 147.

Bewitched? Or Rational and Logical?

Three New Testament scholars in particular have argued this in detail: Gunther Bornkamm, Robert Jewett, and Stanley Stowers.[18] Bornkamm points out that Paul regularly used "the reason theology of the Hellenistic synagogue appropriated and developed [as] a fixed type of missionary preaching."[19] Paul also, he says, speaks of reason "in order to convict the hearer of his guilt before God," and "makes rich use of concepts and moral directives long familiar to the rational ethics of paganism (Phil. 4:8)."[20] We have already noted some of the weighty arguments of Pannenberg on this subject.

In the light of Paul's positive evaluations of reason, rationality, and logic, his reference to illogicality and sheer inconsistency as "being bewitched" becomes less puzzling. Even apart from his diatribe style, Paul's very strong language against sloppy or irrational assumptions among Christians becomes wholly understandable.

---

18. Bornkamm, "Faith and Reason in Paul," 29–46; Jewett, *Paul Anthropological Terms*, 358–90; and Stowers, "Paul on the Use and Abuse of Reason."

19. Bornkamm, "Faith and Reason," 31.

20. Bornkamm, "Faith and Reason," 35 and 41.

Bibliography

Adeney, Walter F. *Thessalonians and Galatians: The Century Bible.* London: Caxton, 1910.
Allison, Dale C. "The Pauline Epistles and the Synoptic Gospels." *New Testament Studies* 28 (1982) 1–32.
Allo, E-B. *Saint Paul: Première Épitre aux Corinthiens.* Paris: Gabalda 1956.
———. *Saint Paul: Seconde Épître aux Corinthiens.* Paris: Gabalda, 1936.
Ambrosiaster. *Commentaries on Galatians-Philemon.* Edited by Gerald Bray and Thomas Oden. Downers Grove, IL: IVP Academic, 2009.
Anselm. *Why God Became Man.* In *A Scholastic Miscellany*, edited and translated by E. R. Fairweather, 100–146. London: SCM, 1956.
Aquinas, Thomas. *Commentary on Saint Paul's First Letter to the Thessalonians and the Letter to the Philippians.* Albany, NY: Magi, 1969.
———. *Summa Theologiae.* 60 vols. Latin and English. Oxford: Eyre and Spottiswoode, 1963.
Arminius, James. *The Works of James Arminius.* 10 vols. CD ROM, Bible Truth Forum, from 1875.
Athanasius. *Four Discourses against the Arians.* In *NPNF*, ser. 2, vol. 4.
———. *Letters* 6.5 and 10.11. In *NPNF*, ser. 2, vol. 4.
Augustine. *City of God.* In *NPNF*, ser. 1, vol. 2, 1–511.
———. *Confessions.* Oxford: Oxford University Press, 1991.
———. *The Letter of Petilian the Donatist.* In *NPNF*, ser. 1, vol. 4.
———. *On Christian Doctrine.* In *NPNF*, ser. 1, vol. 1.
———. *On the Holy Trinity.* In *NPNF*, ser. 1, vol. 3.
Bailey, D. S. *Homosexuality and the Western Christian Tradition.* London: Longmans Green, 1955.
Bailey, Kenneth E. "Paul's Theological Foundation for Human Society: 1 Cor. 6:12–20 in the Light of Rhetorical Criticism." *Near East School of Theological Re*view 3 (1980) 27–41.
Barr, James. *The Semantics of Biblical Language.* Oxford: Oxford University Press, 1961.
Barrett, C. K. *The Epistle to the Romans.* London: Black, 1957.
Barrett, C. K. *Commentary on the First Epistle to the Corinthians.* 2nd ed. London: Black, 1971.
———. *The Pastoral Epistles.* Oxford: Clarendon, 1963.
———. *Second Epistle to the Corinthians.* London: Black, 1973.
Bartchy, S. Scott. *Mallon chrēsai: First-Century Slavery and the Interpretation of 1 Cor. 7:21.* SBLDS, 11. Missoula: Scholars, 1973.

Bibliography

Barthes, Roland. *Mythologies*. London: Vintage, 1993.
Barton, Stephen. "Paul's Sense of Place: An Anthropological Approach to Community Formation in Corinth." *New Testament Studies* 32 (1986) 229–46.
Bauckham, Richard. *Gospel Women: Studies of the Named Women of the Gospels*. Grand Rapids: Eerdmans, 2002.
Baugh, S. M. "A Foreign World: Ephesus in the First Century." In *Women in the Church: An Interpretation and Application of 1 Timothy 2:9–15*, edited by Andreas J. Köstenberger and Thomas R. Schreiner, 25–64. 3rd ed. Wheaton, IL: Crossway, 2016.
Beare, F. W. "The Epistle to the Ephesians." In *Interpreter's Bible*, vol. 10. Nashville: Abingdon, 1953.
Behm, J. "*glōssa*." In *TDNT*, vol. 1, edited by Gerhard Kittel and G. Friedrich, 722–24. Grand Rapids: Eerdmans, 1968.
Bell, Richard H. *Provoked to Jealousy: The Origin and Purpose of the Jealousy Motif in Romans 9–11*. Tübingen: Mohr, 1994.
Bengel, J. A. *Gnomon Novi Tetamenti*. 1773. Reprint. Stuttgart: Steinkopf, 1866.
Best, Ernest. *The First and Second Epistles to the Thessalonians*. London: Black, 1972.
———. *One Body in Christ*. London: SPCK, 1955.
Betz, Hans Dieter. "2 Corinthians 6:14—7:1: An Anti-Pauline Fragment?" *Journal of Biblical Literature* 92 (1973) 88–108.
———. *Der Apostel Paulus und die sokratische Tradition*. Tübingen: Mohr, 1972.
———. *Galatians: A Commentary on Paul's Letter to the Churches in Galatia*. Philadelphia: Fortress, 1979.
Black, Matthew. *Romans*. NCB. London: Oliphants, 1973.
Blair, H. J. "First Corinthians 13 and the Disunity at Corinth." *Theological Education* 14 (1983) 69–77.
Bleek, F. "Über die Gabe des *glōssais lalein* in der ersten christlichen Kirche." *Studien und Kritiken* 2 (1829) 3–79.
Bligh, John. *Galatians: A Discussion of St. Paul's Epistle*. London: Paul, 1969.
Blue, Bradley B. "The House Church at Corinth and the Lord's Supper: Famine, Food Supply, and the Present Distress." *Criswell Theological Review* 5 (1991) 221–39.
Bornkamm, Günther. "Faith and Reason in Paul." In *Early Christian Experience*, 29–46. London: SCM, 1969.
———. "Lord's Supper and Church in Paul." In *Early Christian Experience*, 123–60. London: SCM, 1969.
Brauch, Manfred. *Hard Sayings of Paul*. London: Hodder & Stoughton, 1990.
Brichto, Herbert. *The Problem of "Curse" in the Hebrew Bible*. SBLMS. Philadelphia: Fortress, 1963
Briggs, Richard. *Words in Action: Speech-Act theory and Biblical Interpretation*. Edinburgh: T. & T. Clark, 2001.
Bruce, F. F. *1 and 2 Corinthians*. London: Oliphants, 1971.
———. *1 & 2 Thessalonians*. WBC 45. Waco, TX: Word, 1982.
———. "The Curse of the Law." In *Paul and Paulinism: Essays in Honour of C. K. Barrett*, edited by M. D. Hooker and S. G. Wilson, 27–36. London: SPCK. 1982.
———. *The Epistle to the Galatians: A Commentary on the Greek Text*. NIGTC. Exeter, UK: Paternoster, 1982.
———. *Paul: Apostle of the Free Spirit*. Exeter, UK: Paternoster, 1977.
Brunner, Emil. *Natural Theology*. 1948. Reprint. Eugene, OR: Wipf and Stock, 2002.
Bultmann, Rudolf. *The Second Letter to the Corinthians*. Minneapolis: Augsburg, 1985.

Bibliography

———. *Theology of the New Testament*, Vol. 1. London: SCM, 1952.
Burton, Ernest de Witt. *A Critical and Exegetical Commentary on the Epistle to the Galatians*. ICC. Edinburgh: T. & T. Clark, 1921.
Cadbury, H. J. "A Qumran Parallel to Paul." *Harvard Theological Review* 51 (1958) 1-2.
Calvin, John. *Second Epistle to the Corinthians and the Epistles to Timothy, Titus, and Philemon*. Edinburgh: St Andrew, 1963.
Caird, George B. "The Descent of Christ in Eph. 4:7-11." In *Studia Evangelica*, Vol. 2, edited by F. L. Cross, 535-45. Berlin: Akademie, 1964.
———. *The Language and Imagery of the Bible*. London: Duckworth, 1980.
———. *Principalities and Powers: A Study in Pauline Theology*. Oxford: Oxford University Press, 1956.
Calvin, John. *1 and 2 Thessalonians*. Edited by Alister McGrath and James Packer. Wheaton, IL: Crossway, 1999.
———. *Calvin's Commentaries: Romans*. London: Forgotten Books, 2007.
———. *The First Epistle of Paul to the Corinthians*. Edinburgh: Oliver and Boyd, 1960.
———. *The Institutes of Christian Religion*. 2 vols. Beveridge ed. London: Clarke, 1957.
———. *The Second Epistle of Paul to the Corinthians*. Edinburgh: Saint Andrew, 1964.
Cambier, J. "La Chair et L'esprit en 1 Cor. 5:5." *New Testament Studies* 15 (1968-69) 221-32.
Campbell, R. Alistair. "Baptism and Resurrection (1 Cor. 15:29)." *Australian Biblical Review* 47 (1999) 43-52.
Childs, Brevard. *Myth and Reality in the Old Testament*. London: SCM, 1962.
Chrysostom, John, *Homilies on 1 Corinthians*; (Eng., NPNF, ser.1, vol. 12)
———. *Homilies on Romans*. NPNF, ser. 1, vol. 13.
———. *Homily on Thessalonians*. NPNF, ser. 1, vol. 13.
———. *Homilies on Timothy and Titus*. NPNF, ser. 1, vol. 13.
Clark, S. B. *Man and Woman in Christ in Christ: An Examination of the Roles of Men and Women in the Light of Scripture and Social Sciences*. Ann Arbor, MI: Servant, 1980.
Clavier, H. "La Sante de l'Apotre Paul." In *Studia Paulina in honorem Johannis de Zwaan*, edited by J. N. Sevenster and W. C. van Unnik, 66-82. Haarlem: Bohn, 1953.
Clement of Alexandria. *Stromata*. ANF, vol. 2.
Collange, J. F. *Enigmes de la deuxième épître de Paul aux Corinthiens. Etude exegetique de 2 Cor. 2,14—7,4*. Cambridge: Cambridge University Press, 1972.
Collins, Raymond F. *First Corinthians*. Collegeville, MN: Glazier/Liturgical, 1999.
Conzelmann, Hans. *1 Corinthians: A Commentary*. Hermeneia. Philadelphia: Fortress, 1975.
Crafton, J. A. *The Agency of the Apostle*. JSNT Suppl. 96. Sheffield, UK: JSOT, 1991.
Craig, C. T. "The First Epistle to the Corinthians." In *The Interpreter's Bible*, vol. 10. Nashville: Abingdon, 1953.
Cranfield, C. E. B. *A Critical and Exegetical Commentary on the Epistle to the Romans*. ICC. 2 vols. Edinburgh: T. & T. Clark, 1975 and 1979.
Currie, S. D. "'Speaking in Tongues': Early Evidence outside the NT." *Interpretation* 19 (1965) 274-94.
Cullmann, Oscar. *Christ and Time*. London: SCM, 1955.
———. *The State in the New Testament*. London: SCM, 1963.
Danby, Herbert. *The Mishnah*. Oxford: Oxford University Press, 1933.
Dautzenberg, Gerhard. *Urchristliche Prophetie. Ihre Erforschung, ihre Voraussetzungen im Judentum und ihre Struktur im ersten Korintherbrief*. Stuttgart: Kohlhammer, 1975.

Bibliography

———. "Zum religionsgeschichtlichen Hintergrund der DIAKRISEIS PNEUMATÔN (1 Kor. 12,10)." *Biblische Zeitscrift* NF 15 (1971) 93-104.
Davies, W. D. "Paul and the Law." In *Paul and Paulinism: Essays in Honour of C. K. Barrett*, edited by M. D. Hooker and S. G. Wilson, 4-16. London: SPCK, 1982.
Delling, Gerhard. *Paulus' Stellung zu Frau und Ehe*. Stuttgart: Kolhammer, 1931.
Deluz, Gaston. *A Companion to 1 Corinthians*. London: Darton, Longman, & Todd, 1963.
Deming, W. *Paul on Marriage and Celibacy: The Hellenistic Background of 1 Corinthians 7*. SNTSM 83. Cambridge: Cambridge University Press, 1995.
Denney, James, *The Death of Christ*. London: Hodder and Stoughton, 1902.
———. *The Epistles to the Thessalonians*. Expositor's Bible. London: Hodder & Stoughton, 1892.
Dibelius, Martin, and Hans Conzelmann. *Die Patoralbriefe*. 4th ed. Tübingen: Mohr, 1966.
Dodd, C. H. *Gospel and Law*. Cambridge: Cambridge University Press, 1951.
Dungan, D. L. *The Sayings of Jesus in the Churches of Paul*. Oxford: Blackwell, 1971.
Dunn, James D. G. *The Epistles to the Colossians and to Philemon: A Commentary on the Greek Text*. Exeter, UK: Paternoster, 1996.
———. *Jesus and the Spirit: A Study of the Religious and Charismatic Experience of Jesus and the Earliest Christians*. London: SCM, 1975.
———, ed. *Paul and the Mosaic Law*. Tübingen: Mohr, 1996.
———. *Romans 1-8*. WBC. Dallas: Word, 1988.
———. *Romans 1-16*. WBC. Dallas: Word, 1988.
———. *The Theology of Paul the Apostle*. Edinburgh: T. & T. Clark, 1998.
Eckstein, H.-J. *Der Begriff Syneidēsis bei Paulus*. Tübingen: Mohr, 1983.
Edwards, T. C. *A Commentary on the First Epistle to the Corinthians*. Greek text, 2nd ed. London: Hodder & Stoughton, 1885.
Ellis, E. Earle. *Prophecy and Hermeneutic in Early Christianity*. Grand Rapids: Eerdmans, 1978.
Elliott, Neil. "Romans 13:1-7 in the Context of Imperial Propaganda." In *Paul and Empire: Religion and Power in Roman Imperial Society*, edited by R. A. Horsley, 184-204. Harrisburg, PA: Trinity, 1997.
Engels, Donald. *Roman Corinth: An Alternative Model for the Classical City*. Chicago, University, 1990.
Epp, Eldon Jay. *Junia the First Woman Apostle*. Minneapolis: Fortress, 2005.
Erasmus. *Opera Omnia: in Epist. Pauli ad 1 Cor.*
Eriksson, Anders. *Traditions as Rhetorical Proof: Pauline Argumentation in 1 Corinthians*. Coniectanea Biblica, New Testament series 29. Stockholm: Almqvist & Wiksell, 1998.
Eusebius. *Ecclesiastical History*. NPNF, ser. 2, vol. 1.
Evans, Donald D. *The Logic of Self-Involvement*. London: SCM, 1963.
Fee, Gordon. "II Corinthians 6:14—7:1 and Food Offered to Idols." *New Testament Studies* 23 (1977) 140-61.
———. *The First Epistle to the Corinthians*. NICNT. Grand Rapids: Eerdmans, 1987.
———. "Issues in Evangelical Hermeneutics, III: The Great Watershed." *Crux* 26 (1990) 31-37.
Ferrari, M. Schiefer. *Die Sprache des Leids in den paulinischen Peristasenkatalogen*. Stuttgart: Katholisches Bibelwerk, 1991.
Findlay, G. G. *The Epistles to the Thessalonians: Cambridge Greek Testament*. Cambridge: Cambridge University Press, 1925.

Bibliography

———. "St. Paul's First Epistle to the Corinthians." In *The Expositor's Greek Testament*, vol. 2, edited by W. R. Nicholl. 1900. Reprint. Grand Rapids: Eerdmans, 1961.

Fiorenza, Elizabeth Schüssler. *In Memory of Her: A Feminist Reconstruction of Christian Origins*. New York: Crossroad, 1983.

Fitzgerald, J. T. *Cracks in an Earthen Vessel: An Examination of Catalogues of Hardships in the Corinthian Correspondence*. SBL Diss 99. Atlanta: Scholars, 1988.

Fitzmyer, Joseph. "A Feature of Qumran Angelology and the Angels of 1 Cor. 11:10." In *Paul and Qumran*, edited by J. Murphy-O'Connor, 31–48. London: Chapman, 1968.

———. "Qumran and the Interpolated Paragraph in 2 Cor. 6:14—7:1." In *Essays on the Semitic Background of the New Testament*, 205–17. London: Chapman, 1971.

———. *Romans: A New Translation with Introduction and Commentary*. AB. New York: Doubleday, 1992.

Floyd Filson. "Second Corinthians: Exegesis." In *The Interpreter's Bible*, vol. 10. Nashville: Abingdon, 1953.

Foh, Susan. *Women and Word of God: A Response to Biblical Feminism*. Philipsburg: Presbyterian and Reformed, 1979.

Forbes, Christopher. *Prophecy and Inspired Speech in Early Christianity and Its Hellenistic Environment*. Tübingen: Mohr, 1995.

Foschini, B. M. "Those Who Are Baptised for the Dead: 1 Cor. 15:29." *Catholic Biblical Quarterly* 12 (1950) 260–76 and 379–88.

Foucault, Michel. *The History of Sexuality*. 3 vols. London: Pantheon, 1977.

Frame, James E. *The Epistles of St Paul to the Thessalonians*. ICC. 1912. Reprint. Edinburgh: T. & T. Clark, 1988.

Furnish, Victor P. *II Corinthians: A New Translation with Introduction and Commentary*. AB. New York: Doubleday, 1984.

———. "Homosexual Practices in Biblical Perspective." In *The Sexuality Debate in American Churches 1988-1995*, edited by J. J. Carey, 253–91. Lewiston, CA: Mellen Press, 1995.

Gadamer, Hans-Georg. *Truth and Method*. 2nd ed. London: Sheed & Ward, 1989.

Gardner, Paul. *The Gifts of God and Authentication of the Christian*. Eugene, OR: Wipf and Stock, 2017.

Giblin, C. H. *The Threat to Faith*. Rome: Analecta Biblica, 1967.

Gillespie, Thomas. *The First Theologians: A Study in Early Christian Prophecy*. Grand Rapids: Eerdmans, 1994.

Godet, F. *Commentary on St Paul's First Epistle to the Corinthians*. 2 vols. 4th ed. Edinburgh: T. & T. Clark, 1915.

Gooch, P. D. "Conscience in 1 Corinthians 8 and 10." *New Testament Studies* 33 (1987) 244–54.

Goodman, Felicitas D. *Speaking in Tongues: A Cross-Cultural Study of Glossolalia*. Chicago: University Press, 1972.

Grosheide, F. *Commentary on the First Epistle to the Corinthians*. NICNT. 2nd ed. Grand Rapids: Eerdmans, 1954.

Grudem, Wayne. *The Gift of Prophecy*. Washington, DC: University Press of America, 1982.

Gundry, Stanley. "'Ecstatic Utterance' (NEB)?" *Journal of Theological Studies* 17 (1966) 299–307.

Gundry-Wolf, Judith. "Gender and Creation in 1 Cor. 11:2–16: A Study in Paul's Theological Method." In *Evangelium, Schriftauslegung, Kirche,* Festschrift für Peter

Bibliography

Stuhlmacher, edited by J. Adna, S. J. Hafemann, and O Hofius, 151–71. Göttingen: Vandenhoeck & Ruprecht, 1997.

Guthrie, Donald. *New Testament Introduction*. 2nd ed. London: IVP, 1974.

———. *The Pastoral Epistles*. London: Tyndale, 1957.

Habermas, Jürgen. *Knowledge and Human Interest*. London: Heinemann, 1978.

———. *The Theory of Communicative Action*. 2 vols. Cambridge: Polity, 1984, 1987.

Haimo of Auxerre. *Two Mediaeval Apocalyptic Commentaries*. Kalamazoo, MI: Western Michigan Mediaeval Institute, 2002.

Hall, David R. *The Unity of the Corinthian Correspondence*. London: T. & T. Clark/Continuum 2003.

Hanson, Anthony T. *The Pastoral Letters*. Cambridge: Cambridge University Press, 1966.

Harris, Murray J. *The Second Epistle to the Corinthians: A Commentary on the Greek Text*. NIGTC. Grand Rapids: Eerdmans, 2002.

Harris, Rendle. In *Expositor* 7 (1906) 305–11.

Harris, W. H. *The Descent of Christ: Ephesians 4:7–11 and Traditional Hebrew Imagery*. Leiden: Brill, 1996.

Harris, W. V. "'Sounding Brass' and Hellenistic Technology." *Biblical Archaeologist Reader* 8 (1982) 38–41.

Hays, Richard B. "Awaiting the Redemption of our Bodies: The Witness of Scripture concerning Homosexuality." In *Homosexuality in the Church: Both Sides of the Debate*, edited by J. S. Siker, 3–77. Louisville, KY: Westminster John Knox, 1994.

———. *Echoes of Scripture in the Letters of Paul*. New Haven: Yale, 1989.

———. *First Corinthians*. Interpretation. Louisville: Knox, 1997.

Heinrici, C. F. G. *Das erste Sendschreiben des Apostel Paulus an der Korinther*. Berlin: Hertz, 1880

Hempel, J. "Die Israelitischen Anschauungen von Segen und Fluch im Lichte altorientalscher Parallelen." *Zeitschrift der Deutschen Morgenländischen Gesellschaft* 4 (1925) 20–110.

Henry, Matthew. *Expositions of the Old and New Testaments*. 6 vols. London: Bohn, 1851.

Héring, Jean. *The First Epistle to the Corinthians*. London: Epworth, 1963.

———. *The Second Epistle to the Corinthians*. London: Epworth, 1967.

Hill, David. *Greek Words and Hebrew Meanings*. Cambridge: Cambridge University Press, 1967.

———. *New Testament Prophecy*. London: Marshall, 1979.

Hippolytus. *Treatise on Christ and the Antichrist*. ANF, vol. 5.

Hodge, Charles. *The First Epistle to the Corinthians*. Reprint. London: Banner of Truth, 1958.

Hofius, O. "The Lord's Supper and the Lord's Supper Tradition: Reflections on 1 Cor. 11:23b–25." In *One Loaf, One Cup: Ecumenical Studies on 1 Corinthians 11 and Other Eucharistic Text*, edited by B. Myer, 75–115. Macon, GA: Mercer, 1993.

Hooker, Morna D. "Authority on her Head: An Examination of 1 Cor. 11:10." *New Testament Studies* 10 (1964) 410–16.

Horrell, David. "The Lord's Supper at Corinth and in the Church Today." *Theology* 98 (1995) 196–202.

Howard, J. K. "Baptism for the Dead: A Study of 1 Cor. 15:29." *Evangelical Quarterly* 37 (1965) 137–41.

Bibliography

Hubbard, Moyer. "Kept Safe through Childbearing: Maternal Mortality, Justification by Faith, and the Social Setting of 1 Timothy 2:15." *Journal of the Evangelical Society* 55 (2012) 743–62.

Hughes, Kevin L. *Constructing Antichrist: Paul, Biblical Commentary and the Development of Doctrine in the Middle Ages.* Washington, DC: University Press of America, 2005.

Hughes, Philip E. *Paul's Second Epistle to the Corinthians.* NICNT. London: Marshall, 1962.

Hurd, John C. *The Origin of 1 Corinthians.* London: SPCK, 1965.

Jeremias, Joachim. *The Central Message of the New Testament.* London: SCM, 1965.

Jerome. *Letters. NPNF,* ser. 2, vol. 6.

Jewett, Robert. *Paul's Anthropological Terms.* Leiden: Brill, 1970.

———. *Romans: A Commentary.* Hermeneia. Minneapolis: Fortress, 2007.

Jones, O. R. *The Concept of Holiness.* London: Allen & Unwin, 1961.

Jowett, Benjamin. *The Epistles of St. Paul to the Thessalonians, the Galatians and the Romans.* London: Murray, 1859.

Johnson, L. T. "Tongues." In *ABD* vol. 6, 597–98.

Judge, E. A. "The Conflict of Educational Aims in New Testament Thought." *Journal of Christian Education* 9 (1966) 32–45.

———. "Paul's Posting in Relation to Contemporary Professional Practice." *Australian Biblical Review* 16 (1968) 37–50.

Kamlah, R. *Die Form der katalogischen Paränese im Neue Testament.* WUNT 7. Tübingen: Mohr, 1964.

Käsemann, Ernst. *Commentary on Romans.* London: SCM, 1980.

———. "The Cry for Liberty in the Worship of the Church." In *Perspectives on Paul,* 122–38. London: SCM, 1971.

———. "Die Legitimität des Apostels." *Zeitschrift für die neutestamentliche Wissenschaft* 41 (1942) 33–71.

———. *New Testament Questions of Today.* London: SCM, 1969.

———. "The Pauline Doctrine of the Lord's Supper." In *Essays on New Testament Themes,* 108–35. London: SCM, 1964.

Kearsley, R. A. "Women in Public Life in the Roman East." *Tyndale Bulletin* 50 (1999) 189–211.

Keener, Craig S. *Paul, Women, and Wives: Marriage and Women's Ministry in the Letters of Paul.* Peabody, MA: Hendrickson, 1992.

Kelly, J. N. D. *The Pastoral Epistles.* London: Black, 1963.

Kevan, Ernest F. *The Grace of Law: A Study in Puritan Theology.* London: Carey Kingsgate, 1964.

Kistemaker, S. J. *1 Corinthians.* NTC. Grand Rapids: Baker, 1993.

Klein, William W. "Noisy Gong or Acoustic Vase? A Note on 1 Cor. 13:1." *New Testament Studies* 32 (1986) 286–89.

Kleinknecht, H. "*pneuma.*" In *TDNT,* vol. 6, edited by Gerhard Kittel and G. Friedrich, 345–48. Grand Rapids: Eerdmans, 1968.

Köstenberger, Andreas J., and Thomas R. Schreiner, eds. *Women in the Church: An Interpretation and Application of 1 Timothy 2:9–15.* 3rd ed. Wheaton, IL: Crossway, 2016.

Kramer, W. W. *Christ, Lord, and Son of God.* London: SCM, 1966.

Kroeger, Catherine, and Richard Kroeger. "Strange Tongues or Plain Talk?" *Daughters of Sarah* 12 (1986) 10–13.

Bibliography

Kruckenberg, S. *The Symphony Orchestra and Its Instruments*. New York: Crescent and Gothenberg, 1993.

Kuhn, H-W. "Anathema." In *Exegetical Dictionary of the New Testament*, vol. 1, edited by H. Balz and G. Schneider, 81. Grand Rapids: Eerdmans, 1994.

Lactantius. *Constitutions of the Holy Apostles*. In *ANF*, vol. 7.

———. *Institutes* 17. In *ANF* vol. 7.

Lang, F. *Die Briefe an die Korinther*. NTD 7. Göttingen: Vendenhoeck & Ruprecht, 1994.

Leenhardt, Franz J. *The Epistle to the Romans*. London: Lutterworth, 1961.

Lefkowitz, M. R., and M. B. Fant. *Women's Life in Greece and Rome: A Source Book in Translation*. Baltimore: Johns Hopkins, 1982.

Lietzmann, Hans. *An die Korinther*. 4th ed. Tübingen: Mohr, 1949.

Lightfoot, J. B. *Notes on Epistles of St. Paul: From Unpublished Commentaries*. London: Macmillan, 1896.

Lincoln, Andrew T. *Ephesians*. WBC. Dallas: Word, 1990.

———. *Paradise Now and Not Yet*. Cambridge: Cambridge University Press, 1981.

———. "The Use of the O.T. in Ephesians." *Journal for the Study of the New Testament* 14 (1982) 18–24.

Long, Frederick. "'The God of This Age' (2 Cor. 4:4) and Paul's Empire-Resisting Gospel at Corinth." In *The First Urban Churches: Vol. 2: Roman Corinth*, edited by James R. Harrison and Laurence L. Welborn, 219–69. Writings from Greco-Roman Supplement Series. Atlanta: SBL, 2016.

Luther, Martin. "1 Corinthians 15." In *Luther's Works*, vol. 28. Saint Louis: Concordia, 1973.

———. *The Bondage of the Will*. London: Clarke, 1957.

———. *Commentary on Romans*. 1954. Reprint. Grand Rapids: Kregel, 1976.

———. *Luther's Works*, vol. 35, *Word and Sacrament*. Saint Louis: Concordia, 1960.

———. *Selections from His Writings*. Edited by John Dillenberger. New York, 1961.

Macchia, Frank D. "Sighs Too Deep for Words: Towards a Theology of Tongues." *Journal of Pentecostal Theology* 1 (1992) 47–73.

Malherbe, Abraham J. *Paul and the Thessalonians: The Philosophic Tradition of Pastoral Care*. Philadelphia: Fortress, 1987.

Marshall, I. Howard. *1 and 2 Thessalonians*. NCBC. Grand Rapids: Eerdmans, 1983.

———. *Last Supper and Lord's Supper*. Exeter, UK: Paternoster, 1980.

Martin, Dale B. *The Corinthian Body*. New Haven: Yale University Press, 1995.

Martin, Ralph P. *2 Corinthians*. WBC. Dallas: Word, 1991.

———. *Colossians and Philemon*. NCB. London: Oliphants, 1974.

Menaud, P. H. "L'Echarde et L'Angel Satanique." In *Studia Paulina in honorem de Zwaan*, edited by J. N. Sevenster and W. C. van Unnik, 163–71. Haarlem: Bohn, 1953.

Metzger, Bruce. *A Textual Commentary on the Greek New Testament*. 2nd ed. Stuttgart: UBS, 1994.

Meyer, H. A. W. *The Epistles of the Philippians and* Colossians. Edinburgh: T. & T. Clark, 1873.

Mitton, C. Leslie. *Ephesians*. NCB. London: Oliphants, 1976.

Moffatt, James. *The First Epistle of Paul to the Corinthians*. London: Hodder and Stoughton, 1938.

Moo, D. J. "What Does It Mean Not to Teach or to Have Authority Over Men? (1 Tim. 2:11–15." In *Recovering Biblical Manhood and Womanhood*, edited by John Piper and Wayne Grudem, 179–93. Wheaton: Crossway, 1991.

Bibliography

Moore, A. L. *1 and 2 Thessalonians*. NCB. London: Nelson, 1969.
Moores, John D. *Wrestling with Rationality in Paul*. SNTMS 82. Cambridge: Cambridge University Press, 1995.
Morris, Leon. *The Cross in the New Testament*. Exeter, UK: Paternoster, 1965.
———. *The First and Second Epistles to the Thessalonians*. NICNT. Grand Rapids: Eerdmans, 1959.
Moule, C. F. D. *The Epistles to the Colossians and to Philemon*. Cambridge Greek Testament. Cambridge: Cambridge University Press, 1962.
———. "The Judgment Theme in the Sacraments." In *The Background of the New Testament and Its Eschatology: In Honour of Charles Harold Dodd*, edited by W. D. Davies and D. Daube, 464–81. Cambridge: Cambridge University Press, 1956.
Moulton, J. H., and G. Milligan. *The Vocabulary of the Greek New Testament Illustrated from the Papyri and Other Non-literary Sources*. London: Hodder & Stoughton, 1952.
Mounce, William D. *Pastoral Epistles*. WBC. Nashville: Nelson, 2000.
Munck, Johannes. *Paul and the Salvation of Mankind*. London: SCM, 1959.
Münster, Thomas. "Sermon Before the Princes." In *Spiritual and Anabaptist Writers*, edited by G. H. Williams, 47–70. LCC 25. London: SCM, 1957.
Murphy-O'Connor, Jerome. *1 Corinthians*. Oxford: Albatross, 1997.
———. "1 Cor. 11:2–16, Once Again." *Catholic Biblical Quarterly* 50 (1988) 265–74.
———. *Paul: A Critical Life*. Oxford: Oxford University Press, 1997.
———. "Sex and Logic in 1 Cor. 11:2–16." in *Catholic Biblical Quarterly* 42 (1980) 483–85.
Neil, William. *Thessalonians*. London: Hodder & Stoughton, 1950.
Neufeld, Dieter. *Re-conceiving Texts as Speech-Acts: An Analysis of 1 John*. Leiden: Brill, 1994.
Neufeld, Vernon H. *The Earliest Christian Confessions*. Grand Rapids: Eerdmans, 1963.
Nicholl, C. R. *From Hope to Despair in Thessalonica*. Cambridge: Cambridge University Press, 2004.
Niebuhr, H. Richard. *The Kingdom of God in America*. 1937. Reprint. London: The Wesleyan University Press, 1988.
Niebuhr, Reinhold. *The Nature and Destiny of Man*. 2 vols. London: Nisbet, 1941.
Nietzsche, Friedrich. *Complete Works, Vol. 9: The Dawn of Day*. Mineola, NY: Dover, 2007.
———. *Complete Works, Vol. 16: The Antichrist*. London: Penguin, 1991.
Nock, A. D. *St Paul*. London: Butterworth, 1938.
Nygren, Anders. *Commentary on Romans*. London: SCM, 1952.
O'Brien, Peter T. *Colossians, Philemon*. WBC. Nashville: Thomas Nelson, 1982.
O'Donovan, Oliver. *The Desire of Nations: Discovering the Roots of Political Theology*. Cambridge: Cambridge University Press, 1996.
———. *The Ways of Judgment*. Grand Rapids: Eerdmans, 2005.
Olshausen, Hermann. *St Paul's Epistles on the Galatians, Ephesians, Colossians and Thessalonians*. Edinburgh: T. & T. Clark, 1856.
Origen. *Against Celsus*. In *ANF*, vol. 4.
Oster, Richard. "When Men Wore Veils to Worship: The Historical Context of 1 Cor. 11:4." *New Testament Studies* 34 (1988) 481–505.
Padgett, Alan. "Wealthy Women at Ephesus: 1 Timothy 2:8–15 in a Social Context." *Interpretation* 41 (1987) 19–31.
Pannenberg, Wolfhart. *Basic Questions in Theology*, vol. 2. London: SCM, 1971.
———. *Systematic Theology*, vol. 2. Grand Rapids: Eerdmans, 1994.

Bibliography

———. *Systematic Theology*, vol. 3. Grand Rapids: Eerdmans, 1998.
Payne, P. B. "The Interpretation of 1 Timothy 2:11–15." In *What Does Scripture Teach the Ordination of Women?* Edited by W. L. Liefeld, D. Moo, and P. B. Payne, 96–115. Minneapolis: Evangelical Free, 1986.
Pedersen, J. *Israel: Its Life and Culture*. 2 vols. Oxford: Oxford University Press, 1926.
Pelagius. *Expositions of the Thirteen Epistles of St Paul*. Cambridge: Cambridge University Press, 1926.
Peterson, Brian N. "A Possible Precedent for Paul's Teaching on Divorce (and Remarriage?) in 1 Corinthians 7:10–15." *Tyndale Bulletin* 69 (2018) 43–62.
Philo. *The Confusion of Tongues*. Loeb Library, vol. 4.
———. *The Heir of Divine Things*. Loeb Library, vol. 4.
———. *The Migration of Abraham*. Loeb Library, vol. 4.
———. *On Flight and Finding*. Loeb Library, vol. 5.
———. *On the Life of Moses*. Loeb Library, vol. 6.
Pierce, C. A. *Conscience in the New Testament*. London: SCM, 1955.
Plank, Karl A. *Paul and the Irony of Affliction*. Atlanta: Scholars, 1987.
Plummer, Alfred. *A Critical and Exegetical Commentary on the Second Epistle of Paul to the Corinthians*. ICC. Edinburgh: T. & T. Clark, 1915.
Pomeroy, Sarah B. *Goddesses, Whores, Wives, and Slaves: Women in Classical Antiquity*. New York: Schocken, 1975.
Poole, Matthew. *Commentary on the Bible*, vol. 3. London: Banner of Truth, 1963.
Porter, Stanley E. "What Does It Mean to Be 'Saved by Childbirth' (1 Tim. 2:15)?" *Journal for the Study of the New Testament* 49 (1993) 87–102.
Raeder, Maria. "Vikariastaufe in 1 Cor. 15:29?" *Zeitschrift für neutestamentliche Wissenschaft und die Kunde der älteren Kirche* 46 (1955) 258–61.
Reid, James. "Second Corinthians: Exposition." In *The Interpreter's Bible*, vol. 10. Nashville: Abingdon, 1953.
Richard, Earle J. *First and Second Thessalonians*. Sacra Pagina. Reprint. Collegeville, MN: Glazier, 2007.
Ricoeur, Paul. *Freud and Philosophy: An Essay on Interpretation*. New Haven: Yale, 1970.
———. *Interpretation Theory: Discourse and the Surplus of Meaning*. Fort Worth: Texas Christian University Press, 1976.
Rigaux, Beda. *Saint Paul: Les Épitres aux Thessaloniciens*. Paris: Gabalda, 1956.
Rissi, Mathias. *Die Taufe für die Toten: Ein Beitrag zur paulinischen Tauflehre*. Zurich: Zwingli Verlag, 1962.
Robinson, J. A. T. *The Body: A Study in Pauline Theology*. London: SCM, 1952.
Robinson, J. Armitage. *St Paul's Epistle to the Ephesians*. 2nd ed. London: Macmillan, 1907.
Rousselle, Aline. "Body Politics in Ancient Rome." In *A History of Women in the West, Vol. 1, From Ancient Goddesses to Christian Saints*, edited by G. Duby and M. Perot, 296–337. Cambridge: Harvard, 1992.
Ruse, Michael. *Homosexuality: A Philosophical Inquiry*. Oxford: Blackwell, 1988.
Ryle, Gilbert. *Dilemmas*. Cambridge: Cambridge University Press, 1954.
Räisänen, Heikki. *Paul and the Law*. WUNT 29. Tübingen: Mohr, 1983.
Samarin, W. J. *Tongues of Men and Angels: The Religious Language of Pentecostalism*. New York: MacMillan, 1972.
Sand, Alexander. *Der Begriff 'Fleisch' in den Paulinischen Hauptbriefen*. Regensburg: Pustet, 1967.
Sanders, E. P. *Paul, the Law, and the Jewish People*. Philadelphia: Fortress, 1983.

Bibliography

Sanders, J. Todd. "A New Approach to 1 Cor. 13:1." *New Testament Studies* 36 (1990) 159–87.
Sandnes, K. O. *Paul—One of the Prophets?* WUNT ii, 43. Tübingen: Mohr, 1991.
Schlatter, A. *Die Korintherbriefe Ausgelegt für Bibelleser.* Stuttgart: Calwer, 1962.
Schlier, Heinrich. *Principalities and Powers in the New Testament.* New York: Herder, 1961.
Schmithals, W. "The Corpus Paulinum and Gnosis." In *The New Testament and Gnosis: Essays in Honor of Robert McL Wilson,* edited by A. H. B. Logan, 107–24. Edinburgh: T. & T. Clark, 1983.
———. *Gnosticism in Corinth.* Nashville: Abingdon, 1971.
———. "Zwei Gnostishe Glossen." *Evangelische Theologie* 18 (1958) 552–64.
Schnackenburg, Rudolf. "Baptism for the Dead." In *Baptism in the Thought of St Paul,* 95–103. Oxford: Blackwell, 1964.
Schneider, J. "*olethros.*" In *TDNT,* vol. 5, edited by Gerhard Kittel and G. Friedrich, 167–71. Grand Rapids: Eerdmans, 1968.
Schrage, Wolfgang. *Der erste Brief an die Korinther.* 4 vols. Neukirchen-Vluyn: Neukirchener, 1991–2001.
———. *The Ethics of the New Testament.* Edinburgh: T. & T. Clark, 1988.
Schreiner, T. R. "An Interpretation of 1 Timothy 2:9–15: A Dialogue with Scholarship." In *Women in the Church,* edited by A. J. Köstenberger, 105–54. Grand Rapids: Baker, 1995.
Schweizer, Eduard. "*sōma*" In *TDNT,* vol. 7, edited by Gerhard Kittel and G. Friedrich, 1024–94. Grand Rapids: Eerdmans, 1968.
Scroggs, Robin. *The New Testament and Homosexuality.* Philadelphia: Fortress, 1983.
Sevenster, J. N. *Paul and Seneca.* Leiden: Brill, 1961.
Sevenster, J. N., and W. C. van Unnik, eds. *Studia Paulina in honorem Johannis de Zwaan.* Haarlem: Bohn, 1953.
Simpson, E. K. *The Pastoral Epistles: Greek Text with Introduction and Commentary* London: Tyndale, 1954.
Snodgrass, Klyne. *Ephesians.* NIV Application. Grand Rapids: Zondervan, 1996.
Spicq, C. *Agapē in the New Testament.* 3 vols. London: Herder, 1963.
———. *Les Épitres Pastorals.* Paris: Gabalda, 1947.
Stählin, G. "*orgē, orgizimai.*" In *TDNT,* vol. 5, edited by Gerhard Kittel and G. Friedrich, 382–447. Grand Rapids: Eerdmans, 1968.
Stanton, Graham N. "The Law of Moses and the Law of Christ: Gal. 3:1—6:2." In *Paul and the Mosaic Law,* edited by James D. G. Dunn, 99–116. Grand Rapids: Eerdmans, 2001.
Stein, R. H. "Is It Lawful for a Man to Divorce His Wife?" *Journal of the Evangelical Theological Society* 22 (1979) 115–21.
Stendahl, Krister. "Glossolalia—The N.T. Evidence." In *Paul among Jews and Gentiles,* 109–24. London: SCM, 1976.
———. "Paul and the Introspective Conscience on the West." In *Paul among Jews and Gentiles,* 78–96. Philadelphia: Fortress, 1976.
Stewart, J. S. *A Man in Christ.* London: Regent, 1935.
Stowers, Stanley. "Paul on the Use and Abuse of Reason." In *Greeks, Romans, Christians,* edited by D. L. Balch et al., 253–86. Minneapolis: Fortress, 1990.
Swidler, Leonard. *Women in Judaism.* Metuchen, NJ: Scarecrow, 1976.
Tasker, R. V. G. *The Second Epistle of Paul to the Corinthians.* London: Tyndale, 1958.
Taylor, Vincent. *The Atonement in New Testament Teaching.* London: Epworth, 1940.

Bibliography

Tertullian. *Against Marcion.* In *ANF*, vol. 3.
———. *On Modesty.* In *ANF*, vol. 4.
———. *On the Veiling of Virgins.* In *ANF*, vol. 3.
Thatcher, Adrian. *Liberating Sex: A Christian Sexual Theology.* London: SPCK, 1993.
Thayer, John H. *A Greek-English Lexicon of the New Testament.* 4th ed. Edinburgh: T. & T. Clark, 1901.
Theissen, Gerd. *Psychological Aspects of Pauline Theology.* Edinburgh: T. & T. Clark, 1987.
Theodore of Mopsuestia. *Epistolas B. Pauli Commentarii.* Cambridge: Cambridge University Press, 1880.
Theodoret. *Interpetatio Ep. 1 ad Cor.* In *Patrologia Graeca*, vol. 82, edited by J-P. Migne. Paris: Migne, 1864.
Thielicke, Helmut. *Theological Ethics, Vol. 2: Politics.* Grand Rapids: Eerdmans, 1979.
Thierry, J. J. "Der Dorn im Fleische (2 Kor. XII 7–9)." *Novum Testamentum* 5 (1962) 301–10.
Thiselton, Anthony C. *1 Corinthians: A Shorter Exegetical & Pastoral Commentary.* Grand Rapids: Eerdmans, 2006.
———. "Curse." In *New International Dictionary of the Bible*, Vol. 1, 810–12. Nashville: Abingdon, 2006.
———. *Discovering Romans: Content, Interpretation, Reception.* London: SPCK, 2016.
———. *The First Epistle to the Corinthians: A Commentary on the Greek Text.* Grand Rapids: Eerdmans, 2000.
———. "The 'Interpretation' of Tongues: A New Suggestion in the Light of Greek Usage in Philo and Josephus." *Journal of Theological Studies* 30 (1979) 15–36.
———. "The Logical Role of the Liar Paradox in Titus 1:12, 13: A Dissent from the Commentaries in the Light of Philosophical and Logical Analysis." *Biblical Interpretation* 2 (1994) 207–23.
———. "The Meaning of Sarx in 1 Cor. 5:5." *Scottish Journal of Theology* 26 (1973) 204–28.
———. "Realized Eschatology at Corinth." *New Testament Studies* 24 (1978) 510–26.
———. "The Supposed Power of Words in the Biblical Writings." *Journal of Theological Studies* 25 (1974) 283–99.
———. *Thiselton on Hermeneutics: Collected Works and New Essays.* Aldershot, UK: Ashgate, 2006.
———. *Understanding Pannenberg: Landmark Theologian of the Twentieth Century.* Cascade Companions. Eugene, OR: Cascade, 2018.
Thornton, L. S. *The Common Life in the Body of Christ.* 3rd ed. London: Dacre, 1950.
Thrall, Margaret E. *1 and 2 Corinthians.* Cambridge: Cambridge University Press, 1965.
———. "The Pauline Use of *Syneidēsis*." *New Testament Studies* 14 (1967) 118–25.
———. "The Problem of II Corinthians 6:14—7:1 in some Recent Discussion." *New Testament Studies* 24 (1977) 132–48.
Towner, P. H. "Gnosis and Realized Eschatology in Ephesus (of the Pastoral Epistles) and the Corinthian Enthusiasm." *Journal for the Study of the New Testament* 31 (1987) 95–124.
Travis, Stephen. *Christ and the Judgment of God.* 2nd ed. Milton Keynes, UK: Paternoster, 2008.
Trible, Phyllis. *Texts of Terror: Literary-Feminist Readings of Biblical Narratives.* Philadelphia: Fortress, 1984.
Turner, Max. "Spiritual Gifts Then and Now." *Vox Evangelica* 15 (1985) 7–64.

Bibliography

Vasey, Michael. *Strangers and Friends: A New Exploration of Homosexuality and the Bible.* London: Hodder & Stoughton, 1995.
Verhey, Allan. *The Great Reversal.* Grand Rapids: Eerdmans, 1984.
Vidu, Adonis. *Atonement, Law, and Justice.* Grand Rapids: Baker Academic, 2014.
Vielhauer, P. *Oikodomē: Das Bild vom Bau in der Christlichen Literatur.* Heidelberg: Karlsruh-Durlael, 1940.
Vögtle, A. *Die Tugend- und Lasterkataloge im Neue Testament.* Münster: Aschendorff, 1936.
Wall, Robert. *1 and 2 Timothy and Titus.* Two Horizons. Grand Rapids: Eerdmans, 2012.
———. "Pauline Authorship and the Pastoral Epistles: A Response to Stanley Porter." *Bulletin for Biblical Research* 5 (1995) 125–28.
Wedderburn, A. J. M. *Baptism and Resurrection.* Reprint. Eugene, OR: Wipf and Stock, 2011.
Wehmeier, Gerhard. *Der Segen im Alten Testament: Eine Semasiologische Untersuchung der Wurzel brk.* Basel: Reinhardt, 1970.
Weinel, Heinrich. *Die Wirkungen des Geistes und der Geister im nachapostolichen Zeitalter bis auf Irenaeus.* Freiburg: Mohr, 1899.
Welborn, L. L. *Paul, the Fool of Christ: A Study of 1 Corinthians 1–4 in the Comic-Philosophical Tradition.* London: T. & T. Clark, 2005.
———. "The Runaway Paul." *Harvard Theological Review* 92 (1999) 115–63.
Wesley, John. *Notes on the New Testament.* 1754. CD-ROM, Bible Truth Forum.
Westcott, B. F. *Saint Paul's Epistle to the Ephesians: The Greek Text.* London: MacMillan, 1906.
Whiteley, D. E. H. *The Theology of St Paul.* 2nd ed. Oxford: Blackwell, 1972.
———. *Thessalonians.* Oxford: Oxford University Press, 1969.
Wibbing, S. *Die Tugend- und Lasterkataloge im Neue Testament und ihre Traditionsgeschichte.* Berlin: Töpelmann, 1959.
Wiedemann, Thomas. *Greek and Roman Slavery.* London: Broom Helm, 1981.
———. *Slavery, Greece and Rome: New Surveys 19.* Oxford: Oxford University Press and the Classical Association, 1997.
Williams, Cyril G. *Tongues of the Spirit: A Study of Pentecostal Glossolalia and Related Phenomena.* Cardiff: University of Wales, 1981.
Williams, G. H., ed. *Spiritual and Anabaptist Writers.* LCC 25. London: SCM, 1957.
Wimbush, V. L. *Paul the Worldly Ascetic: A Response to the World and Self-Understanding according to 1 Corinthians 7.* Macon, GA: Mercer, 1987.
Windisch, Hans. *Paulus und Christus: Ein biblisch-religiongeschtlicher Vergleich.* Leipzig: Heinrich, 1934.
Winger, M. "*By What Law? The Meaning of Nomos in the Letters of Paul.* SBLDS. Atlanta: Scholars, 1992.
Wink, Walter. *Engaging the Powers: Discernment and Resistance in a World of The Politics of Jesus.* Augsburg: Fortress, 1992.
———. *Naming the Powers: The Language of Power in the New Testament.* Philadelphia: Fortress, 1984.
———. *Unmasking the Powers: The Invisible Forces That Determine Human Existence.* Philadelphia: Fortress, 1986.
Winter, Bruce. "Secular and Christian Responses to Corinthian Famines." *Tyndale Bulletin* 40 (1989) 86–106.

Bibliography

———. "Social Mobility:1 Cor. 7: 21–24." In *Seek the Welfare of the City*, 145–63. Grand Rapids: Eerdmans, 1994.
Wire, Antoinette. *The Corinthian Women Prophets*. Minneapolis: Fortress, 1990.
Witherington, Ben. *1 and 2 Thessalonians: A Socio-Rhetorical Commentary*. Grand Rapids: Eerdmans, 2006.
———. *Conflict and Community in Corinth*. Grand Rapids: Eerdmans, 1995.
———. *Jesus, Paul, and the End of the World*. Carlisle, UK: Paternoster, 1992.
———. *Women in the Earliest Churches*. Cambridge: Cambridge University Press, 2003.
Wittgenstein, Ludwig. *Philosophical Investigations*. 2nd ed. Oxford: Blackwell, 1967.
———. *Tractatus Logico-Philosophicus*. London: Routledge, 1961.
Wolff, C. *Der erste Brief des Paulus an die Korinther*. Leipzig: Evangelische Verlagsanstalt, 1996.
Wright, David. "Homosexuality: The Relevance of the Bible." *Evangelical Quarterly* 61 (1989) 291–300.
Wright, N. T. "The Letter to the Romans." In *The New Interpreter's Bible*, Vol. 10. Nashville: Abingdon, 2002.
Yarbrough, O. Larry. *Not Like the Gentiles: Marriage Rules in the Letters of Paul*. Atlanta: Scholars, 1985.
Yoder, John. *The Politics of Jesus*. 2nd ed. Grand Rapids: Eerdmans, 1994.

Index of Names

Abraham, 49
Adam, 14, 72
Adeney, W. F., 184
Alison, Dale, C., 86
Allo, E-B., 46, 129, 148,
Ambrose, 125
Ambrosiaster, 58, 64, 129, 157, 181
Andronicus, 56
Anselm, 30, 95
Antiochus Epiphanes, 184, 186
Aquila, 56, 57
Aquinas, Thomas, 65, 129, 142, 145, 149, 157, 158, 190
Aretas, King, 161
Aristotle, 110, 120
Athanasius, 125, 181
Augustine, 13, 14, 15, 37, 65, 111–12, 125, 142, 169, 176, 177, 181
Austin, John, L., 109

Bailey, D. S., 134–35, 138
Bailey, Kenneth, 136
Balaam, 50, 109
Balthasar, Hans Urs von, 37
Barr, James, 135
Barrett, C. K., 10, 28, 43, 45, 59, 61, 90, 91, 118, 128, 129, 143, 147, 165, 166, 175
Bartchy, S. Scott, 128,
Barth, Karl, 116
Barthes, Roland, 66
Barton, Stephen, 59
Basil of Caesarea, 125, 181
Baugh, S. M., 74
Beare, F. W., 69

Behm, J., 148
Belial, 177
Bengel, Albrecht, 50, 59, 166, 174
Benjamin, 153
Best, Ernest, 32, 186
Betz, Hans-Dieter, 23, 57, 91, 166, 188
Beza, Theodore, 45, 46, 142
Blair, H. J., 103
Bleek, F., 145, 147
Bligh, John, 24, 25, 57,
Blue, Bradley, 80–82, 84,
Bonnington, Mark, 135
Bornkamm, Gunter, 20, 142, 156, 189, 191
Boswell, John, 134, 138
Bousset, W., 169, 184
Bradley, F. H., 128
Brauch, Manfred, 16, 46, 58, 107–8, 132, 141,
Brichto, Herbert, 109
Briggs, Richard S., 109
Bruce, F. F., 5, 20, 23, 24, 26, 56, 59, 78, 86, 146, 177, 180, 184, 186, 188, 189
Brunner, Emil, 126, 127
Bullinger, Heinrich, 45, 88, 157
Bultmann, Rudolf, 10, 43, 91, 100, 114, 142, 151, 175, 176
Burgess, Anthony, 5
Burton, Ernest de Witt, 23, 57,

Cadbury, Henry J., 65,
Caird George B., 20, 35, 80, 81, 82, 84, 124, 126, 183
Cajetan, 65

Index of Names

Calvin, John, 11, 14, 15, 50, 103, 125, 157, 158, 166, 182
Cambier, J., 169
Campbell, R. Alistair, 47
Cantor, Georg, 119
Carrington, Philip, 134
Celsus, 120, 124
Charles, R. H., 184
Childs, Brevard, 183
Chrysostom, John, 46, 59, 120, 124, 129, 145, 149, 169, 176, 181
Clark, Stephen B., 73
Claudius, 56, 127, 177, 180, 185
Clavier, H., 168
Clement of Alexandria, 33, 120,
Cocceius, Johannes, 45, 46
Collange, J. F., 91
Collins, Raymond F., 44, 46, 65, 66, 78, 86, 87, 102, 104, 128, 129, 132, 143,
Congar, Yves, 37,
Conzelmann, Hans, 46, 118, 128, 129, 134, 146,
Cornelius, 149
Crafton, J. A., 165
Craig, C. T., 106
Cranfield, Charles E. B., 7, 10, 50, 127, 174
Cromwell, Oliver, 169
Cullmann, Oscar, 80, 124, 126, 134, 186
Currie, S. D., 145, 148
Cybele, 105
Cyril of Jerusalem, 33

Danby, Herbert, 50
Daniel, 184
Danker, Frederick, 7, 11, 59, 81, 110, 141, 169
Darby, J. N, 90, n.2
Dautzenberg, Gerhard, 145, 147
Davies, J. G., 145, 149
Davies, W. D., 5, 6, 86,
Delling, Gerhard, 82
Deluz, Gaston, 58, 115
Deming, Will, 81, 82, 129,
Denney, James, 11, 27, 157–58
Dibelius, Martin, 19, 118,

Dionysius of Halicarnassus, 147
Dionysius, 105
Dodd, C. H., 10, 28, 29, 97, 134, 174
Driver, S. R., 36,
Dungan, D. L., 86
Dunn, James D. G., 5, 13, 20, 25, 26, 27, 30, 32, 33, 50, 111, 127, 148, 156, 173
Dürr, L., 109

Easton, B. S., 134
Eckstein, H-J., 100
Edwards, T. C., 150
Ellis, E. Earle, 145
Engels, Donald, 178
Engelsen, N. I. J., 148
Ephrem of Syria, 64
Epimenides of Crete, 120
Epp, Eldon Jay, 56
Erasmus, 46,
Ericksson, Anders, 109–10
Ernesti, J. A., 147
Estius, 65, 149
Eubilides of Miletus, 118
Euodia, 55
Euripides, 151
Eusebius, 125
Evans, D. D., 109
Eve, 73
Ezekiel, 184
Ezra, 89

Fant, Maureen B., 67
Fee, Gordon, 44, 73, 76, 78, 88, 91, 118, 128, 143, 146,
Ferrari, M. S., 162
Filson, Floyd V., 91, 92
Findlay, G. G., 47, 169, 184
Fitzgerald, J. T., 162
Fitzmyer, Joseph, 6, 10, 11, 50, 51, 65, 67, 111, 173
Foh, Sarah, 72
Forbes, Christopher, 105, 148, 149, 156
Foschini, B. M., 45
Foucault, Michel, 135
Frame, J. E., 184
Freud, Sigmund, 135, 137

Index of Names

Furnish, Victor, 42, 91, 134, 136, 138, 175, 176
Fyall, Robert, 135

Gadamer, Hans-Georg, 137
Gaius (Caligula), 180, 183, 186
Gardner, Paul, 100
Garr, Alfred G., 150
Garr, Lilian, 150
Gillespie, Thomas H., 155–57
Godet, F., 59, 142,
Gooch, Peter, 100
Goodman, Felicitas D., 150
Gordon, Robert, 109–10
Gregory I, 14,
Grether, O., 109
Grim, J. H. and Thayer, J.H., 110
Grosheide, F. W., 45, 105, 129,
Grotius, 65
Grudem, Wayne, 148
Gundry, Robert, 145, 149
Gundry-Wolf, Judith, 66
Guthrie, Donald, 57, 62,

Habermas, Jürgen, 133, 137
Haimo of Auxerre, 182
Hall, David, 163
Hamaan, J. G., 190
Hanson, Anthony, 61, 72, 118, 121,
Harnack, Adolf von, 29
Harris, Murray, 161, n.1, 163, 175
Harris, Rendle, 118
Harris, W. V., 35, 104, 105
Hays, Richard, 46, 65, 135, 143,
Heinrici, C. F. G., 58, 103, 145, 147,
Hempel, Johannes, 109
Henry, Matthew, 157
Heraclitus of Ephesus, 118
Herder, J. G., 147, 190
Héring, Jean, 58, 65, 88, 146, 155–56, 163,
Hill, David, 28, 155–57
Hippolytus, 180, 181
Hodge, Charles, 149
Hofius, O., 143
Holtzmann H. J., 99
Hooker, Morna, 64, 67
Horrell, David, 143

Horsley, Richard A., 100
Hosea, 89
Howard, J. K., 47,
Hubbard, Moyer, 74
Hughes, Philip E., 91, 92, 169, 170
Hurd, J. C., 65, 78, 87
Hymenaeus, 169

Irenaeus, 33, 88, 89, 176

Jacob, 109
Jereboam, 50
Jeremias, Joachim, 27, 50,
Jerome, 111, 120, 149, 169
Jewett, Robert, 7, 50, 100, 111–12, 123, 126, 151, 174, 191
Joel, 57
John the Baptist, 149
Johnson, Bill, 45
Johnson, L. T., 150
Jones, O. R., 87
Josephus, 20, 1, 180
Jowett, Benjamin, 183
Judge, E. A., 163
Junia, 55, 56,
Justin, 87, 142

Kamlah, E., 134
Kant, Immanuel, 37
Keener, Craig, 75
Kelly, J. N. D., 61, n.28, 118,
Kevan, Ernest F., 4
Kildahl, J. P., 150
Kistemaker, Simon J., 65, 146
Klein, W. W., 104–05, 106,
Kleinknecht, K. T., 148, 162
Knight, George, 118
Köstenberger, Andreas J., 74
Kroeger, C. and R., 5
Kümmel, W.G., 10, 20, 142,
Käsemann, Ernst, 8, 10, 50, 112, 113, 142, 146, 151, 174

Lactantius, 124, 125, 181
Lambert, Ian, 177
Laurin, R. L., 105
Leenhardt, F., 10
Lefkowitz, Mary R., 66

Index of Names

Lenski, R. C. H., 105
Leo I, 14,
Lewis, C. S., 45,
Lietzmann, Hans, 46, 134
Lightfoot, J. B., 88, 169, 184, 189
Lincoln, Andrew, 35,
Lohmeyer, Ernst, 19,
Lohse, Eduard, 20, 32,
Lombard, Peter, 65, 129, 142
Long, Frederick, 176–78
Luther, Martin, 10, 15, 45, 125, 136, 182, 190
Lydia, 55

Macchia, Frank D., 146, 151
Malherbe, Abraham, 186
Manasseh, 50
Manson, T. W., 28
Marcion, 176, 181
Maritain Jacques, 37,
Marshall, I Howard, 73, 143, 183
Martin, Dale B., 44, 66, 78, 129, 130,
Martin, Ralph P., 21, 32, 91, 92, 165, 170
Marx, Karl, 103
Mary, 73
Matthew, 184
Menaud, P. H., 170
Metzger, Bruce, 58,
Meyer, H. A. W., 31, 65, 150
Mitton, Leslie, 34, 3, 68, 71,
Moffatt, James, 58, 105, 106
Molièrre, Jean-Baptiste, 135
Moore, Arthur L., 185
Moores, John, 110
Morris, Leon, 27, 185
Moses, 8, 35, 153–54
Moule, C.F.D., 19, 31, 83, 143,
Moulton, J. H. and Milligan, G., 110
Mounce, William, 60, 61, 62, 76 n.21,
Mowinckel, S., 109
Müller, Ulrich, 155
Mummius, Lucius, 105
Munck, Johannes, 49
Münster, Thomas, 125, 157
Murphy-O'Connor, Jerome, 47, 56, 66, 87, 88,
Murray, John, 11

Napoleon, 169
Nehemiah, 89
Neil, William, 185
Nero, 85, 126, 176–78, 183
Neufeld, Dieter, 108
Neufeld, Vernon, 108
Nicuum, Curt, 58
Niebuhr, H. Richard, 96
Niebuhr, Reinhold, 126
Nietzsche, Friedrich, 103
Nock, A. D., 115,
Nygren, Anders, 10, 11, 95, 174

O'Brien, Peter, 21, 22, 31, 32,
O'Donovan, Oliver, 126–27
Olhausen, Hermann, 33, 183
Origen, 33, 120, 121, 124, 149, 176, 181
Oster, Richard, 66

Padgett, Alan, 62,
Pannenberg, Wolfhart, 12, 15, 126–27, 137, 156, 158, 189–90
Parmenides, 118, 121
Parry, St John, 46
Payne, Philip, 58
Pedersen, J., 109
Pelagius, 65, 129, 169, 182
Peter, 57, 184
Peterson, Brian, 85, 89
Philetas, 169
Phillips, J. B., 104, 168
Phillips, Obe, 125, 182
Philo, 151, 153
Phoebe, 55, 57
Photius, 46, 129, 149
Pierce, C. A., 99, 100
Plato, 20, 151
Plank, K. A., 162
Plummer, Alfred, 42, 165, 168, 170, 175, 176
Plumptre, Edward, 169
Plutarch, 147
Poole, Matthew, 88
Porter, stanley, 75,
Priscilla, 55, 56, 57,
Pythagoras of Samos, 118

Quinn, J. D., 118

Index of Names

Raeder, Martin, 47,
Rahner, Karl, 14, 37
Ramsay, Sir William, 169
Reid, James, 92
Richard, Earle J., 187
Rigaux, Beda, 180
Ringgren, H., 109
Risssi, Matthias, 45
Ritschl, Albrecht, 29
Robertson, A. T., 118
Robertson, A., and Plummer, A., 59, 88
Robinson, J. A. T., 114,
Robinson, J. Armitage, 36, 69, 71,
Rousselle, Aline, 66, 85
Ruse, Michael, 135
Ryle, Gilbert, 119
Räisänen, Heikki, 5

Samarin, W. J., 150
Sanders, E. P., 5
Sanders, J. Todd, 106
Sandnes, K. O., 156
Schlatter, A., 44, 97
Schleiermacher, Friedrich, 29,
Schlier, Heinrich, 124, 126
Schmithals, Water, 46, 91
Schnackenburg, Rudolf, 45,
Schoeps, Hans-Joachim, 5, 25, 169
Schrage, Wolfgang, 65, 78, 81, 83, 87, 143
Schreiner, Thomas, 61, 74, 75, 76,
Schweitzer, Albert, 82, 142
Scott, E. F., 118
Scroggs, Robin, 134–36, 138
Searle, John, 109
Selwyn, E. G., 134
Seneca, 85
Simpson, E. K., 121
Snodgrass, Klyne, 35, 69–71,
Socinus, Faustus, 29
Soden, Hans von, 46
Spicq, C., 100, 103,
Stanton, Graham, 5
Stein, R. H., 88
Stendahl, Krister, 12, 15, 16, 150
Stowers, Stanley, 191
Stuart, J. S., 27,
Stählin, G., 13, 97,

Suetonius, 130
Syntache, 55

Tacitus, 84
Tasker, R. V. G., 91, 164, 175
Tertullian, 64, 65, 88, 145, 148, 169, 176, 180
Thatcher, Adrian, 136
Theissen, Gerd, 135, 145
Theodore of Mopsuestia, 169, 182
Theodoret, 65, 129, 149, 169
Theophylact, 46, 129,
Thielicke, Helmut, 126
Thiselton, Anthony C., 108, 109, 119, n.7, 119, 137, n.24, 152–53
Thornton, Lionel, S., 33
Thrall, Margaret, 91, 100, 175
Tiberius, 176, 177
Tillich, Paul, 37
Titus, 183
Toplady, Augustus, 30
Towner, P. H., 62, 118
Travis, Stephen, 163
Trible, Phyllis, 63
Turner, Max, 156
Tyconius, 181

Ullmann, Stephen, 82

Vasey, Michael, 136
Verhey, Allen, 134
Vespasian, 177
Vielhauer, Philipp, 156
Virgil, 151
Vitellius, 183
Vitruvius, 104
Vögtle, A., 134

Wall, Robert W., 61, n.28, 62, 73,
Wedderburn, A. J. K., 46
Wehmeier, Gerhard, 109
Weiss, Johannes, 46, 134,
Welborn, L. L., 162, 163
Wendland, H-D., 4
Weymouth, Richard, F., 168
Wesley, Charles, 30
Wesley, John, 157
Westcott, B. F., 34, 35, 36, 69, 71,

Index of Names

Whiteley, D. E. H., 3, 11, 13, 24, 27, 28, 32, 42, 185
Wibbing, Siegfried, 134
Wiedemann, Thomas, 129
Williams, Cyril, 148
Wimbush, V. L., 80, 81–84,
Windisch, Hans, 31, 163
Winger, M., 5
Wink, Walter, 124, 126
Winter, Bruce, 80, 81, 82, 84, 129, 177
Wire, Antoinette, 65, 82, 87
Wischmeyer, O., 103
Witherington, Ben, 59, 80, 81–84, 88, 142, 147, 180, 187
Wittgenstein, Ludwig, 118, 121
Wolff, Christian, 143
Wolters, Al, 75
Wright, David, 135
Wright, N. T., 3, 4, 8, 10, 48, 50, 112, 170, 174

Yarbrough, Larry, 82
Yarbrough, Robert, 75
Yoder, John H., 124

Zedekiah, 154
Zeilinger, F., 32
Zeno of Elea, 118, 119
Zeus, 118, 120
Ziesler, J. A., 50
Zimmerli, W., 109
Zwingli, Ulrich, 157

Index of Main Biblical Passages Discussed in Canonical Sequence

Rom. 1:18: How can the God of love reveal his wrath against ungodliness and wickedness? 95

Rom. 5:20: Did God give the law to increase sin? 7

Rom. 7:6; 10:4: Are Christians antinomians? 3

Rom. 7:7; 7:22: "If it had not been for the law, I would not have known sin"; yet "I delight in the law," 9

Rom. 8:28: Bland, progressive optimism about everything? 173

Rom. 11:26: Will all Israel be saved? 48

Rom. 13:1: Is obedience to the state unconditional? 123

Rom. 12:20: "Heaping burning coals on their heads" – Is this a Christian sentiment? 111

1 Cor. 5:5: Death penalty for immorality? with no second chance? 113

1 Cor.6:9–11: Who inherits the kingdom of God? 132

1 Cor. 7:1: Is it really "well for a man not to touch a woman"? 78

1 Cor. 7:10–15: Is an abandoned Christian spouse free to remarry? 85

1 Cor. 7:17–24: Remaining in slavery? 128

1 Cor. 7:29: What is the "appointed time" that suggests that people should live as if they had no spouse? 81

1 Cor. 8:12: What are a wounded conscience and a weak conscience? 99

1 Cor. 11:10: Why should women choose their head-covering "because of the angels?" 64

1 Cor. 11:28–30: Self-Examination before communion and "not discerning the Lord's body," 141

1 Cor. 13:1: Loveless brass, and a flourish of cymbals? 104

1 Cor. 13:7: Does love Involve utter credulity? 102

1 Cor. 14:1, 3, 29–40, and 1 Thess. 5:20: What kind of thing is prophesying in Paul? 155

1 Cor. 14:5: Should all Christians speak in tongues? 145

1 Cor. 14:34; 1 Tim. 2:11–14, Should women not be permitted to Speak? 55

1 Cor. 15:29: Baptism for the Dead? 44

1 Cor. 16:22; Gal. 1:8–9: Curses by Paul, 107

2 Cor. 4:4: Who is the "the god of this world"? 175

2 Cor. 5:17: Has everything old passed away and everything become new? 41

2 Cor. 6:14: How can Christians be mismatched with unbelievers? 90

Index of Main Biblical Passages Discussed in Canonical Sequence

2 Cor. 11:33: Why boast about "being let down in a basket through a window in the wall? 161

2 Cor. 12:1–2: Why not boast about visions and being caught up in the third heaven? 164

2 Cor. 12:7: What was Paul's "thorn in the flesh"? 168

Gal. 3:1: Bewitched? Or rational and logical? 188

Gal. 3:13: How can Christ be a curse for us? 23

Eph. 4:10: Did Christ "descend into the lower parts of the earth"? 34

Eph. 5:22: Should wives be expected "to be subject to their husbands"? 68

Phil. 3:6: How can Paul claim to be "as to righteousness under the law, blameless? 12

Col. 1:15–17: What is the meaning of "In Christ all things hold together" and related Christological titles? 19

Col. 1:24: Is Christ's work not "finished and sufficient"? 30

2 Thess. 2:3,7: Who is "the lawless one," and what is "the mystery of lawlessness"? 179

1 Tim. 2:15: Can childbearing ever relate to salvation? 72

Titus 1:12–13: Is the epistle to Titus incurably racist? 117

www.ingramcontent.com/pod-product-compliance
Lightning Source LLC
Chambersburg PA
CBHW022017220426
43663CB00007B/1108